T0392244

SCHOOL ENVIRONMENT IN
NIGERIA, GHANA AND THE PHILIPPINES

Prof. Irene A. Boateng
Dr. Princewill I. Egwuasi
Dr. Jake M. Laguador
Dr. Ohene B. Apea
Dr. Ngozika A. Oleforo

authorHOUSE®

AuthorHouse™
1663 Liberty Drive
Bloomington, IN 47403
www.authorhouse.com
Phone: 1 (800) 839-8640

Published by AuthorHouse 03/08/2017

ISBN: 978-1-5246-7458-8 (sc)
ISBN: 978-1-5246-7457-1 (e)

Library of Congress Control Number: 2017903424

Print information available on the last page.

Contents

QUALITY ASSURANCE ISSUES

HIGHER EDUCATION ISSUES

MANAGEMENT ISSUES

BUSINESS ISSUES

LIBRARY AND INFORMATION TECHNOLOGY ISSUES

SPECIAL EDUCATION ISSUES

GLOBALISATION ISSUES

SCIENCE ISSUE

About the Editors

Professor Irene A. Boateng is the former Dean, School of Business, Valley View University Accra, Oyibi, Ghana. An erudite scholar, she has published copiously in both national and international journals.

Dr. Princewill I. Egwuasi is of the University of Uyo, Uyo, Nigeria. He is currently the Business Editor of three reputable journals, an international reviewer to several global online and print journals. His areas of specialization are English Education and Educational Management and Planning. A recipient of the Nigerian Merit Gold Award for Productivity 2011 and Nigerian Hall of Fame Awards 2013, Dr. Egwuasi has over 30 publications in both national and international journals. He is the initiator of the book on *School Environment in Nigeria and the Philippines,* published in 2015.

Dr. Jake M. Laguador is currently the Dean, Postgraduate School, Lyceum of the Philippines University, Batangas-City, Philippines and *Research Journal Editor,* Lyceum Engineering Research Journal, Lyceum of the Philippines University. He is also the Associate Editor of Asia Pacific Journal of Education, Arts and Science. He has published several papers in reputable international journals.

Dr. Ohene B. Apea is currently a lecturer in Applied Chemistry and Biochemistry Department, University for Development Studies, Navrongo, Ghana. He is a research and development consultant with particular emphasis on Programme Planning and Execution, Product Design and Development. Dr. Apea is a consultant to ON GHANA LIMITED and Managing Editor of Novel Publications.

Dr. Ngozika A. Oleforo is currently a Senior Lecturer in the Department of Curriculum Studies, Educational Management and Planning, University of Uyo. An astute scholar who has published several journal articles in referred journals, both in Nigeria and the Overseas. She has received several awards due to her contribution in human resources development.

Preface

This publication on *School Environment in Nigeria, Ghana and the Philippines* is a continuation of our maiden publication on *School Environment in Nigeria and the Philippines*, published in February, 2015. The philosophy being that since there is a shift from globalization to internationalization of education, there is the urgent need to revisit some topical issues in our school environment towards the realization of an internationalized qualitative teaching and learning. It is therefore, based on this, that the Education International 7th World Congress Meeting in Ottawa, in July, 2015, recognized that the quality of teaching and learning is enhanced by an environment which is supportive and ensures the safety and health of learners and teachers.

The inclusion of Ghana in this edition is a conviction of the strategic position of the country's educational system, not only as a fast and dynamic developing economy in the African continent, but one with an enviable educational culture. In this edition, all the articles are theoretically, conceptually and/or empirically assembled to address diverse but all-important facets of the school environment in Nigeria, Ghana and the Philippines, with a view of proffering solutions, suggestions and recommendations to several questions that may have arisen over time, not to ignore the contributions to existing knowledge and literature of the academia. The articles were also subjected to international peer reviews and went through insightful scrutiny for standardization.

It is the utmost belief of the editors, that this book would become a food for thought to other countries of the world that sincerely require the best in their educational system, hence, the editors welcome more collaborations, especially from Asian and African countries.

Editors

Acknowledgment

The production of this academic project would not have been possible without the benevolence of the Almighty God, through whose grace, wisdom was bestowed on the initiator of the project, Dr. Princewill I. Egwuasi, of the University of Uyo, Nigeria, to visualize this work. From the maiden edition to the present, several individuals and institutions shall be continually acknowledged for their roles in making the book a reality. The Lyceum of the Philippines University, Batangas-City, Philippines, South Asia, is worthy of recognition. Through its Director of Research, Dr. Norma L. Menez and Dean, Postgraduate School, Dr. Jake M. Laguador, the university has continued to support this vision.

We are also indebted to Professor Irene A. Boateng of Valley View University, Accra, Oyibi, Ghana and Dr. Ohene B. Apea of University for Development Studies, Navrongo, Ghana, for accepting to collaborate with us by being part of the editors. To Dr. Ngozika A. Oleforo of the University of Uyo, Uyo, Nigeria, we say thank you for contributing to the realization of this second edition.

Finally, the Book Coordinator is appreciative of all the efforts of the chapter contributors to this publication and wishes to thank them immensely for believing in our commitment and genuine dedication to this course. Not forgetting the unquantifiable expertise of Princess Joan I. Egwuasi, CNA, who designed the book.

At this point, we state categorically that the views and findings as expressed in this book are strictly those of the authors.

Princewill I. Egwuasi *Ph.D*
Book Coordinator

List of Contributors

Prof. Irene Akuamoah Boateng
School of Business
Valley View University Accra, Oyibi
Ghana

Ohene Boansi Apea *Ph.D*
Applied Chemistry and Biochemistry Department
University for Development Studies, Navrongo
Ghana

Inuwa Magaji
Department of General Studies
Isa Kaita College of Education Dutsin-ma
Nigeria

Mahmud HalliruBakori
Department of Curriculum and Instruction
Isa Kaita College of Education Dutsin-ma
Nigeria

Justina Ekwuru *Ph.D*
Faculty of Education
Imo State University
Owerri
Nigeria

Collins Owusu-Ansah
Office of International Relations
University of Education
Winneba
Ghana

Deborah Afful
Division of Human Resources
University of Education
Winneba
Ghana

Jojoe Annan
Admissions Office
College of Ghanaian Languages, Ajumako
Ghana

Jurji N. Gomos
Department of Sociology
Faculty of Social Sciences
Plateau State University, Bokkos
Nigeria

Felix D. Tappi
Department of Educational Foundations
FCE Pankshin
Nigeria

Chiaka P. Denwigwe *Ph.D*
Faculty of Education
University of Calabar
Nigeria

A. D. Oghiagbephan *MISPON, MCASSON, MNISEP, MASSE*
Department of Educational Psychology
College of Education
Warri
Nigeria

Martha O. Egbro
Biology Department
College of Education
Warri
Nigeria

Ugochukwu K. Agi
Department of Foundations and Management
Faculty of Education
Ignatius Ajuru University of Education, Rumuolumeni
Port Harcourt
Nigeria

Joy-Telu Hamilton-Ekeke *Ph.D*
Department of Teacher Education
Niger Delta University,
Wilberforce Island
Nigeria

Michael O. Ogundele *Ph.D*
Department of Educational Foundations
Faculty of Education
University of Jos
Nigeria

Jake M. Laguador *Ed.D*
Graduate School,
Lyceum of the Philippines University,
Batangas City, Philippines

Alhassan Iddrisu
University for Development Studies
Tamale
Ghana

Rahmat M. Tinja
School of Education
Federal College of Education (Technical)
Potiskum
Nigeria

Tijani O. Abdulgaffar
School of Education
Federal College of Education (Technical)
Potiskum
Nigeria

Regina N. Azunwena *Ph.D*
Department of Home Economics & Hotel Management
Ignatius Ajuru University of Education
Port Harcourt
Nigeria

Ngozika. A. Oleforo *Ph.D*
Department of Curriculum Studies
Educational Management and Planning
University of Uyo, Uyo
Nigeria

Petronilla O. Owen
Department of Curriculum Studies
Educational Management and Planning
University of Uyo, Uyo
Nigeria

Frank. O. Udukeke
Department of Vocational Education
University of Uyo, Uyo
Nigeria

Angela E. Abba
University of Uyo, Uyo
Nigeria

Kingsley E. Nwachukwu *Ph.D*
Department of Early Childhood and Special Education
University of Uyo, Uyo
Nigeria

Eme Ndeh *Ph.D CLN*
College of Education
Afaha Nsit
Nigeria

Mbuotidem Umoh *Esq.*
Law Librarian
University of Uyo, Uyo
Nigeria

Godfrey O. Ebohon
School of Secondary Education (Language Programmes)
Federal College of Education, Kontagora
Nigeria

Harrison G. Ugbijeh
School of Secondary Education (Language Programmes)
Federal College of Education
Kontagora
Nigeria

Michael Ademola
School of Secondary Education (Language Programmes)
Federal College of Education
Kontagora
Nigeria

Agbaje A. Agbaje *Ph.D*
Department of Educational Foundations
Guidance and Counselling
University of Uyo
Nigeria

Efon U. Inyang
University of Uyo, Uyo
Nigeria

Mercy Ebong *Ph.D*
University of Uyo Library
Uyo
Nigeria

Etido E. Nelson
University of Uyo Main Library
Uyo
Nigeria

Godwin B. Afebende
Department of Library and Information Science
University of Calabar
Nigeria

Stella N. Nwosu *Ph.D*
Institute of Education
University of Uyo, Uyo
Akwa Ibom State
Nigeria

Gibson Okworo *Ph.D*
Dept. of Educational Technology and Library Science
University of Uyo, Uyo
Akwa Ibom State
Nigeria

Emekpe O. Omon
Department of Visual Arts and Technology
Cross River University of Technology
Calabar, Cross Rivers State
Nigeria

Ogechi C. Okonkwo *Ph.D*
Department of Foundations and Counselling
Imo State University
Owerri, Imo State
Nigeria

Joan I. Egwuasi *CNA*
Department of Accounting
University of Uyo, Uyo
Nigeria

Chioma l. Ikeanyionwu
Federal College of Education (Technical)
Umunze
Nigeria

Rita N. Udoye *Ph.D*
Federal College of Education (Technical)
Asaba
Nigeria

Guidelines for Authors

The Project Co-ordinator and Board of Editors welcome scholarly articles on *Contemporary Issues in School System of Africa and Asia* for publication in its 3rd edition of a book titled, **"SCHOOL ENVIRONMENT IN AFRICA AND ASIAN PACIFIC"**. It is an international book with editors from Universities in Africa and Asian Pacific, which aims at showcasing the educational system of the two continents.

Interested contributors are to abide by the following instructions;

- Submit an online copy of manuscript(s), including abstract and references, in MS Word format to dr.princewilluniuyoedu@gmail.com
- The title page of the article should carry the authors' names, status/rank and address, place of work and affiliations.
- Abstract of not more than 250 words.
- Manuscripts are received on the understanding that they are original and unpublished works of the author(s) not considered for publication elsewhere.
- Current APA style of referencing should be maintained.
- Author(s) e-mail addresses and phone numbers should accompany the paper.
- Figures, tables, charts and drawings should be clearly drawn and the position marked in the text.
- Pay a publication fee of $200.00 only.
- All manuscripts should reach the Project Co-ordinator on or before 31st March, 2017.

Dr. Princewill I. Egwuasi
Department of Curriculum Studies,
Educational Management and Planning
University of Uyo, Uyo
Akwa Ibom State
Nigeria
dr.princewilluniuyoedu@gmail.com
+2348038955075, +2348094454419

QUALITY ASSURANCE ISSUES

QUALITY ASSURANCE ISSUES

1

Quality Assurance Mechanisms for Sustainable Development of Nigerian and Philippine Education

Michael O. Ogundele *Ph.D* & Jake M. Laguador *Ed.D*

Abstract

Quality Assurance (QA) is a way of life, gearing towards achieving desired performance target beyond the minimum requirements. It directs organisations and even academic institutions in a certain course of action that could provide sustainable development in economic, social and political dimensions. Nigeria and the Philippines are both developing countries that need to strengthen QA to ensure delivery of instruction and not suffer from the challenges being encountered by the entire nation. This article reviewed some of the existing policies of the governments and private entities in establishing suitable approaches to measure performance in all levels of education system. Giving its background on assessment, would provide basic idea that Quality Assurance really exists in both countries trying to enhance its commitment towards quality.

Key Words: *Quality Assurance, Mechanisms, Sustainable Development*

Introduction

Education is a veritable instrument for a sustainable national development. No nation toys with the issue of education of her citizen. However the changing roles of education have necessitated the processes in teaching and learning to always call for quality control and assurance in their educational provision. The interplay of market forces would have driven the quality of products and services in higher education to a stable and acceptable market equilibrium (Padua, 2003). Any Quality Assurance mechanism either locally or internationally recognized that is being utilized and adopted by the HEIs must reflect on the quality of their graduates which is one way of measuring the performance of an institution (Dotong & Laguador, 2015a). Olatunji (2010) stated that the type of education provided will enable individual citizen to meet up the various changes and challenges in the society, the author noted that no institution can afford to be competitive if their products and services are not well improved upon. Education in Nigeria is faced with the problems of incessant strikes, inadequate facilities and equipment, truncated school calendars and regular disruption of the academic programmes, cultism, social violence vandalism, examination malpractices, inferiority of certificates awards, sexual harassment, child labour, perpetration of unethical issues in the schools unemployment and poverty. Ogundele (2008) however observed that most of the perpetrated evils are caused by the faulty educational system provided by the citizens. The author noted that the education provided in the schools is theoretical and non-cultural in nature and non-technologically oriented.

The Philippine Education is continuously striving to get along with its neighboring countries in South East Asia in providing equally dynamic and competitive quality of education in pursuit to the changing global economic environment. The Philippines is experiencing the phenomenon of mass higher education with the concomitant rise of universities and colleges (public and private) offering a greater diversity of programs, and with varying capacity to deliver teaching and learning services (Corpus, 2003a). The growing number of HEIs in the Philippines calls for attention to strengthen the monitoring and assessing the capability of the academic institutions in providing education based on the standards of accreditation. Licuanan (2012), the Chairperson of Commission on Higher Education (CHED) in the Philippines, identified this as one of the critical areas of concern in higher education.

The problems however require drastic changes in educational system. Federal Republic of Nigeria (2013) therefore noted that education provision today has made it possible for any country to have a steady supply of highly creative citizen that will help in improving the living standard, condition of the general citizens and to solve the global problems therefore there is an urgent need for the Nigerian education to be committed towards improving the quality of her education system in order to meet up with the global challenges. If society is to meet up and be able to conform with the global needs and aspiration, quality assurance must guarantee and the required standard are to be adequately be met.

The concern of quality has been at the core of the motivating forces for enhancing the needed reforms in education. Considering the capability of the government and its educational system to watch over and supervise the operations of HEIs in every aspect of educational management. Ajayi and Adegbesan (2007) described quality as the totality of the features like process, product, services and performance in the customers. It is not only the feature of a finished product or services it focuses on the relationship between the input, internal processes, output and all efforts that eradicate wastes and those that enhance productivity.

Nigeria and the Philippines are both from third world category wherein various similarities and differences in the implementation of quality assurance will be explored that will serve as the basis for further discussion to create mutual cooperation in delivering appropriate services to the youth from the same perspective and experiences.

Concept of Quality Assurance in Education

Quality assurance in the product of the industrial sectors will enhance high patronage in the competitive markets. In Nigeria, the stakeholders and well-meaning Nigerians want quality assurance in Nigerian education products produced. The quality assurance in Nigeria education is therefore measured through conducive environment, students' academic performance, teacher performance, learners' behaviours, efficiency and effective complaisance to the societal norms, ethical value orientation, moral conviction and values, ability defend certificate acquired internal and external efficiency. Quality of education provided is being determined by the quality of the products and the availability of role quality management infrastructure to bring forth well qualified products and outputs (Oyedeji, 2012; Ogundele & Oparinde, 2012).

Nicolas (2014) noted that "Quality assurance is a guarantee to various stakeholders, students and employers that undergraduate and post-graduate programs are relevant and responsive to the developmental, social, intellectual and economic needs of contemporary societies. A QA system will also ensure continuing review of curricula and how these are being implemented, identify current weaknesses and strengths and plan for improvement". The Philippine Commission on Higher Education (CHED) defines quality as the alignment and consistency of the learning environment with the institution's vision, mission and goals demonstrated by exceptional learning and service outcomes and the development of a culture of quality (CHED Memorandum Order No. 46, s. 2012) similar to the practices of other developed countries. Educational programs and projects for student and faculty mobility as well as quality assurance in accordance with the ASEAN Integration assist the local academic institutions in reaching the goal of globalization (Dotong & Laguador, 2015b).

The word quality in educational institution is an elusive word that makes it difficult for researchers and educationists to define in concise language. The term quality was adopted from the industrial sectors where the quality of the products are adequately monitored through adequate supervision, monitoring, motivation in order to encourage high societal patronage at the market place. Dotong and Laguador (2015) stated that quality is the core of any business model to gain reputation and credibility from the local and international community wherein recognition from various accrediting and certifying bodies and agencies provide better opportunity for the organizations to prove their worth and claim for excellence.

QA mechanisms undoubtedly fuel the passion in the hearts of organizational members to move towards higher levels of quality manifestations (Javier, 2015) and failure to acknowledge its different dimensions can diminish the institutional purpose (Jung, et al., 2013). Ogundele and Oparinde (2012) see the quality assurance as a way of preventing wastage, mistake and defects in the products or services and avoiding problems when delivering the services. Sofoluwe (2005) defines quality assurance as planned and systematic actions that are put in place to provide adequate confidence needed to meet the needs and aspirations of clients. This is a systematic review of educational programme that ensure that acceptable standards of education, academic performance that ensure that acceptable standards of education, academic performance and infrastructure are being maintained (Sofoluwe, 2011). The author however stated that basic principles underlying the quality assurance are committeemen, focus, satisfaction, employee empowerment, contours change and transformation organization culture, team work training and retraining opportunities through regular capacity buildings.

Achi (2010) noted that quality assurance focuses on the learners' entry behavior characteristics and teachers' qualifications. To sum up the definition of quality assurance in education, the whole educational system must include the attitudes, objectivism, actions and procedures that enhance the production of the quality products that the institutions in education in the society. For any nation to aspire to a greater height, the educational programme of activities and learning should be adequately planned to enhance the implementation of quality assurance mechanisms in the products of the institutions.

Purposes of Quality Assurance in Education System

Article 1 Section 1 of CHED Memorandum Order No. 46, s. 2012 on the rationale for enhancing Quality Assurance states that Philippine higher education is mandated to contribute to building a quality nation capable of transcending the social, political, economic, cultural and ethical issues that constrain the country's human development, productivity and global competitiveness.

The need for quality assurance in schools cannot be over emphasized. In order to ensure the quality of the educational products in Nigeria, there are major needs in Nigeria's educational system to embrace quality assurance that will serve as an indispensable way for monitoring quality control strategy for every stakeholder. Also quality assurance mechanism will give opportunity for enhancing high standard in Nigeria's education at all levels.

QA Systems in HEIs provide mechanisms, procedures and processes that are systematized and institutionalized. The HEI is protected from arbitrary changes that can be imposed by stakeholders with new interests while the quality cycle becomes integral to the HEI operations (PACU, 2012).

The objective of ASEAN Quality Assurance Network Project is to promote regional harmonization in higher education by developing a QA framework in higher education that develop regional identities which countries could benchmark and align their own QA system of higher education with (PACU, 2012).

Program accreditation in Philippine higher academic institutions serves as a quality assurance mechanism and an approach for external body to monitor the implementation of educational practices to ensure high quality outputs. It is a voluntary procedure of submitting one's curricular offering to evaluation from accrediting agency to prove the institution's capacity in providing above the minimum requirements set by the Commission in Higher Education (CHED). This is one way of demonstrating optimum transparency and integrity in showing one's worth of possessing the character of an excellent university for the future leaders of the country (Laguador, Villas & Delgado, 2014). Padua (2003) noted that accreditation results are generally used for the grant of more autonomy to colleges and universities.

The quality assurance mechanisms assist in the monitoring and supervision of the existing programme implementation strategies in education system. Putting in place the quality assurance mechanism helps to determine the adequacy of the facilities needed for enhancing quality control in the interest of quality assurance in educational levels.

Furthermore, quality assurance aids the effectiveness and efficiency in meeting the organization goals. Samshark (2011) also identified the following purposes for putting in place the quality control as follows: to improve teaching learning processes to enhance public accountability and patronage, to enhance information and market transparency, to enhance equitable distribution of resources in educational system and to provide the guidelines and efficient methods, procedure which will assist the schools to implement predetermined programme of activities that will enhance quality control and assurance in the school system.

Quality Assurance Mechanism in Philippine Schools

The QA in the Philippines is measured through Degree Program Level Accreditation (Padua, 2003) wherein HEIs are voluntary submitting their individual baccalaureate and graduate degree programs to external evaluation of legitimate and registered educational associations or organizations. Accreditation is seen as a system of evaluation based on the standards of an accrediting agency (Corpus, 2003a).

Interests of students and society should be at the forefront of External Quality Assurance Principles and Processes. QA standards, criteria and procedures are developed together with stakeholders;

published in advance and readily accessible to the public; and applied consistently, fairly and with due regard for cultural diversity (PACU, 2012).

One possible assurance mechanism that HEIs can acquire is the Philippine Quality Award which is a national quality award comparable with the Malcolm Baldrige National Quality Award (MBNQA) of the US and those in Europe and Asia ("Background of PQA"). There are 6 HEIs recognized for their Commitment to Quality Management and 2 for Proficiency in Quality Management. The most recent recipients from the academic sector in 2015 are the Colegio de San Juan Letran Manila and the Lyceum of the Philippines Laguna (Dotong & Laguador, 2015a).

The PQA aims "to promote standards in organizational performance comparable to those of leading business abroad, pursuant to the country's effort to be globally competitive; to establish a national system for assessing quality and productivity performance, thus providing local organizations regardless of size, sector and maturity with criteria and guidelines for self-assessment to guide their quality and productivity improvement efforts; and to recognize organizations in both the private and public sector which excel in quality management and overall organizational performance, thus providing Philippine industries with benchmarks and models to emulate" ("PQA Objectives").

Accreditation: The accreditation system in the Philippines started in 1957 through the Philippine Accrediting Association of Schools, Colleges and Universities (PAASCU) which is the oldest and largest accrediting agency in the country when they developed evaluation instruments, trained the accreditors and performed public information about the importance of voluntary accreditation (Arcelo, 2003; Pijano, 2010).

A unique feature of the accreditation system in the Philippines is the government's policy of classifying schools for purposes of progressive deregulation and the grant of other benefits. The levels serve as pathways for colleges and universities as they move on from candidacy to full membership. While CHED policy clearly benefits accrediting agencies, the amount of control it exerts is also a threat to the private voluntary nature of the accreditation system, which is one of its strengths (Pijano, 2010).

There are several accrediting agencies in the Philippines which are all under the umbrella of Federation of Accrediting Agency of the Philippines (FAAP) such as: Philippine Association of Accrediting Agencies of Schools, Colleges and Universities (PAASCU), the Accrediting Association of Chartered Colleges and Universities of the Philippines (AACCUP), the Philippine Association of Colleges and Universities-Commission on Accreditation (PACU-COA), the Association of Christian Schools and Colleges (ACSC).

The Philippine Government through CHED has various initiatives to strengthen the educational system in higher education through introducing the Center of Excellence and Centre of Development as another assessment tool for ensuring quality in offering tertiary degree programs. CHED's Centre of Excellence refers to a department within a higher education institution, which continuously demonstrates excellent performance in the areas of instruction, research and publication, extension and linkages and institutional qualifications" in pursuant to the Higher Education Act of 1994.

Many governments have implemented, or are considering, policies of concentration within national systems to lift the performance of selected universities (Marginson, 2009). Granting recognitions as centers of excellence and development to tertiary institutions is a great initiative from the Philippine Government but the issue on how this program can really uplift the entire educational system of the country is still in question. Because out of 2,299, there are only 97 Philippine HEIs or nearly 4 percent have either COE or COD recognition from CHED as of September 20, 2012 with expiration on May 31, 2014. And most of them are those already high performing HEIs in the country which are voluntarily applying for this recognition but those low performing HEIs still remain unresponsive to the call for application.

System of Measurement: The present system adopts a system of values in the assessment based on the set criteria. Weights are allocated to the different criteria, and evaluation is pursued both qualitatively and quantitatively. The specific tool for evaluation is the accreditation instrument (Corpus, 2013b). PACUCOA and AACCUP have similarities the way accreditation by program is being assessed based on the given criteria: Purposes/Philosophy and Objectives; Faculty; Instruction; Library; Laboratories; Physical Plant & Facilities; Student Services; Organization & Administration; and School and Community/ Social Orientation and Community Involvement

Research Journal Accreditation Service: The Philippine Commission on Higher Education (CHED) promotes mechanisms for notable research publication through its initiative of introducing the Journal Accreditation Service that measures the quality of published papers and articles based on the national standard and peer refereeing system of research journals from any organization or institution in the Philippines. CHED recognizes research journals based on the following evaluation criteria: composition and qualification of the editorial board; recruitment and qualification of the peer-reviewers/external referees; type of refereeing system adopted and overall appearance, timeliness and regularity of the journal.

According to the CMO No. 5 series of 2012, "Publication of research outputs of faculty members of colleges and universities in refereed journals has become a universal requirement for tenure in higher education institutions. This requirement hinges on the assumption that peer-reviewed or refereed journals of research are publications of high quality, credibility and integrity. However, the practice of peer-review and/or refereeing is not uniformly implemented by all higher education institutions thus, giving rise to huge variance in the quality of journals of research published by colleges and universities in the country".

Quality Assurance Mechanisms in Nigerian Schools

Quality assurance is referred to as the mechanisms and the processes used to enhance effective maintenance and the improvement of the educational input process and output of the educational, and to guarantee the standard of the certificate issued in the society.

However, to enhance quality assurance in Nigerian schools at different levels, quality assurance mechanisms came into being. At Nigerian universities, National Universities Commission (NUC) adopted the following mechanisms like accreditation, universities ranking, performance rating, bench marking and the programme verification, research publication mechanisms, board of examiners and institutional discipline.

Ijaiya (2010) also stated that the quality assurance mechanisms for the secondary and primary education programmes in Nigeria are supervision, training opportunities, external examination, performance indicators and institutional ranking and rating.

Generally, in Nigerian educational system, be it higher, secondary or primary education systems, the federal republic of Nigeria (2013) advocated for the quality assurance in her educational programme. Find below the quality assurance mechanisms put in place.

Accreditation: This is one of the major quality assurance mechanisms done through the National Universities Commission. NUC (1999) defined accreditation as the system of evaluating academic programmes. In line with the laid down academic standard; the commission stated that accreditation process focused on the comprehensive examining of the mission, resources and procedures of various programmes of higher education. The aims of accreditation programmes are to ensure adequate provision of the minimum standards. Also to assure that the employers and community, that the university graduates have attained the acceptable level of competency in the areas of their specialization and to ensure that Nigerian universities are ranked high among other universities at the global level. The quality assurance mechanism of accreditation is peculiar to Nigerian higher education institutions and Nigerian distance education system.

It should however be noted that as accreditation is peculiar to the institution of higher learning and distance education, so also the supervision and inspection of schools are peculiar to secondary and primary education. The State and Federal Ministries of Education established inspectorate divisions to supervise and inspect the programme, educational facilities provided, teaching-learning processes, teacher's commitments, qualification, school environment and all those factors that will enhance quality assurance in the product and output. However, in Nigeria, the result of the accreditation and supervision are used by the government for supporting the educational institutions financially as providing the necessary subsidies and help to supply useful data for the educational growth and development.

Performance Indicators: Quantitative measures are put in place to access the achievement of the institutions of higher learning. Through the performance indicators, the institutions are monitored and enable the institutions to work effectively so that they will be ranked and rated high among other universities. It should be noted that in Nigeria, the indicators of quality assurance are students' academic achievement, skills acquisition, accountability, rating of institution, research publication. In both secondary and primary schools, Annual Performance Evaluation Review (APER) forms are used in the performance rating of the teachers. While in Nigerian institutions of higher learning, staff appraisal forms are designed to appraise staff performance and the student-lecturers appraisal forms are available for the students to appraise their lecturers. All the efforts aimed at encouraging high quality assurance in Nigerian education products.

Also, there is teaching-learning mechanism. In Nigerian educational system there are external examiners to scrutinize and moderate school examinations. They review the marked scripts and make a comment in the general results. The external examiners check the lecturers and the teachers during the teaching-learning processes and to correct their discrepancies. The external supervisor or examiners advises on matters relating to teaching, curriculum development, research publications and other academic matters in the school.

Research Publication Mechanism: Since the primary function of educational research is to increase the knowledge of educational practices and phenomena that will aid effective decision making process, effective research conduct will aid progressive, transformation and sustainable national development, supervision, curriculum planning and implementation and effective evaluation of the instructional facilities, teachers, students and environment. However, in a bid to improve research and development in the country and enhance quality assurance in the Nigerian educational system, Okebukola (2004) launched the first Nigeria research and development with the aim of exhibiting innovative research projects and the output. Also for the industry to select outstanding research outputs and to provide avenues to attract support for developmental oriented researches for the organized private sectors and development agencies. However, to encourage high integrity in Nigerian research work and to bring out quality assurance in the research publications, various universities established their university repository whereby every lecturer upload their research works, profiles and other publications on the repository. However, the efforts will expose the institution and individual to the international communities and their qualities will be adequately assured.

Establishment of quality assurance department at the federal, state and local government areas in Nigeria. The basis for this department is to enable adequate monitoring of the various institutions and to ensure that all the efforts in the various educational institutions will aid quality assurance.

Also, programme verification is another mechanism for enhancing quality assurance in Nigerian educational system. The Federal, States and University commissions tried to verify the readiness of the institutions to establish a great programme. This is done by verifying the claim and the available physical and human resources for their readiness. The readiness is conducted by the National University Commission Staff and invited experts in the disciplines.

However, it is important to note that in Nigeria educational institutions, quality assurance mechanisms include self-evaluation, bench marking, ranking, rating, accreditation, survey of students, graduate employers and professional bodies, peer review of the publication and identification of goal practices, setting standard, auditing of progress and assessment of outcomes, bench marking and having examination ethics to enhance quality assurance in the school product.

Indicators of Quality Assurance in Nigerian Schools

In terms of certain specifications like satisfactions, standardization, accountability, prestige credibility in Nigeria educational system, quality of education cannot only be measured based on the quality of the instructional facilities provided in the schools but there are series of indices to which quality assurance of the education is enhanced. Prominent among the indicators or quality assurance in Nigerian schools are

Educational Goals Achievement Evaluation: The philosophy to be enhanced by the Federal Republic of Nigeria (2013) called for free and democratic society, just and egalitarian society, strong and self-reliant nation, great and dynamic economy and land of bright and full opportunity for ill citizens. However, in order to make the philosophy functional, every educational level like primary, secondary, higher education, distance education and special education has their own aims and objectives. The quality assurance is therefore determined by the extent to which the aims and objectives are achieved to enhance the national goals. However, the achievement of the national goals therefore become an indicator that the quality of education is assured in Nigeria. In Nigeria, the educational planning and implementation of the school curriculum is therefore focused on the societal needs and aspiration.

Performance Indicators: These are the quantitative measures which attempt to assess the achievement of educational institutions. For quality assurance to be enhanced in Nigeria education, the institutions monitored the teachers and non-teachers performance and the institution performance. However, in Nigeria, the examination bodies like West African School Certificate Examination (WAEC), National Examination Council (NECO), National Board for Technical and Business Board (NABTEB), National Universities Commissions (NUC) and National Council of Colleges of Education (NCCE) monitor the various institutions and give them effective ranking in order to enhance quality assurance in their products. The Academic Excellence Indicator System (AEIS) set up by the Federal Ministry of Education emphasize on the students achievement and other academic indicators as the basis for the accountability ranking and ratings of the institutions.

Functional Areas of Effectiveness: Goh (2000) identified quality assurance indicators under following functional areas which include teaching and learning experience, research, staff management, record keeping, community services and communication. Effectiveness of these functional areas identified was described as indicators or quality assurance in Nigeria education.

Arikewuyo (2004) observed that the quality assurance in Nigerian education is measured in the ability of the students that are performing well in a standard external examination, their relevance to the needs for the students' community and society. The author therefore concluded that quality assurance is closely related to the quality control which serve as the techniques and activities used to make the requirements met.

Quality Assurance in the Philippine Basic Education System

The Philippine Government has been very active in instilling quality education through providing policies and guidelines for basic education to facilitate the teaching-learning process. This strategy is one way of demonstrating eagerness to present better perspective and approaches on how to deal with quality through various Department of Education Orders (DO).

According to DepEd Order (DO) No. 75, s. 2012, "Under the Basic Education Social Reform Agenda (BESRA), the Department of Education has formulated the Quality Assurance and Accountability Framework (QAAF) to serve as a 'road map' in instilling quality and accountability in the respective operation within the basic education sector" and to implement the desired learning outcomes enhanced by national learning strategies multi-sector coordination, and quality assurance. This move paved the way for the installation of the Quality Management System (QMS) in the Department to ensure delivery of quality basic education. It is a system of processes and tools to be applied so that the desired knowledge, skills, attitudes and values of the students can be attained at some expected level. Furthermore, it is a system that requires coordinated and shared responsibility of the various levels of governance of the Department and all other stakeholders of basic schooling to deliberately bring about quality education. Enclosure No. 1 contains the details on QAAF and QMS (DO no. 44 s. 2010).

The establishment of QMS in the Department is in line with Administrative Order No. 161, "Institutionalizing Quality Management System in Governance", (Enclosure No. 2 amended through Executive Order No. 605, "Institutionalizing the Structure, Mechanisms and Standards to Implement the Government Quality Management Program" (Enclosure No. 3. Said Orders direct all government agencies and government-owned and/or controlled corporations to implement and institutionalize a national quality management system as a strategy to promote transparency and accountability in governance, provide a framework for assessing quality system performance, establish public service quality standards and recognize quality excellence among the government organizations (DO no. 44 s. 2010).

There are always great intentions and objectives behind those orders that only need proper assessment and evaluation after implementation to counter check the quality of outputs against the inputs. The long process of achieving the goals of basic education in the Philippines is still far behind the performance of neighboring countries in Asia.

Determinants of Quality Assurance in the Primary Education System of Nigeria

It is obvious that the philosophical objectives of quality assurance are the decisions of educational programmes to train individuals to achieve competence in a given area of industrial production function. The focus of which, is to prevent problems, strengthen organizational systems, and continually improve performance. Thus, quality assurance is the ability of educational institutions to meet the need of the use of manpower in relation to the quality of skills acquired by their products. With this, the quality of an academic programme becomes a universal concern. This is because the product of one primary school becomes another student in another school (secondary school) or other culture's industrial setting.

Consequently, quality assurance has become an internationalized concept. The UBE reported the first attempt at universalization of quality assurance in primary education across the globe in 2004. The study ranked the primary schools in terms of their productive functions, and the relative efforts on their product. No African primary or Basic Education was ranked, including Nigeria. Since this development, the UBE has heightened its efforts in standardizing the quality of primary education in Nigeria.

To establish and maintain high quality standards, the universities and the UBE have a shared responsibility in addressing the following key areas, are identified by Adedipe, (2007): Minimum Academic Standard; Supervision and Monitoring; Carrying capacity and admission enrolment; Visitation; Impact assessment; Education Research and Development; Publications and research assessment; and Structures, infrastructures and utilities.

Abolade and Newton (2004) observed that the Whole-School Evaluation (WSE) concept/practice is considered as one of the cornerstones of quality- assurance and one way of improving the quality of education, quality assurance in this concept refers to the monitoring and evaluation of performance of the various levels of the education system in achieving the specific goals at each level and overall objectives of the system. To them, quality assurance consists of three programmes, namely: Whole - School Evaluation (WES), Systematic Evaluation (SE), and Quality Management System (QMS).

It is generally believed that the purposes of evaluation in the school system are to: Assess the quality of school using nationally agreed criteria; Increase the level of accountability in the education system; Strengthen the support given to schools by government and other agencies; Provide feedback to stakeholders through a publication of reports resulting from whole school evaluation; and Identify aspects of excellence in schools as well as areas of major under achievement; thus, improve understanding of what makes an effective institution.

Institutional evaluation, according to Kartz (2009) focuses on the following key areas to enhance quality: basic functionality of the school or institution; Leadership, management and communication; governance and relationships; quality of teaching and learning/educator development; Curriculum provision and resources; learner achievement; school or institutional safety, security and discipline; Infrastructure; parents and community.

Problems Militating against Quality Assurance in Nigeria Education

Quality assurance is a way of preventing defects in the products, services and avoiding problems when delivering solutions and services, quality assurance is therefore part of quality management and quality control mechanisms that focuses on providing confidence that quality requirement will be fulfilled. However, the following problems militate against effectiveness of quality assurance mechanisms in Nigerian schools.

Unresolved Ethical Issues in Nigeria Education System: There are so many unethical issues which militate against the integrity of Nigerian educational system Ogundele, Bwoi and Gyot (2015) identified such unethical issues like examination malpractices, drug abuse, in disciplinary behaviours, students' unrest, truncated school calendars, incessant strike, plagiarisms, and sexual harassment. The perpetration of these did not portray the quality assurance in Nigerian certificates.

Over Dependency on Paper Qualifications: Over dependency on the certificates without correspondence in skills acquisition is another problem. Yusuf (2006) and Olanipekun (2002) observed that Nigerian educational quality is affected by the theoretical non-technological orientation and culturally bias that characterized Nigerian education. The problem therefore leads to high rate of unemployment, moral laxity, unethical issues perpetration in the society and socio-economic crises relegated the quality of the educational system in Nigeria.

Politics in Nigerian Education: In Nigeria, politics in all socio-economic sectors had been influencing the quality of the education in Nigeria. Akpa (2015) observed that there are politics in supervision and accreditation.

Job Satisfaction: Abdulkareem, Ogundele and Etejere (2012) identified job satisfaction as one or the problem that militate against quality assurance of Nigerian education system. To the authors, what many teachers take as salary cannot take them home, the job satisfaction is so low, there is also low teacher morale. However, the teachers are no longer performing their duties to the satisfaction of the parents and for enhancing educational goals achievement. It should be noted that low teachers' morale according to Ogundele (2015) does not allow the teachers to perform their duties effectively to enhance quality assurance in the educational system. For instance the teacher can no longer give and mark assignment and test, taking of the teaching-learning process with levity, they no longer performing the students' supervisory role and all quality assurance mechanisms are adequately neglected.

Poor value orientation to quality of the educational system. The value orientation accorded Nigerian education system negates the quality assurance accorded the educational sector. However in Nigeria, due to the high rate of examination malpractices, poor skills acquisition, unemployment, poverty, low practical orientation enables the public to lose hope on the quality assurance on the type of educational provided. For instance, Ogundele, Moronfoye and Oparinde (2012) sited example or unqualified mechanical engineers that could not repair his car unless he carries it to the road side mechanic. The so-called civil engineers cannot construct simple bungalow for himself unless invite road side brick layers. Half-baked teachers had ruined the life of many innocent children because of neglected areas or delivery or quality teaching to her students.

Finally, socio-economic crises in Nigerian society had greatly affected the quality of Nigerian education. Many schools had been closed down, accessibility for quality education had been hampered, many schools have being destroyed through bombs, kidnapping, environmental degradation all the factors had been affecting the quality provision of education in Nigeria and thereby affecting quality assurance in the educational system.

Strategies for Establishing Quality Assurance in Education

The strategies used for quality assurance in education include:

Monitoring: It refers to the process of collecting data at intervals about ongoing projects or programmes within the school system. The aim is to constantly assess the level of performance with a view of finding out how far a set objectives are being met (Ogundele, 2008).

Evaluation: This is a formal process carried out within a school setting. It is based on available data which are used to form conclusions. It could be formative or summative. The aim of evaluation, a quality assurance strategy, is to see how the system can be assisted to improve on the present level of performance (formative) (Ijaiya 2001).

Supervision: Supervision might involve inspection, but it goes beyond inspection and includes attempt at bringing about improvement in the quality of instruction. It involves staff as essential part of the process. It is a way of advising, grinding, refreshing, encouraging and stimulating staff (Olorunmola, 2008)

Inspection: Usually involves an assessment of available facilities and resources in an institution with a view to establishing how far a particular institution has met prescribed standards, it is more of an assessment rather than an improvement induced exercise (Achi, 2010).

Quality control: The issue of quality control cannot be over- emphasized. It is one of the strategies for establishing quality assurance in the inferior education system at all levels. Ojedele (2007) views that; quality control should be of concern to the country in its drive towards technological development. Enhanced teachers' job satisfaction and improved morale through adequate pay, conducive enrolment and effective students' success in their results.

Establishment of quality assurance units: Quality assurance units should be established at the various universities, polytechnics and colleges of education to monitor the quality of the teaching-learning process, research publications and community services of the lecturers in the various educational institutions (Durosaro, 1998).

Periodic Review of Educational Programme: Also, there should be periodic review of educational and academic programmes in Nigeria to meet up with the change and innovation in the society. It should be noted that compatibility of educational programmes with the societal needs and aspirations will definitely reveal the quality assurance needed from education.

Development of Qualified Experts: Attention should be paid to the development of the best qualified experts involved in instructional, scientific research activities, technology transfer and other productive services. The need for technical assistance to develop quality standards is urgent, particularly as regards regulation of e-learning and cross border delivery of tertiary education.

Acceptance and Prompt Implementation of Quality Assurance Mechanisms: All higher education institutions should accept and implement the principles of quality assurance and accreditation in order to guarantee uniformity of academic standards. There is urgent need for the internationalization of education institutions and adopt criteria for recruiting developing and maintaining qualified staff with appropriate background, experience and ethical standards. Job descriptions for lecturers must be clearly specified. Teachers must evaluate regularly by way of improving the quality of teaching, research and maintaining educational standards.

Adequate students and staff motivation: Students should be motivated by providing them with a healthy learning environment (Modern classroom, well-stocked libraries, online educational materials and living quarters), and assists the needy with affordable loans and grants to finance their education.

Conclusion

This article explores the quality assurance mechanisms employed in Nigeria and the Philippines. It shows that there are well established quality assurance mechanisms in Nigeria and the Philippines supported by the government policies and laws protecting the rights of every citizen and the institution to acquire what is due to them and ensure they share experiences in the environment that provides better opportunity for learning. Quality assurance is therefore determined and verified whether the output of Nigerian educational system really meets up the specifications and requirement (Ogundele and Oparinde, 2012).

It is highly respected in the Philippines and Nigeria to extent that all efforts are being put in place to enhance quality assurance in all sectors of the economy including education. They defined strategies and basic frameworks to follow in achieving the objectives set for all levels of education.

QA is a form of measurement that inspires every institution to adhere the national and international standards of accreditation and at the same time, industries keep on trusting the academic institutions with various QA mechanisms that are in placed in the Quality Management System as a proof or seal of quality in products and services.

Quality assurance mechanisms put in place are working well in Nigeria and the Philippines towards enhancing socio-economic transformation, scientific development and bringing about sustainable positive change and innovations in both countries. It serves as a platform to sustain the process of teaching and learning amidst some issues and challenges being encountered by both countries. However, with the quality assurance mechanisms therefore, Nigerian educational system is ranked high among other educational system at the global village. The Philippines is now facing many challenges during the K to 12 transition period in the Education System and QA has a great importance in ensuring its implementation process that could be successful along the way.

The result of reviews of program accreditations serves as baseline information for continuous improvement of any institution that will reflect in the kind of services being provided to its customers. This will serve as a guide for local and international industries and investors to determine the capacity of education system of Nigeria and the Philippines to provide competitive graduates for their demands. Development of human resources through skills training as well as personal and professional growth is also being assured that the people who provide services to the students have adequate capacity to deliver expected results or outcomes. Student development is the primary purpose of QA in educational institutions along with the other factors that influence to the achievement and realization of educational objectives for the holistic growth of future leaders of both countries. The significance of QA could never be taken for granted as well as its strength to describe the extent of quality and excellence.

References

Abdulkareem, A.Y., Ogundele, M. O. & Etejere, P. A. D. (2012). Teachers' Job Satisfaction and Quality Assurance of Secondary Schools in Kwara State. *African Journal of Educational Developmental Studies. 3* (2) 93 – 100.

Abolade, J. A. &, A. A. (2004). *Indicators of Quality Assurance in Nigerian Education.* Ibadan: Newton Press

Adedipe, S. O. (2007). *Fundamental of Educational Studies in Nigeria.* Abuja: Success Press.

Achi, C. N. (2010). Issues of Quality in Nigerian Education System. Retrieved on 15th April 2011 *http://servicesbeprease.com/enhancement/20*

Administrative Order No. 161, Series 2006, "Institutionalizing Quality Management System in Governance", http://www.gov.ph/2006/10/05/administrative-order-no-161-s-2006/

Ajayi, J. O. & Adegbesan, S. A. (2007). Quality Assurance Mechanisms in Nigerian Education: Ways Forward. A Paper Presented at the National Teachers Institute Kaduna on the Teachers' Forum held on 12th September 2007.

Akpa, G. O. (2015). Politics in Supervision as a threat to Quality of Universal Basic Education in Nigeria. A Lead Paper Presented at the National Conference of National Association of Educational Administration and Planning held 7th – 10th October 2015 at University of Benin. Nigeria.

Arcelo, A. A. (2003). In pursuit of continuing quality in higher education through accreditation. *International Institute for Educational Planning, Paris.*

Arikewuyo, J. O. (2004). *Total Involvement in Management. A 21st Century Imperative.* Lagos: Makugma Press.

Background of PQA, http://www.pqa.org.ph/background-pqa.php, date accessed: October 10, 2015.

CHED Memorandum Order (CMO) No. 46 series 2012, Section 6, Policy-Standard to Enhance Quality Assurance (QA) in the Philippine Higher Education through an Outcomes-Based and Typology – Based QA

CHED Memorandum Order (CMO) No. 5, Series of 2012, Revised Guidelines for CHED Accreditation of Research Journals and Providing Incentives Therefor, Commission on Higher Education, Republic of the Philippines.

Corpus, M. T. (2003a). Historical Perspective of the Philippine Quality Assurance System. *Journal of Philippine Higher Education Quality Assurance, 1(1)*

Corpus, M. T. (2003b). Redesigning the Philippine Quality Assurance System. *Journal of Philippine Higher Education Quality Assurance, 1(1).*

DepEd Order (DO) 44, s. 2010 - Adoption of the KRT 3: Quality Assurance and Accountability Framework (QAAF), Department of Education, Republic of the Philippines, url: http://www.deped.gov.ph/orders/do-44-s-2010, date retrieved: March 24, 2016.

DepEd Order (DO) No. 75, s. 2012, Guidelines on the Utilization of the Regional Implementation Support and Enhancement (RISE) Funds, Department of Education, Republic of the Philippines, url: http://www.deped.gov.ph/sites/default/files/order/2012/DO_s2012_75.pdf

Dotong, C. I., & Laguador, J. M. (2015a). Philippine Quality Assurance Mechanisms in Higher Education towards Internationalization. *Studies in Social Sciences and Humanities,* 3(3), 156-167.

Dotong, C. I. & Laguador, J. M. (2015b), Developing and Maintaining an International Climate among Philippine Higher Education Institutions. *Journal of Education and Literature,* 3(3), 107-116.

Durosaro, D. O. (1998). Accountability in Education: Case of Nigeria. In D. O. Durosaro, & J. Fagbamaye, (Eds.) *Nigerian Education Project Monitoring and School Plant Maintenance.* Ibadan: Graphics.

Famro, C. O. (2000). *Goals and Goal Congruence in Nigerian Universities:* Unpublished Ph.D Thesis University of Ilorin, Nigeria.

Federal Republic of Nigeria (2013).*National Policy on Education.* Abuja: NERDC

Goh, T. S. (2000). *Elements of Educational Administration and Planning.* Akure: Raphmore Press.

Ijaiya, N.Y.S (1991). *Educational Supervision.* Ilorin: MygraceRecipo Press.

Javier, E. R. (2015). Quality Assurance Mechanisms towards Organizational Transformation: Best Practices of an Autonomous University in the Philippines. In A. N. Ekpe, I. L. An, J. M. Laguador & N. A. Oleforo (eds.) *School Environment in Nigeria and the Philippines.* USA: Authorhouse.

Jung, I., Wong, T. M., & Belawati, T. (Eds.). (2013). Quality Assurance in Distance Education and e-learning: Challenges and Solutions from Asia. SAGE Publications India.

Kartz, J. J. (2009). Functional Role of Teachers in Enhancing Quality, Assurance in Nigerian Education. *Kaduna Journal of Teachers' Education, 2* (1) 16 – 22.

Laguador, J. M., Villas, C. D., Delgado, R. M. (2014). The Journey of Lyceum of the Philippines University-Batangas towards Quality Assurance and Internationalization of Education. *Asian Journal of Educational Research, 2*(2).

Licuanan, P. (2012). Challenges in Higher Education, url: http://densmaligaya.blogspot.com/, date retrieved: March 6, 2016

Marginson, S. (2009). Open Source Knowledge and University Rankings. Thesis Eleven, 96(1), 9-39. DOI:10.1177/0725513608099118

Nicolas, M. G. (2014). ASEAN Integration and Quality Assurance, ASEAN Integration in UP Forum, url: http://www.up.edu.ph/asean-integration-and-quality-assurance/, date retrieved: March 23, 2016

Ogundele, M. O. (2008). *Funding, Teachers' Job Satisfaction and Students' Academic Performance of Private Secondary Schools in Kwara State, Nigeria.* Unpublished Ph.D thesis, University of Ilorin.

Ogundele, M. O. (2015). Improving Teachers' Morale for Enhancing Quality Assurance of Universal Basic Education in Nigeria. *Journal of Educational Innovator 3* (1) 1 – 6.

Ogundele, M. O., Moronfoye, S. A. & Oparinde, F. O. (2012). Entrepreneurship Education: A Panacea for Educational Transformation in Nigeria. *European Journal of Educational Sciences 1* (1) 52 – 58.

Ogundele, M. O & Oparinde F. O. (2012). Quality Control Mechanism for Administrative Effectiveness of Nigerian Distance Education. *Ila College Education Review* 8 (1) 22 – 28.

Ogundele, M. O., Gyot, K. & Bwoi, P. N. (2015). Towards Resolving Ethical Issues for Enhancing Research Integrity in Nigerian Education. *Asia Pacific Journal of Multi-disciplinary Research* 3 (5) 83 – 90.

Ojedele, P. A. (2007). *Handbook on Educational Management.* Lagos: University Press.

Okebukola, P. (2002). Trends in Nigerian Tertiary Education. Abuja: UNESCO Office.

Olorunmola, S. O. (2008). Ethical Resolution for Enhancing Administrative Effectiveness indicators in Secondary Schools. A Seminar Paper Presented at University of Ilorin on 24th April 2008.

Olatunji, D. A. (2010). *Quality Assurance Indicators in Nigerian Education.* Offa: Adex Concepts.

Oyedeji, N. B. (2012). *Management in Education: Principles and Practices.* Lagos: Aras Press.

Padua, R. N. (2003). International Higher Education Quality Assurance Practices: Situating the Philippine System. *Journal of Philippine Higher Education Quality Assurance,* 1(1).

PACU (2012). Quality Assurance Framework from PACU Academic Management Seminar Series 2012-2013, url: http://pacu.org.ph/wp2/wp-content/uploads/2013/06/Quality-Assurance-Framework-CHED-PACU.pdf

Pijano, C. V. (2010). Quality Assurance and Accreditation: The Philippine Experience, Japan-ASEAN Information Package Seminar, retrieved from: http://www.niad.ac.jp/n_kokusai/pdf/13_no17_paascu_abstract_e.pdf, date accessed: September 29, 2015.

Sofoluwe, A. O. (2011). Quality Assurance Mechanisms in Nigerian Universities. *International Research Journals of Science Management 4* (1) 1 – 10.

Sofoluwe, A. O. (2005). Influence of Managerial Behaviours on Academic Staff Effectiveness of Nigerian Universities. *Abuja Journal of Administration 2* (1) 126 – 141.

Yusuf, L. A. (2006). Examination Malpractice in Nigeria: Causes and Management Strategies. *Ilorin Researcher 4* (1) 44 – 50.

2

Quality School Environment for Qualitative Learners' Performance in Nigerian Schools

Godfrey O. Ebohon, Harrison G. Ugbijeh & Michael Ademola

Abstract

This paper discussed quality school environment for qualitative learners' performance in Nigerian schools. This discourse was based on the premise that the environment is a significant factor in determining the academic performance in schools. To this end, corruption, policy formulation implementation, Nigerian constitution, politicization of administrative heads, social status of teaching profession and attitude to work by teachers were identified as the contending issues. The paper therefore concluded that all principal actors of learning, which are teachers, learners and the environment, must be cooperatively organized as well as funded to achieve the desired goals, while recommending that government should ensure good learning environment at all levels.

Key Words: *Quality, School Environment, Qualitative Learners' Performance, Nigerian Schools*

Introduction

Education is often considered as one the means of passing wisdom, experiences, achievement and other activities of the past generations to the young ones. According to Omoruyi and Osayande (2013), the essence of such transmission is to ensure continuity in knowledge acquisition that can promote growth in all aspects of human endeavour. Each generation leaves behind a cumulative wealth of experience, knowledge, values, skills, aptitude and attitude for succeeding generations. These are to be passed onto other generations in order to promote knowledge acquisition that can facilitate transformation for societal growth and development.

Today, it is no longer news that the issue of poor academic performance of students in Nigeria has been of much concern to government at all levels: federal, state and local governments, parents, teachers and even the students themselves.

There seems to be a sustained public outcry over students' poor performance in public examinations. The public worries are caused by high rate of academic failures among Nigerian students in national examinations such as the West Africa Examination Council (WAEC), the National Examination Council (NECO) National Board for Technical Education (NBTE), Unified Tertiary Matriculation Examination (UTME) and the Nigerian Law School Examination etc. What is really responsible for the backward trend in Nigerian educational system? Any attempt at finding possible answer to this question, would leave one with mirages of problems. Thus, what quickly comes to mind often

19

as one of the responsible factors for poor state of students' performances in this country is the level of quality in the school environment.

The quality of education not only depends on the teachers' ability to perform their duties in the classroom, but also in the effective coordination of the school environment. The physical characteristics of the school have a variety of effects on teachers, students, the learning outcome and learning process. Poor lighting, noise, location of the school, seat arrangement in the class, poor eyesight and poor learning make teaching and learning difficult. Poor maintenance and ineffective ventilation systems lead to poor health among students, which leads to poor academic performance and high rates of absenteeism in the school system. According to Strange and Banning (2001), these factors can adversely affect students' behaviour and lead to higher levels of frustration among teachers and poor learning attitude among students.

The school is the complex set of physical, geographical, biological, social and political conditions that surround an individual or an organism and that ultimately determine (his) its form and the nature of (his) its survival. The environment influences how people live and how societies develop. An extensive amount of research has linked a positive school environment to higher test scores, graduation rates and attendance rates. Every school environment should have conducive atmosphere which would make every student feel relaxed and secure. This is because the physical quality of every school can make negative or positive impacts on students, teachers as well as the learning process (Nebo, Akaeze and Ishaku, 2014).

This study is looking at the school environment as a vital learning place to the educational system with a great impact on teaching and learning at any level that will contribute to great academic performances of learners.

The Concept of Quality School Environment

Quality is referred to as the standard of what is on ground when compared to other things, especially to show how good or bad it is. Quality now becomes a prerequisite for achieving the fundamental goal that is set for educational attainment in schools through the medium of input processes for learners cognitive, affective and psychomotor domains. The overall responsibility of a school environment is to ensure enhanced standard within the system to encourage the learners and the teachers for possible school maintenance of set minimum standards that is widely acceptable judging by the academic performance of learners.

The learning environment is a vital part of the educational system and has a great impact on teaching and learning at any level of education. According to Abdulwahab and Ibrahim (2010), an environment can be likened to "Black Box" and "Engine House" that somehow produce or fail to produce a particular valued educational objective. It is believed that no matter how beautiful and well framed our educational policies are, their fulfillment and attainment of the overall goals and objectives of the educational domains depends largely on the environment within which such policies operate. Quality school environment comprises of a wide range of educational concepts. Among these concepts are physical setting, psychological environment which is created through social contexts and numerous instructions. According to Nebo, Akaeze and Ishaku (2014), the physical environment of school buildings and school grounds are key factors in the overall health and safety of students, staff, and visitors. School buildings and grounds must be designed and maintained to be free of health and safety hazards and to promote learning.

It is believed that a positive or quality school environment is linked to higher test scores, graduation and attendance rates. That is, effective and highly qualified teachers with high expectations for students and good teaching conditions have been a factor to strong academic performance in multiple studies. Peer support for achievement oriented behaviours, such as studying or participating in class, is also strongly tied to positive school climate and academic achievement. Take for instance, a classroom that is overcrowded, or large as the case may be or a classroom that is not properly furnished or where the furniture is so rough; a school with poor lighting system or a school environment that is so polluted with carbon monoxide, when all these factors are inconsistent with the proper school environment, students academic performance will definitely drop. In view of the above, Lyons (2001) opined that these factors can affect the behavior of students adversely, leading to high levels of frustration among teachers and lower jobs satisfaction. All these factors interact to hinder the learning process and perpetuate the shortage of teachers.

According to Aremu and Bulus (2014), some of the entrances and environs of most school in Nigeria today are highly repellent with old dilapidated structures, inadequate teaching- learning facilities such as lecture theatres and classrooms. In most cases, the available classrooms and halls are grossly inadequate and overcrowded thus creating an unconducive atmosphere for teaching and learning. Environment of this nature becomes ill-motivating to both the teachers and the learners. The resultant effect is low output in students' performance.

Students' Academic Performance

This is the outcome of learning or education. It is the extent to which students have achieved the educational goals. This cannot be seen unless measured by or through examination or continuous assessment. According to Ward, Stocker and Murray-ward (1996), there is no general agreement on how it is best tested or which aspects are most important procedurally when measuring students' performance.

Whatever has been adduced for students poor or good performance still leaves much to be desired. A lot have been done in order to understand the influence of students and school characteristics on test scores. Students' achievement variables aggregated to the school level have been used greatly to describe the school output, while variables describing aggregation of properties of classrooms within schools have been studied more or less in school analyses.

Large classes are often perceived as one of the major obstacles to ensuring quality education outcome. In spite of this, large classes have become unavoidable reality in Nigerian schools today. This is as a result of inadequate funding and absence of political will to provide a sufficient number of teachers, schools and classrooms that will ensure good performance of students. But the truth is that students' academic performances have nothing to do with large class. According to Shaaba (2011), the fact still remains, perhaps because many assume that learning occurs in proportion to class size such that the smaller the class, the more students learn. However, research shows that class size does not automatically correlate with students learning. Students in large classes can learn just as well as those in small ones. What counts is not the size of the class, but the quality of the teaching. Evidence shows that students place emphasis on the quality of teaching than class size (UNESCO 2006:1).

Quality school environment provides for conducive teaching and learning process. In general, for students to achieve academic success they must attend and be engaged in school; and school environment can influence both attendance and engagement. Quality school environment will encourage school discipline policies that emphasize relational or restorative, as opposed to punitive, justice and are considered clear, fair and consistently enforced by students are related to higher student attendance to class rates and engagement. Relational responses to students' negative behaviours should be encouraged such that sensitive, individualized and emphasized character strengths as means of preventing future misbehavior, a common practice within schools with positive climate. This can be achieved when responses rely upon staff members' positive relationship with students to understand the current situation and be positioned as trusted mentors in the students' eyes. A quality school environment presupposes that the personnel and materials on ground should be such that can project positive students achievement in their academic performances, vis-à-vis policies and protocols that must ensure that students are given adequate protections like food, sanitation, safe water supply, healthy air, good electricity supply, safe play ground, violence prevention and emergency response, among other issues that relate to the physical environment of the schools. With all these in place, students' performances will be in the increase.

Qualitative Education

The right to quality education is at the very heart of UNESCO'S mission and by implication very fundamental to member states like Nigeria. Given the general need for quality education everywhere and considering the shortage of educational facilities in Nigeria, the issue of qualitative education becomes quite topical. Quality in education requires a change in attitudes and psychological orientation of educational administrators and teachers who are the direct beneficiaries of qualitative change; and the client of the educational industry, namely, parents and employers in both government and private sectors of the economy. According to Bassey (2005), qualitative change is more basic and fundamental; it affects the very essence of the educational system. It requires more than a decree or a legislative instrument to effect a qualitative change in education.

Quality in education does not only consist of good teaching, but also good learning. This is influenced by the conditions obtained in the school, health nutrition, parents' attitude, living levels of families, the cultural and religious views prevailing in a community and above all, the goals of education. In the National Policy on Education (2004), the Nigerian philosophy of education is based on the following:

- The development of the individual into a sound and effective citizen
- The full integration of the individual into community
- The provision of equal access to educational opportunities for all citizens of the country at the primary, secondary and tertiary levels both inside and outside the formal school system.

The policy on qualitative education should be defined in a clear term for the educational institutions that are expected to produce or develop the individual into a sound and effective citizen. An individual who has an intellectual understanding of his cultural roots in the country's (Nigeria) environment should be aware of his political right under the constitution, his civic responsibility and role in the family. He must also be an individual that will be appreciative of the direction of social change and development taking place around him and adequately prepare to contribute his quota to the areas of national development to which the education he had acquired has best fitted him.

Government should also be aware that working towards qualitative education is not a cheap exercise, either in terms of the human development or materials and fiscal resources. The school environment at this point becomes the melting pot for a qualitative education in Nigeria. This process therefore requires adequate attention from all stakeholders in the society as education is globally recognized as the nerve centre that is indispensible to any nation. Thus, there is the need to readdress the challenges confronting this sub-system for optimum competence, quality and productivity required for the desired development sought for as failure will continually lead to retrogression.

Factors Militating Against Quality School Government in Nigeria

There is no doubt that quality school environment will help the Nigerian nation to pursue qualitative education that will in turn help in the high performance of students in their academic pursuit.

It is a general belief that education or quality education is conceived as the primary instrument within a state for fulfilling the hopes and aspirations of the people. In Nigeria today, there are so many factors that have marred the achievement of quality school environment that would have helped in the betterment of qualitative education in Nigeria. The most critical amongst these myriad of problems are:

- Corruption
- Policies formation/implementation
- The Nigerian constitution
- The politicization of administrative head
- Social status
- Attitude towards work.

Corruption: This is perhaps, the most troubling issues in Nigeria as of today, not because it is new, but because it has refused to yield to all manners of medication. According to Ebohon (2015), corruption has exerted greater costs on the development process of Nigeria in these ways: one, it weakens the institutional capacities of the state by eroding public confidence and promoting inefficiency. Two, it causes severe distortion in the efficient allocation of resources and often manifests as a form of re-distribution of money from the poor to the rich.

Today, this evil has become the epitome of whatever is right particularly in the public sector. Corruption is now synonymous with Nigerians. People are greedy; they want more and more of everything, so much so that when construction work is awarded, it is done shabbily and with this, the project does not survive the test of time. Corruption has now become a capsule that has encapsulated the system so much that in all facets of the lives of Nigeria, corruption is seen. That is why the lack-of-fund syndrome has become a national anthem. Even the little that is provided, the school administrators do not manage it well. The resultant effect of this are always lack of facilities, dilapidated structure and lack of capacity building in Nigerian institutions.

Policy: Policy can be defined as a framework of action that embraces both the process and the end result thus providing guideline to nations towards achieving defined goals.

Policies formulation/ implementation: This should be people oriented to provide a universal access to quality education for the people to attain full potentials and contribute to the entire process of the development of an independent and integrated personality. This encompasses training and acquisition of special skills, knowledge attitudes and values needed by an individual to be responsible and which would enable him to contribute his own quota to the growth of the society of which he belongs. Nigerian educational policy today is still dancing round the colonial era, where educational pursuit was to be closer to the white and not for skills improvement.

The government constantly changes our educational policies without involving educational experts. As a result, implementation becomes a problem. Ministers of education in this country are very good at copying ideas and foreign policies from various developed countries across the globe without first considering what the impact will be. They do that often without studying and knowing what it has cost such countries to formulate and operate such policies. According to Uya (2011), the present state of education in Nigeria is antithetical to the country's quest for good governance, sustainable development and impartation of skills needed by an individual to live a meaningful life as well as to adjust to his immediate environment and the ultimate world he finds himself.

The Nigerian Constitution: The Nigerian constitution puts education under the concurrent list. This implies that federal, state and local governments can legislate on education as long as it is not inconsistent with the constitution. This action has brought the problem of funding and major conflict in the management and administration of education at all levels in Nigeria. The constitution had created a problem on the funding of education, because the federal government cannot dictate to the state government how to manage primary, secondary and tertiary schools within its jurisdiction. The resultant effect of this today is what is now known as either educational backward state or educational disadvantaged state.

Politicization of administrative head: The day to day running of these schools is in the hands of the administrators. Presently in Nigeria, appointment of heads of educational institutions, from the headmasters to the vice-chancellors, has been politicized. They are appointed or recommended based on their political party's affiliations. This has adversely affected the learning environment, because most of these administrators mismanage the funds meant for educational development of schools in their care. And like the proverbial bird dancing by the road side, their drummers are always within the corridors of power to provide protections from being prosecuted.

Social Status: The non recognition of teaching as a highly rewarding profession by the Nigerian society has also become a major factor of discouragement for most people who desire to become professional teachers. The world conference of organization of Teaching Profession of 1996 as reported by Osa- Edeh (2012) observes that the status of teaching profession in Africa is low and this is coupled with inadequate recruitment. Recruitment exercise has been heavily politicized both in federal and state owned schools. In recruitment exercises, most of the Council chairmen, law makers, officials of Federal Character Commission and others do insist their candidates be employed whether they are qualified or not. This is not helping the system. Alternatively, some prefer to use teaching as a stepping stone, while seeking for a greener pasture (Aremu & Bulus, 2014). This unhealthy perception of the society as well as unethical reactions of some people within the profession towards teaching further compounds its low rating and pose a big challenge of entry into it. Those who are motivated to go into it are looked down as not being well to do or low in intelligence.

Attitude towards work: Attitude makes a difference; it can affect whether you attain a goal or give up; whether a tragic event brings out the best in you or the worst. Ovwigbo (2008) stated that attitude is how individual or group considers and reacts to work, his views and reactions towards colleagues, superiors, contents of the job and the condition of work. It also includes the disposition of individual or group towards another person, group, idea, policy or event.

In Nigeria today, there are more of negative attitudes towards work, which has led to what is now known as poor maintenance culture. Majority of us handle our personal properties and belongings carefully. But as long as that thing belongs to government, we are no longer careful. While we maintain our individually acquired properties, those of the government are left to rot away. Even where they are maintained the cost of maintenance is so high. Nigerians must seek to development positive attitude to work so that sustainability of the country's development will be evident. Government work, properties and responsibility should be carried like our own personal belongings instead of the shoulder carrying style.

Conclusion

Quality school environment for qualitative learners' performance in Nigerian schools is achievable if adequate attention is paid to the issues discussed so far in this discourse by the relevant stakeholders in the society. Education is the bedrock of any given society, as well as a vital tool for nation building. Development is found to be linked to the quality of education of a given society or system. This, therefore, has made education an issue in global discourse. For Nigeria to achieve quality in education, all principal actors of learning which are teachers, learners and the environment must be cooperatively organized as well as funded.

Recommendations

Based on the conclusion above, the following points are therefore recommended as necessities for the improvement in the academic performances of Nigerian learners.

- Government at various levels must be ready to find a good learning environment and teaching aids that will facilitate the successful development of the overall goals and objectives of the learners' educational domains (cognitive, affective and psychomotor). Unless this is done urgently, hope for quality human capacity development for Nigeria's future may remain an illusion.
- There should be motivation from the part of the administrators and government; because positive attitude change is a responsibility that employee must proactively work towards. Therefore, there should be a concerted effort to making sure that institutions develop globally. The importance of motivation is that it gets the individual started and moving towards developing a positive attitude that keeps him or her going.
- Since every school curriculum contents contain set of values expected to be transmitted to the younger ones through education, such curriculum contents in the public and private schools should reflect more on areas related to development such as peace promotion, security,

honesty, transparency, accountability and tolerance. With all these in place, corruption will be reduced to its barest minimum.

- Government at all levels should concentrate on restructuring our primary school system, considering the structure-collapse of Nigerian education system. If a structure or building is faulty, the engineers start from the base. Primary education remains the foundation upon which all other levels of education are deeply or firmly rooted. Thus, primary education in this country demands better attention of all the stakeholders in all ramifications in order to prevent other levels (secondary and tertiary levels) leaning on it from a complete ruin.

- Government at all levels should ensure that qualified, intelligent, competent and hardworking teachers are employed to take charge and teach at all levels of our educational institutions. This would ensure effective management of educational programmes and resources directed towards meeting the expectations and needs of the society through effective teaching, planning, monitoring and evaluation of all the learning processes.

References

Abdulwahab, R. S. and Ibrahim, F. N. (2010). Effects of school environment as a determining factor to learning: Implication on the growing child. *Journal of Association of Organism Educators*, 7 (1) 189-194.

Aremu, O. D. and Bulus, G. B. (2014). Teacher education in Nigeria and the prevailing challenges. *Kontagora Journal of Education* (KONJE) 14 (1), 14-19.

Bassey, J. E. (2006). Qualitative education as an instrument in nation building. *Adult and Non-formal Education in Nigeria: Emerging Issues,* Nigeria National council for Adult Education (NNCAE), 118-126.

Ebohon, G. O. (2015). Corruption in Nigerian society, education and technology: The Nexus. *World Educators Forum*, 7(1), 231-238.

Lyons, B. J. (2001). *Do school facilities really impact a child's education? An introduction to the issues.* Available at @ sdpl.coe.uga.educ./.../ Lyons. html.

Nebo, J., Akaeze, P. and Ishaku, D. (2014). Quality environment and academic performance in Nigerian schools. Being a paper presented at the 4th Biennial National Conference, organized by COEASU, North/Middle Belt Zone, held at Federal College of Education, Zuba, Abuja from 13th – 17th October, 2014.

Omoruyi, P. F. E. O. and Osayande, E. I. (2013). Appropriate strategies for enhancing teachers' competence for quality teaching/performance in the 21st century Nigeria. *Nigeria Journal of Adult and Lifelong learning,* 2(1), 135-145.

Osa-Edeh, G. I. (2012). The role of teacher education in Nigeria. *Journal of Education Research and Development*, 7(3), 242-246.

Ovwigbo, M. Y. (2008). *Practice guide to management of organization in Nigeria*. Benin City: Justice-Jeeo Press and Publisher Limited.

Shaaba, M. M. (2011). Promoting students' learning in large group classroom teaching. Being a paper presented at the First Maiden Staff Seminar organized by staff Seminar Organizing Committee, Federal College of Education, Kontagora, Niger State, 23rd August, 2011.

Strange, C. C. and Banning, J. H. (2001). *Educating by design, creating campus learning that works.* San Francisco, C A: Jossey-Bass.

UNESCO (2006). *Practical tips for teaching large class.* A teacher's guide.

Uya, E. O. (2011). Governance education and the state of the nation. Being a paper presented at Mary Hanney Girls Secondary School Golden Jubilee Anniversary, 5th November, 2011.

Ward, A. Stocker H. W. and Murray-Ward, M. (1996). *Achievement and ability tests- definition of the domain, educational measurement 2*, University Press of America. pp 2-5.

3

Quality Girl-Child Education and the Actualization of Vision 20:2020 Objectives in Nigeria

Rahmat M. Tinja, Tijani O. Abdulgaffar & Regina N. Azunwena *Ph.D*

Abstract

The global worry about female/women education is premised on the increasing demand for over all societal development. Thus, showing no concern about female education is building a bad society characterized by armed robbery and other social vices. No matter how beautiful and articulated a developmental vision is packaged, without quality education devoid of gender affiliation, it would not see the light of the day. It is on this foundation that this chapter discusses the place of quality education for girl child in the attainment of vision 20:2020 objectives in Nigeria. Certain challenges confronting girl child education were examined. In view of this, the paper concludes with recommendations such as creation of awareness through media on the importance of girl child education for national development.

Key Words: *Quality, Girl Child Education and Vision 20:2020 objectives*

Introduction

The world past and present experiences have shown that education is a pre-condition to social, economic and political development of any nation in this era of globalization. It is the bedrock and only instrument for socio-economic and technological survival yet known in the world of mankind. This is why global attentions are on education for all to liberate the minds of the citizens and empower them for a fruitful and harmonious living. However, despite the due recognition given to education, there are issues that have become universal concern in educational provision for the citizenry. Thus, the issues of access, quality education and gender imbalance focusing on girl child education remain an educational discourse. Girl-child education is highly inevitable most especially now that a target has been set for overall national development. Thus, Nigeria's inspiration to be among the 20 biggest economies by the year 2020 becomes a mirage without quality education for all. Therefore, the main aim of this chapter is to discuss what constitute quality education, Girl-child education and the importance of Girl-child education in the achievement of human development objectives encapsulated in vision 20:2020 in Nigeria with a view to suggest the way forward for improvement.

Quality Education

The term "quality education" expresses the different or differences between two things of the same characteristics. Accordingly, Abubakar (2010) opines that "relative terms such as worth, better, value, superior, acceptable are applied to judge quality. Dimson in Tijani, Musa and Abubakar (2010) visualizes quality as the degree of excellence or level in a product or a grade of achievement or standard against which to judge others or the degree of worth or fitness for purpose". Besides, quality education can be seen as the process of imparting worth-while knowledge, skills, attitudes and values which make the individual learners become useful members of the society. Quality education is all embracing phenomenon comprising the input, process and output. Musa (2010) identifies the criteria used in assessing the quality of education as follows: the school enrolments (a measure of access), quality (education being available to all sub-groups); retention rates; the number of teachers available (teacher-pupil ratio); and their qualifications; quality and efficiency of administrative structures and personnel; budgetary allocations to education; availability of classrooms; library and laboratories; availability of text books and instructional materials; examination results; examination and administration malpractices; employers assessment of the performance of graduates; work place behaviour and output.

From the foregoing, one is convinced that issues of quality in education enterprise is indeed all embracing that could not be based on one parameter assessment. No wonder therefore that Igwe in Dimson cited by Tijani, Musa and Abubakar (2010) describes quality in education as "elusive". Achieving quality education in any given society largely depends on the existing socio-cultural values of the nation.

Girl Child Education

Education is undoubtedly a fundamental right of al citizens not only in Nigeria but the world over irrespective of sex, age and economic status of the citizens. This underscores the fact that education is generally recognized as a core factor of development. Girl Child education refers to the process of imparting qualitative and quantitative knowledge and competences in female siblings with a view to enhancing their future life careers as basis to contribute their quota to national transformation. Girl chid education covers adequate training which goes beyond writing, reading and calculation, but over all knowledge and skills which bothers on the development of their total capacities intellectually, physically, socially, economically, technologically, politically; and other wise, all in attempt to prepare them for future challenges. The global interest in girl child education is premised on the fact that girls of today are potential women, house makers, house managers and the future custodians of societal values, therefore, losing sight or concern on their education points to future disaster.

According to Davies in Okenwa (2009) women constitute more than fifty percent of adult population in many countries of the world, but it is disheartening that majority of them are illiterate and under-educated even though majority of them are intelligent and hardworking. Gone were the days when female education is seen as irrelevant. In this modern economy, Girl-child education is increasingly seen as a necessary impetus to nation building. Therefore, Okam (2002) affirms that Girl should have equal access to education as the boys. He emphasizes that the training of girls for the purpose of fulfilling their roles as women should form a common "core" curriculum to which all female children should be exposed. The implication of this assertion is that for female children/women to carry out their traditional roles or functions in the family efficiently and effectively, they need appreciable degree of education, hence the need for quality Girl-child education is not a misplaced priority.

Vision 20:2020 Objectives

It is a known fact that for a country to develop there must be certain plan in form of programme and policies statement to be vigorously pursued to bring about the desired change. This must be first conceived in form of a vision. Thus, a vision can be summarised to be a prediction of the type of future one desires, that of course, has a link with the present situation. Bulus (2010) views it as a description or prediction of the future that stems from the present to reach the presumed forecast. It is an effort made for strategic planning that identifies goals and objectives and the means and methods to achieve them. Having stated this, vision 20:2020 focuses on world development plan to foster development from all angles. Nigeria's vision 20:2020 is an economic and political frame work to place the country among the 20 most developed countries in the world in the year 2020.

It is a comprehensive approach to stimulate socio-economic growth in the country. To realize this, Nigerian government has put in place certain programmes such as the implementation of Universal Basic Education, Millennium Development Goals and the 7-point Agenda of the previous administration. Thus, accomplishment of these programmes would lay a sound foundation for this vision. According to Ndubisi and Abimbola in Tijani, Musa and Abubakar (2010) twenty nine thematic areas are identified as scope of this vision covering different sectors of the Nigerian economy. These are:- Agriculture, business, environment, corporate governance and social responsibility, culture and tourism, education, employment opportunities, energy, finance sectors, foreign policy, health, human development, judiciary and rule of law, Niger Delta and regional development, manufacturing, media and communication, security, science, technology and innovation, solid minerals, sport, trade and commerce, transport, urban and rural development, water and sanitation.

It is a desire by the Nigerian government to be the largest economics in the world able to consolidate its leadership role in Africa and establish itself as a significant player in the global economic and political arena (FRN, 2008).The vision was predicted on the premise of the prospects of the Nigeria's economic realities that require prudent management of the resources to transform Nigeria into a greater power by the year 2020 (Bulus, 2010). To achieve the above, Bulus believes that Nigeria will need to enhance her socio-economic and political development performance based on the following parameters:-

- A peaceful, harmonious and stable democracy;
- a sound, stable and globally competitive economic;
- adequate infrastructure service that support the full mobilization of all economic sector;
- modern and vibrant education system which provides for every Nigerian the opportunity and facility to achieve his maximum potential and provides the country with adequate and competent manpower;
- a healthy sector that supports and sustains a life expectancy of not less than70 years and reduces to the barest maximum, the burden of infectious diseases such as malaria, HIV/AIDS and other diseases;
- a modern technologically enable agricultural sector that fully exploits the vast agricultural resources of the country;
- ensure national food security and contributes significantly to foreign exchange earnings.

Based on the above exposition, the place of qualitative education is highly uncompromisable. It is a core determinant of the achievement of this human development goal. Therefore, government at all levels has to make effort beyond mere proclamation of education for all and building of empty structures. Adequate funding, provision of infrastructural facilities, employment of qualified and sufficient teachers, effective monitoring control, etc., should therefore be put in place as basic achievement mechanism to arrive at the much desired destination.

Girl Child Education and Vision 20:2020

The role of girl child education in achieving the objectives of this vision as identified above cannot be underestimated. This is because any country that neglects intellectual development of her teeming population would not smell social advancement, not to talk of experiencing it. Without any doubt, women occupy a strategic position in the society. They are the home managers, child bearers and custodians of socio-political and cultural values of any nation. Therefore, their exposure to formal education serves as impetus towards achieving the vision of this magnitude. Similarly, the Nigeria Education Research Development Council in Wasony (2009) asserts that women constitute half of the population......and permanent change is often best achieved through them. Moreover, the popular adage that "behind any successful man, there must be a woman" is a pointer to the significant role girl child education can play in the national transformation.

Quality child education prepares the child intellectually and socio-economically to contribute her talent, time and resources to nation building which constitutes the central focus of this vision. When girl child is exposed to a formal education, the socialization process of the Nigerian children which is essential in any meaningful development is assured. Education as an agent of social change is a medium through which girl child, having assumed adulthood, can participate actively on an equal footing with their male counterparts and meet the requirement of a diverse labour market and also defend and fight for their fundamental rights when violated. In the same vein, Aliyu in Wasony (2010) opines that "with the education of women, the education of children is assured. Because children come in contact with their mothers, they give the children home educational background on which the foundation of the school education is built".

The global demands of a modern world requires the nation to pay attention to training and development of its citizens irrespective of gender affiliation to attain national progress for which vision 20:2020 is hinged. Quality female education for all citizen helps in no small measure to determine the achievement of not only this vision, but any future developmental framework meant for the advancement of mankind as they interact with their socio-physical environment. Therefore, effort should be made by the Nigerian government at all levels to promote access and quality education for girl child or women for the benefits of all. Quality education for female children equips them for responsible womanhood. It is an assured medium of their economic empowerment which allows them to contribute their token towards achieving sustainable national development.

Challenges of Girl-Child Education

There has been a greater concern to promote female education in Nigeria. This informed her frequent educational reforms which are geared towards access to education by the citizens. However, many female children are out of school compared to the enrolment of their male counterparts most especially, in the northern part of the country. Available statistics on male-female enrolment reveals a proportion of 55.12% for male and 44.88% for female (National Statistics, 2005). There are several factors responsible for this; some of them are

a. Economic Challenges: Many people in Nigeria today live below poverty level. This has brought untold hardship to many families, despite the free nature of Universal Basic Education; some parents cannot afford sending send their male children to school and allow female to engage in one economic activity or the other to argument their financial status. A research conducted by Haruna and Mwada (2009) reveals that, out of the two hundred hawkers, fifty were male while 150 were female. This means that 150 female children were out of school to contribute to the economic status of their parents. Accordingly, Okenwa (2009) asserted that "in some families a daughter may be sacrificed to pay for an expensive education for the sons.

b. Cultural Challenges: Some people are still conserving the notice that girl child education is a mere wasting of resources. Since female children are expected to get married, their education would certainly end up in the kitchen. In addition, it is believed that educated women could be disrespectful to their husbands. Indabawa (2004) held that "the socio-cultural expectation of women and the priority given to the future roles as mothers and wives has strong negative bearing on their educational opportunities"

c. Religious Issues: Religion has certain influence in our daily activities. The belief of many Muslim with specific reference to the northern Nigeria is that Girl-child education (western) is a threat to Islamic religion. Therefore, for the fear of sexual harassment and unwanted pregnancy, they prefer marrying their female child at an early stage. In this point of view, Jiya in Okenwa (2009) opined that people hold the belief that young girl should marry early especially in northern part of Nigeria. In the same vein, Okenwa argued that some parents prefer Islamic education for their daughters for fear that western education promotes values and behaviours of women which are contrary to Islamic cultural norms such as exposing their hair and body, etc.

d. Domestic Activities: Another factor militating against Girl-child education has to do with household task. The young girls are seen as helpmates for mothers. They are kept out of school to care for their young siblings or anyone who is sick and also run the home as a mother (Okenwa, 2009).

Conclusion

This paper has considered girl child education as an instrument for the realization of vision 20:2020. In Nigeria, the access to quality education by all citizens is a precondition for national development most especially, in a democratic and diverse cultural values society such as ours. Therefore, for Nigeria to be among 20 most developed economic countries in the year 2020, socio-cultural challenges responsible for the imbalance in gender educational enrolment must be tackled with all seriousness it deserves. Equally, quality education for the citizen at all level would serve as added advantage to her social transformation.

Recommendations

From the foregoing, the following recommendations are put forward for consideration:

- To ease the economic problem of girl education, government should provide free uniform, reading and writing materials for the female children. This would motivate them to develop interest in schooling.
- Religious leaders should emphasize the important of girl child education to their members.
- Necessary awareness should be created by the government at all levels on the media about the relevance of girl child education to socio-economic and political development of the nation.
- Community leaders and educated elites should collaborate to organize adult education classes for drop out female child/women.

References

Abubakar, A. U. (2010). Enhancing Teacher Quality through Qualitative Teacher Education. A Paper Presented at the 7th National Conference of Primary and Tertiary Teacher Education Association (PATTEAN).

Bulus, I. (2010). Technical Teacher Education: A Road Map to Achieving Vision 20:2020. A Convocation Lecture delivered at the Federal College of Education (Technical) Potiskum.

Federal Republic of Nigeria (2008). Concept of Nigerian's Vision 20:2020 Abuja: Government Press.

Grace, I. L. (2009). Challenges and Future of Women in Nigeria. A Paper Presented at the Annual National Conference of the Association of Nigerian Teachers (ASSONT). Benue State University.

Haruna, A. & Mwada, M. (2009). Causes and Effects of Hawking among Children in Potiskum Local Government Area of Yobe State. *Journal of Languages, Arts and Social Sciences Education.* 1(1). 45-55.

Indabawa, S. A. (2004). Some Socio-economic Determinants of Girl Child Involvement in Education in Nigeria. Unpublished M.Ed Thesis, Faculty of Education, University of Ibadan.

Musa, B. (2010). Quality Education for Sustainable Development in Nigeria. *Journal of Qualitative Education.* 1(1), 55-67.

Okam, C.C. (2002). *Reading in New Development in Education: Issues and Insights.* Jos: Deka Publication.

Okenwa, O. M. (2009). Social Cultural Factors impeding the Participation of Women in Higher Education in Nigeria. *Knowledge Review: A Multidisciplinary Journal.* 19(4), 68-79.

Tijani, O. A., Musa, Y. I. & Abubakar, M. A. (2010). Social Studies Education: A Distinctive Value for the Attainment of Vision 20:2020 in Nigeria. *Approaches in International Journal of Research Development,* 4 (1), 92-95.

4

School Environmental Factors and Students' Academic Achievement in Civic Education in Aba Education Zone

Ngozika A. Oleforo *Ph.D*, Petronilla O. Owen, Frank O. Udukeke & Angela E. Abba

Abstract

*T*he purpose of the study was to determine the relationship between school environmental factors and students' academic achievement in civic education in Aba educational zone. The correlational research design was adopted for the study. Instrument entitled School Environment Questionnaire (SEQ) was used for data collection. The sample was 112 principals and teachers drawn from the total population of 2001 teachers and principals. Three research questions and three hypotheses were posed to guide the study. Pearson's Product Moment Correlation (PPMC) was employed for data analysis in order to provide answers to the research questions. The findings reveal that a substantial relationship exist between library facilities and students' academic achievement in civil education, very strong relationship between class size and students' academic achievements; and moderate positive relationship exist between seats/desks and students' academic achievement in civic education in Aba Educational Zone. It was concluded among others that the lesser the number of students in a classroom, the more academic performance will improve. Among the recommendations made is that the Abia State Ministry of Education should ensure that schools in Aba Educational Zone are well provided for in terms of library facilities, seats and desks.

Key Words: *School environmental factors and academic achievement.*

Introduction

Civic education, as one of the new subjects introduced at the secondary school level in Nigeria, is very important. It plays a significant role in the development of a nation. This is because the development of any nation hinges on good and effective citizens. No nation can thrive beyond the civic and traits demonstrated by her citizens. Civic education is concerned with the development of values, social norms, skills and democratic ideas in the citizens. Utulu (2011) stated that civic education becomes very relevant since it essentially seeks to introduce learners to the process of democratic socialization by promoting support for democratic behaviours and values among citizens. The introduction of civic education has been extolled by many stakeholders of education. However, for the laudable objective of introducing the subject to be achieved, it must be taught in a conducive environment.

Environment means everything that surrounds an individual. To Oniyama and Amroma (1998), environment means physical, ecological, economic and socio-cultural surrounding conditions which influence an individual. Arising from the above definition of environment, we can derive different types of environment. They include; home environment, social environment and school environment. The school environment, which include; classroom, laboratories, libraries technical workshops, teaching methods, seats and desks and so on are the variables that affect students' academic achievement. Hence, the school environment remains an important area that should be studied and well-managed to enhance students' performance.

The issue of poor academic achievement of students in Nigeria has been of much concern to various stakeholders such as government, parents, teachers and students. Ajao (2001) stated that the quality of education does not only depend on the quality of teachers, but also on the effective coordination of the school environment. The extent to which students' learning can be enhanced depending on some school environmental variables such as library facilities, class size and seats/desks.

Library is an essential service in the school. Sanders (2006) maintained that the educational process functions in the world of books. The school library provides comprehensive services to students and teachers in all discipline in order to enhance academic performance. The chief purpose of a school library is to make available to the students books, periodicals, films, work of arts and other produced materials. The importance of library has been reiterated by the Federal Government of Nigeria (2013) when she stated that every State Ministry of Education needs to provide fund for the establishment of libraries in her educational institution and to train librarian and library assistants. As a resource, it occupies a central and primary place in any school system. Ola (2000) found that well-equipped library is a major quality which enhances good learning and achievement of high educational standard. However, Shodium (2007) argued that school libraries may not be effective if they are not well-equipped with up-to-date books and materials.

In another development, the number of learners in a class to a large extent determines the quality of learning that would take place. In recognition of this fact, Federal Government of Nigeria (2013) recommended that the teacher-student ratio should be 1.35. Buttressing the importance of a manageable class size, the Nigeria Conference of Principals of Secondary Schools (NCOPSS) recommended a maximum of forty (40) students per class for better control and effective management. In this light, Ezewu (1997) found that interaction influence on learning vary according to the size of the group when a classroom is overcrowded, learning will be frustrated. Overcrowding implies too many students in a classroom or learning environment. In most urban schools, classes are overcrowded due to insufficient classroom blocks. Overcrowding of the classroom has effect on learning. One of such effects, is that, the teacher will be unable to give adequate attention to the learners. Since the learners are too many, those needing special attention will not be recognized and attended to. This affects students learning adversely.

Furthermore, classroom seats and desks are major infrastructures that facilitate students' academic achievement in secondary schools. Odili (2003) stated that inadequacy of seats and writing desks is one of the problems militating against effective classroom organization and management when students sit on the floor during civic education class; their achievement could be affected negatively. The academic achievement of students represents performance outcomes that indicate the extent to which a person has accomplished specific goals that were the focus of activities in instructional environment. Observation in recent times seems to show that students' achievement in the secondary schools in Nigeria is on the decline in various subjects including civic education. Hence the researchers were interested in investigating the relationship between school environment factors and students' academic achievement in civic education.

Research Questions

The following research questions guided the study.

- What is the relationship between availability of library facilities and SS2 students' achievement in civic education Aba North Educational Zone?
- What is the relationship between class size and SS2 students' achievement in civic education Aba North Educational Zone?
- What is the relationship between Seats/Desks and SS2 students' achievement in civic education Aba Educational Zone?

Research Methodology

The correlational research design was adopted for the study. Correlation research is mainly concerned with achieving a fuller understanding of a complexity of phenomenon such as behavioural pattern by studying the relationship between the variables which the researcher hypothesized as being related (Cohen, Manion and Morrison, 2004). Correlational research became appropriate for the study because the research intended to investigate a presumed relationship between school environment factors and students' academic performance in civic education in Aba Educational Zone. The study was carried out in Aba Education Zone of Abia state situated in South East of Nigeria. The population of the study comprised all 2001 teachers and principals in public secondary schools in Aba education zone of Abia State. The sample comprised one hundred and twelve principals and teachers drawn from the ninety-five (95) public secondary schools in Aba educational zone by means of stratified random sampling technique.

The research instrument which was entitled School Environmental Factors Questionnaire (SEFQ) was used to obtain information for the study. The instrument contained 30 items. The instrument was validated by three validates in the Department of Test and Measurement, University of Uyo. Cronbach's Alpha reliability formula was employed to determine the internal consistency of the instrument and a reliability coefficient of .77 was obtained. The Pearson Product Moment Correlation (PPMC) was used in answering the research questions. The research questions were answered in terms of direction of the relationship thus: from -1 to -0 was negative relationship; and from 0 to +1 was positive relationship. The magnitude of the relationship was interpreted using the following descriptors of correlation values by Davis (1971) as presented by Thomas (2007) and Essien (2014): .00 to .09 = negligible; .10 to .29 = weak; .30 to 49 = moderate; .50 to 69 = substantial .70 to 1 = very strong.

Results

The results of the study are presented according to the research questions 1-3.

Research Question One

What is the relationship between availability of library facilities and SS2 students' achievement in civic education in Aba Educational Zone?

Table 1: The PPMC Analysis of the Relationship between Availability of Library Facilities and SS2 Students' Achievement in Civic Education

n= 112

Variables	$\sum X$	$\sum X^2$	$\sum XY$	r	r^2
	$\sum Y$	$\sum Y^2$			
Library Facilities	4194	155358			
			145722	.63	.3969
Students Achievement	3932	138312			
Substantial positive relationship					

The analysis on Table 1 shows a correlation coefficient (r) of .63. This indicates that a substantial positive relationship exists between availability of library facilities and students' academic achievement. It implies that the more library facilities are made available for students use, the more their academic achievement will improve substantially. The strength of linear association (r^2) of .3969 implies that 39.69 percent of SS2 students' academic achievement in Abia Education Zone is associated to library facilities.

Research Question Two

What is the relationship between class size and SS2 students' achievement in civic education in Aba Educational Zone?

Table 2: The PPMC Analysis of the Relationship between Class Size and SS2 Students' Achievement in Civic Education.

n=112

Variables	$\sum X$	$\sum X^2$	$\sum XY$	r	r^2
	$\sum Y$	$\sum Y^2$			
Library Facilities	6964	45831			
			63118	.86	.73976
Students Achievement	7630	528688			
Very strong positive relationship					

Table 2 shows the PPMC analysis of the relationship between class size and SS2 students' academic achievement in civic education in Aba Education Zone. The analysis yielded a correlation coefficient of .86 which is described as a very strong positive relationship. This implies that the lesser the number of students in classroom, the higher the academic achievement will be. The strength of linear association between class size and SS2 students' academic achievement ($r^2 = .7396$) indicates that 73.96 percent of students' academic achievement is attributed to class size.

Research Questions Three

What is the relationship between seats/desks and SS2 students' achievement in civic education in Aba Educational Zone?

Table 3: PPMC Analysis of the Relationship between Class Size and SS2 Students' Achievement in Civic Education.

n=112

Variables	ΣX	ΣX^2	ΣXY	r	r^2
	ΣY	ΣY^2			
Library Facilities	3976	145264			
			139068	.48	.2304
Students Achievement	3918	138510			
Moderate positive relationship					

The analysis on Table 3 yielded a correlation coefficient(r) of .48. This shows a moderate positive relationship between availability of seats/desks in classroom and students' academic achievement in Aba Educational Zone. It means that academic achievement would improve moderately as more seats and desks are provided for use in the classroom by students. The analysis also reveals the strength of linear association (r^2) of .2304 which implies that availability of seats and desks would enhance students' academic achievement by 23.04 percent in Aba Educational Zone.

Discussion of Findings

The study reveals that a substantial positive relationship exists between availability of library facilities and students' academic achievement in Aba Educational Zone. This result is supported by the findings of Ola (2000) who found that well-equipped library is a major facility which enhances good learning and achievement of higher educational standard. The researchers wish to observe that availability of library facilities such as books, periodicals, journals, gazettes, internet resources among others can help to improve students' reading culture thus, enhancing their academic performance in civic education.

The study reveals that a very strong positive relationship exists between class size and students' academic achievement in civic education in Aba Educational Zone. This finding is in line with the finding of Ezewu (1997) who found that interaction influence on learning varies according to the size of the group. Overcrowded classrooms present too many distractions. There would be too much background noise. This distracts the attention of the learners and consequently affects students' academic achievement negatively. When the class size is too large, the teacher would not be able to give adequate attention to the learners. Since the learners are too many, those needing special attention may not be recognized and attended to. In this situation, some students engage in informal discussion, chatting, playing computer games and so on as the lesson is going on. However, when the class-size is small, the teacher will be able to carry each and every student along. Of course, this will enhance students' performance in civic education. It will help students to thoroughly acquaint themselves with the process of governance and how to be well-cultured individuals in the society.

Seats and desks have been found in the study to have a moderate positive relationship with students' academic achievement in civic education in Aba Educational Zone. This finding is corroborated by the findings of Inyang (2013) who found significant relationship between availability of classroom facilities and students' academic performance when seats and desks are available for students to seat on and write. Students learning become less-tedious as they comfortably take notes and complete their class work on time. However, when seats and desks are lacking in the classroom, learning would be frustrated as students will resort to sitting on widows and floor. Students will feel very uncomfortable as they will find it difficult to take notes, complete class work and maintain needed attention.

Conclusion

Based on the findings of the study, it was concluded that students achieve higher in civic education where library facilities are available and up-to-date. The lesser the number of students in a classroom, the more academic achievement in civic education will improve and finally, students in school where seats and desks are available for use, tend to achieve higher academically than their counterpart in schools where there are no seats and desks.

Recommendations

Based on the findings and conclusions, the following recommendations are made:

- Abia State Ministry of Education should ensure that schools in Aba Education Zone are well provided for in terms of library facilities, seats ad desks. This will make students feel comfortable as they engage in their learning activities. This will help to ensure that students' academic achievement is enhanced significantly in civic education.
- The Abia State Government through the Officials of the Ministry of Finance should ensure increased budgetary allocations to secondary schools in Aba Educational Zone. This will ensure that funds are made available to various schools for the acquisition of library facilities seats and desks.
- The Officials of the Abia State Ministry of Education should carryout regular supervision. This will enforce suitable and acceptable student-teacher ratio and make appropriate recommendations to the Government on how best to maintain suitable and acceptable student-teacher ratio. It will go a long way to ensure that students' achievement in civic education is considerably enhanced.

References
Adenipekum, O. (2010).Government Drives Tertiary Institutions to Develop New Teacher Education Programmes Vanguard, 29th April.

Azabanwan, C. (2010). Integrating Civic Education in school and Strategy for Implementation. *Nigerian Observer Online*, October 16.

Alao, A. (2012). *Ethics and Religious Conflicts and their Implications for National Security in Nigeria.* Ondo: Olajesu.

Cohen, L, Manion, L. & Mornson, K. (2004). *Research Methods in Education (5ᵗʰ Edition).* London: Routledge Folmer.

Cronbach, L. & Shavelson, R. J. (2004). My current thought on co-efficient alpha and successor procedures. *Educational and Psychological Measurement,* 64(2): 391-418.

Davis, R. A. (2001). *Educational Management:* A Basic Text. Lagos: Prospects Publications.

Essien, E. O. (2014). Job Characteristics and Work Ethnic of Technical Teachers in Akwa Ibom State. An Unpublished Ph.D Thesis in the Department of Vocational Education, University of Uyo, Uyo.

Ezewu, E. E. (1997). The map of social-psychological factors of human learning in school. In E. E. Ezewu (ed.). Social-*psychological Factors in Human Learning in Schools.* Onitsha: Leadway Books Limited.

Federal Republic of Nigeria, (2013). *National Policy of Education.* Lagos: NERDC.

Ola, J. R. (2000). The Place of School Library in the New 6-3-3-4 Educational System. *Teachers Journal*, Ondo State. ANCOPSS (2ᴺᴰ edition), Ibadan, Evans Brother Nigeria Publisher.

Odili, J. N., Oniyama, E. E. and Dittimiya, A. L. (1995). *Child Development Psychology.* Warri: COEWA Publishers.

Oniyama, E. E. and Amroma, T. M. (1998). *Fundamentals of Human Learning.* Warri: COEWA Publishers.

Sanders, H. A. (2006). 'School Library' Encyclopedia Education Presented at the Faculty of Education University of Ibadan, Ibadan.

Thomas, C. (2007). *Though questions, good answers: Taking control of any interview.* Sterling Virginia: Capital Books Inc.

Utulu, R. E. (2011). Civic Education Democracy and Nation Building in Nigeria: Conceptual Perspective. *Nigeria Journal of Social Studies*, 14(1):21-38.

Williams, A., Persual, U. L. and Turner V. N. (2008). The role of the laboratory in science teaching: Neglected aspects of research. *Review of Education,* 2(2):85-142.

5

Innovative School Environment and Academic Growth in Nigeria

Justina Ekwuru *Ph.D*, Emekpe O. Omon & Ogechi C. Okonkwo *Ph.D*

Abstract

This chapter discussed an innovative school environment and academic growth in Nigeria. As a conceptual discourse, the paper examined the concept of school environment, its meaning and characteristics. Furthermore, a distinctive stance was made for an all-embracing school environment which is innovative in nature towards the realization of the goals and philosophies of schools of the establishment of schools as agents of transformation. In the end, the paper concluded that education cannot be seen as a vital instrument for transformation, among others, without the school environment playing its expected roles. Recommendations, among others, were that government and private owners of schools at all levels should provide adequate funding and infrastructural facilities to cater for the development of the school environment.

Key Words: *Innovative, School Environment, Academic Growth*

Introduction

The school is a society in its own right, just as the community and nation are societies with a network of interpersonal relationships. The school is a close society where members of the society interact with one another. The school society exists so that some members (teachers and administrators) may direct the behavior and learning of students of the society. Most of the student's day is spent in the school. School experiences give dramatic effects on their learning behavior. School factors are more predictive of academic success than the family socio-economic background. A child's socio-economic background may exert marginal effects if the school environment is a good one. But if the school is a poor one, even the socially advantaged child may not enjoy academic excellence. Thus the extent to which a child can go in his/her school performance is dependent on a couple of variables (Fagbamiye 2007).

School environment is also known as learning environment. Learning is described as a change in behavior due to motivation. Behaviour itself is an indication of learning. Environment to a large extent influences learning. The extent to which a child could reach in academic attainment is depended upon the existence of certain environmental conditions. It is important to know that people tend to derive a sense of well-being from a pleasant environment. School environment, which includes the classrooms, libraries, laboratories, technical workshops, teachers' quality, school management, teaching methods, peers etc., are variables that affect students academic performance (Oluchukwu, 2000). Hence, the school environment remains an important area that should be studied and well managed to enhance students' academic performance. The issue of poor academic performance of students has been of much concern to the government, parents, teachers and even students themselves. The quality of education not only depends on the teachers as reflected in the performance of their duties, but also in the effective co-ordination of the school environment (Okonkwo & Okoye, 2008)

School environment is an essential aspect of educational planning. School environment which include instructional spaces planning, administrative places planning, conveniences planning, accessories planning, the teachers, as well as the students themselves, are essential in teaching-learning process. The extent to which student learning could be enhanced depends on their location in the school compound, the structure of their classroom, availability of instructional facilities and accessories. It is believed that a well planned school will gear up expected outcomes of education that will facilitate good social, political and economic emancipation, effective teaching and learning process and academic performance of the student. School environment is where children need safe, health and stimulating environment in which to grow and learn. During the school year, children can spend 6 to 8 hours at the school where the environment plays a significant/critical role in child development. More of the time is spent in the school yard or travelling to and from school.

Students' Academic Growth in an Enabling Environment

The school environment is of paramount importance in shaping and reshaping intellectual ability. However, supportive and favourable school environment enriched with enough learning facilities and favourable climate makes students more comfortable, more concentrated on their academic activities that result in high academic performance. A proper and adequate environment is very much necessary for a fruitful learning of the child. The favourable school environment provides the necessary stimulus for learning experiences. The children spend most of their time in school, and this school environment is exerting influence on performance through curricular, teaching techniques and relationship (Fagbamiye 2007). However, educational institutions are intimately linked with society as a whole. They are the temple of knowledge and agent of social change and transformation. The general condition of our schools, colleges and universities are a matter. It plays a significant role in the development of the personality of the students. As the students spend most of their life at school, the school environment is highly responsible for the inculcating of high value into them. Therefore, students being a backbone of every nation need a healthy school environment that supports them to perform well.

Okon (2005) in an article, "the role of the supportive school environment in promoting academic success" postulates that the school environment has broad influence on students' learning and growth, including a significant aspect of their social, emotional and ethical development. When students find their school environment supportive and caring, they are less likely to become involved in substance abuse, violence and other problem behavior. The research indicated that supportive schools foster positive connectedness, outcomes by promoting students sense of belongingness or community. Therefore, building in a school community is a means of fostering academic success. Students who experience their school as a caring community become more motivated, ambiguous and engage in their learning.

Another research by Oworye (2011) showed that there is a significant difference between the academic achievement of students in rural and urban secondary schools as measured by Senior

School Certificate Examinations (SSCE). To him, the geographical location has a significant influence on the academic achievement of students. He also pointed out that uneven distribution of resources, poor school mapping, facilities, problem of qualified teachers refusing appointment or not willing to perform well in isolated villages, lack of good roads, poor communication, and nonchalant attitude of some communities to school among others are some of the factors contributed to a wide gap between rural and urban secondary schools. Schools located in rural areas lack qualified teachers and lack social amenities. Also, the study has proved that students in urban areas had better academic achievement than their rural counterpart. In other words, students in urban locations have a very high advantage of favourable learning environment that apparently enhances their academic performance.

Each of us was born with our hereditary potentials and limitations into a set of surroundings and conditions. These factors interact continuously from birth until death. Thus, the child's environment is made up of all the forces that influence his/her growth and development, his/her behaviour and the realization of his potentials, intellectual and otherwise. The natural characteristic of a child is set up by heredity while environment helps to influence it for better or for worse. According to Idowu (2001), the child who comes from a remote village for instance, behaves differently from a child who comes from a city. This is the effect of environment. Good or criminal behavior is learnt from a good or criminal environment respectively. A stimulating environment affects positively a child's rate of growth and learning effectiveness. Good feeding, adequate physical exercises and clean habits positively affect the rate of learning (Denga 2006). Thus, two children who are bore of the same parents and happen to have similar intellectual potentiality but who are reared in different environments (one rich and the other poor) will certainly exhibit a significant difference in the rate of educational achievement in favour of the child reared in a rich and conducive environment. Thus, environment helps the inherited potentialities to mature and actualize.

Environment can be defined as those aspects of the organism's surroundings to which it responds at a given time (Denga, 2006). Thus, environment can be physical or psychological. According to Idowu (2001), the physical environment provides opportunities and may also limit experiences. Everything in the child's world that he/she can see, hear, taste, smell, touch or feel gives some influence on his/ her development and learning behavior. Thus, the home in which the child lives, the neighbourhood where he/she plays, the school he attends, the company he/she keeps and the community in which he/she grows up bear a lot of influence on his/her learning behavior (Idowu, 2001).

By Dictionary definition, environment is defined as surroundings, circumstances or influences. Capitalizing on this, Mallum and Haggai (2000) opined that environment is the surrounding in which the child learns. It is also a truism that learning does not take place in a vacuum but within a context. The context for the child in this sense is the environment or surrounding. Environment is a term which is used to refer to all the complex factors other than genetic which influence the individual from the time of conception to death (Okonkwo and Stilwell 1981). Generally, learning occupies an important place in the life of any individual. Learning equally cannot take place without a person; interaction, environment and behavioural change. They all constitute the pre-requisite for learning. Okonkwo and Stilwell (1981) described the real learning environment as that part of the real world which directly affects the responses of the child.

Innovation and the School Environment

The concept of innovation is relatively new in the Nigerian educational system. However, the concept cannot be totally separated from education. According to Tijani, Nura and Muhidden (2014), this is based on the premise that achievement of any educational goal depends largely on innovation, hence, it can be seen as the introduction of new ideas into a particular system for positive performance.

In another development, the exposition and definition of David (2011) in Sylvanus and Idowu (2013) cited in Tijani, Nura and Muhidden (2014), sees the concept of innovation as the deliberate identification and application of ideas, information, imagination and initiative in deriving greater different values and results from educational resources and to generate useful product. No wonder Tijani, Tijani and Umar (2012) posited that innovation is all-embracing learning experiences.

Every school must be innovative in its sense, bearing in mind, the peculiarities, realities and practicalities of its environment. The philosophies behind innovation in education, which include: development in science and technology; dynamic nature of knowledge; societal demands for quality education; malfunction of the existing curriculum contents; and research findings, cannot be achieved in a non-conducive school environment. The schools in all ramifications must be ready and willing to allow for innovations.

Conclusion

It is an established fact that education innovation in Nigeria has always been failing to beat the equilibrium with the expected result for effective impact on the beneficiaries, with special emphasis on the students. As an agent through which education can achieve its role as a vital instrument for transformation, means of livelihood, civilization, human resources development, among other things, the environment of schools have what it takes to play this very important function, which of course, is in the innovativeness of the school environment.

Recommendations

Based on the stance of this discourse, the following recommendations are made:

- The government and private owners of schools should provide adequate funding and infrastructural facilities to cater for the development of the school environment.
- Provision of well-equipped digital school environment.
- The school should be internationalized through its curriculum and other services.
- The introduction of entrepreneurship ideas in all facets of education.

References

Denga, D. I. (2006). *An Introduction to Foundations of Education*. Calabar: Advanced Publishers and Printing.

Fagbamiye, E. O. (2007). Inequalities in Nigeria Education: Towards Genuine Revolution in Education. *Logos Education Review, I*(1)

Idowu, A. I. (2001). Overview of Total Environment of the Adolescent and its Effect on His/Her Total Behaviour. Text of a Guest Lecture delivered at the Occasion of Training Workshop for Guidance Counsellors and Youth Workers at Abeokuta, Ogun State, February 2001.

Mallum, J. and Haggai, M.(2000). *Educational Psychology: Classroom Practice.* Jos: Deka Publications.

Okon, S. E. (2005). *The School and Nigerian Society.* Ibadan: University Press Limited.

Okonkwo, R. U. N. & Okoye, R. O. (2008). *The Learning Environment of the Nigeria Child.* Awka Publication of the Nigerian Society for Educational Psychologists (NISEP). Erudition Publishers.

Okonkwo, W. J. & Stilwell, W. E. (1981). *Psychology for Teachers and Students.* New York: McGraw-Hill.

Tijani, O. A., Tijani, M. R. and Umar, K. M. (2012). Curriculum Innovation in Primary Teacher Education: Prospects and Challenges in Nigeria Primary Schools. *Journal of Pristine.*

Tijani, O. A., Nuru, B. M. and Muhidden, A. A. (2014). Innovation in Education: Key to Achieving the 21st Century Global Economic Transformation Agenda in Nigeria. A Paper Presented at the 1st International Conference of the Association for Progressive and Alternative Education, held in Akwa Ibom State University, Obio Akpa Campus between 12th – 16th May, 2014.

HIGHER EDUCATION ISSUES

6

Enhancing Academic Quality and Standards in Higher Education Admissions: The Case of University of Education, Winneba (UEW)

Collins Owusu-Ansah, Deborah Afful & Jojoe Annan

Abstract

*E*ducation, and for that matter higher education, has been the mainstay of modern nations and economies. As more higher education institutions spring up, competition for intake also comes to the fore. Higher education institutions determine their own entry requirements and admission policies, which of course, are designed within the framework of the directives given by accreditation boards. Such admission policies and entry requirements differ between institutions and courses. This paper seeks to discuss the issue of quality assurance in higher education, stakeholders in the quality game and the importance of higher education. It further explores the various admission processes and makes recommendation for improving the online Application Process.

Key Words: *Academic Quality, Standards, Higher Education Admissions*

Introduction

Education has in recent years, been at or near the top of the public's concerns and it has been a major priority for every nation. Today, the focus is turning to higher education (including both two-year and four-year colleges and universities). The growing importance of higher education has attracted greater public attention and concern. Immerwahr (1998) intimated from a research conducted by the Public Agenda in February 1998 in which 700 Americans were surveyed nationwide that:

- Americans believe that higher education is more important than it ever has been, both as a key to a middle-class lifestyle and as a resource for the local economy.
- Because higher education has become so important, Americans are convinced that no qualified and motivated student should be denied an opportunity to go to a college or university merely because of the price.
- While many Americans are still worried about access to higher education, concerns about students being shut out of a college education have decreased significantly in the last five years.

- The public believes that what a student gets out of a higher education is a function of what he or she puts into it.
- The public is opposed to policy proposals that limit access to higher education or raise the amount families will have to pay, but has not come to a consensus on how society should pay for access to higher education.

In a quest to ensure access to all, however, there is the need to ensure that the academic quality and standards in higher education are maintained. Quest for excellence and learner satisfaction represents a historic commitment and foundation of important higher education milestones relating to Quality and Accountability. At a training workshop organized by the National Tempus Office of Lebanon, it was revealed that, in the medieval age, universities were dedicated to the spirit of learning (EUA Publications, 2007). It came to light again that, in recent days, they need to cover not only learning, but also research and entrepreneurial activities. This expansion of activities reveals the need to develop Quality Management (QM). Consequently, the role of the selection process (that is, the admission process), is critical in ensuring the quality and standards required.

In Ghana, apart from the standards put in place by the quality assurance bodies such as National Accreditation Board (NAB) and National Council for Tertiary Education (NCTE) to ensure quality in higher education, each institution has its own internal policies and mechanisms for ensuring the fulfillment of its mandate as credible higher education institution (Seniwoliba, 2014) and University of Education, Winneba is no exception.

The Origins of Quality Assurance in Higher Education

The issue of Quality Assurance has always been an important issue. Originating from business, Quality Assurance has now been a key factor in education as well as other public sectors (ESIB, 2001). Quality is an important attribute for the receiver as it creates value about the product/service. Of course, quality is also the means by which business/service providers are able to differentiate themselves from their competitors. Since businesses are usually considered leaders in quality assurance, non-business organisations such as educational institutions can benefit from the important lessons learnt by business. It should be envisaged that adaptation of the most successful and relevant strategies would help educational institutions in creating higher standards of quality in education.

Quality Assurance (QA) clearly emerged as a principal business methodology in the Western World throughout the 1950's and in the early 1960's (ESIB, 2001). The concept of quality assurance is not a new one, but elusive. The generally accepted criterion of quality in higher education is probably "fitness for purpose" as it just carries the discussion one step further to the question "what is the purpose of higher education?" Indeed, it is the different perceptions about the purpose of higher education that lends itself to the varying concepts of what quality should be as far as higher education is concerned.

The European Commission's Training Manual (2007) defines Quality Assurance as "an all-embracing term referring to an ongoing, continuous process of evaluating (assessing, monitoring, guaranteeing, maintaining and improving) the quality of a higher education system, institution or program." 'Quality assurance' is a generic term in higher education which lends itself to many interpretations: It is not possible to use one definition to cover all circumstances. In the glossary at the website of INQAAHE, assurance of quality in higher education is described as a process of establishing stakeholders' confidence that provision (input, process and outcomes) fulfils expectations or measures up to threshold minimum requirements. Quality Assurance may be described as the systematic, structured and continuous attention to quality in terms of maintaining and improving quality.

Issue of Quality

Quality means different things to different people. According to Green (1994) as quoted in SALT (2012), a distinction has been made as follows:

Quality as excellence

In the concept, the emphasis is on high-level standards. We talk of being the best or being excellent. Thus, promoting quality simply means promoting excellence.

Quality as fitness of purpose

Within this concept of quality, the question we normally ask is whether the university is able to achieve its formulated goals. This quality concept is improvement-oriented.

Quality as a threshold

In this view, quality is seen as meeting the threshold requirements. This quality concept often forms the basis for accreditation decisions. The problem is that it is not always clear what basis quality is. Setting threshold standards might also hinder innovations. Compliance with the threshold standards does not stimulate innovations.

Quality as added value

This concept emphasizes what happens to the students. Education is about doing something to the student. Quality means the value added to the student during education and training. The basic question is "what has he/she learnt?"

Quality as value for money

This focuses on efficiency and measures outputs against inputs. The concept is connected with accountability.

Satisfaction of the Client

With the rise of the concept of the "student as a consumer", quality is described as "something that has quality when it meets the expectations of the consumer, quality is the satisfaction of the client.

On the other hand, an academic will especially look at quality as a good academic training based on good knowledge transfer, good learning environment and a good relationship between training and research.

Quality assurance (QA) is one of the main tools that contribute to the development of trust between Higher Education Institutions (HEIs) which in turn is key to fostering cooperation in Higher Education (HE) at institutional, regional and national level.

Stakeholders in the Quality Game

It is believed that the notion of quality varies from industry to education. Whereas in the industry, quality is easily linked to the product, in the educational sector, what constitutes the "product" as well as the "client" is not clear. The question is whether the "graduate" is the "product" or the "programme" offered is the "product". Higher Education has several stakeholders and all of them have their own views on quality. Some of such stakeholders are:

- The State or Government
- Employment Agencies or Professional Bodies
- Academic World
- Students
- Guardians or Parents
- Society in general

It is interesting to note that because these have varying views on quality, they also have their own requirements or expectations. Whereas one stakeholder will stress the "product", another will lay emphasis on the processes involved in the production.

Definition of Higher Education

Higher education includes 'all types of studies, training or training for research at the post-secondary level, provided by universities or other educational establishments that are approved as institutions of higher education by the competent State authorities' (UNESCO, 1998, Pg. 1). Specifically, higher education is education provided by universities, colleges, and other institutions that award academic degrees. Higher education includes both the undergraduate (i.e., college) and the graduate (or postgraduate) levels. Higher education includes most professional education and is strongly vocationally or professionally oriented.

Importance of Higher Education

The importance of Higher education cannot be under-estimated as it has an important role both for the student, as an individual, and also for the society in which one lives. According to Heather (2007) & Kezar et al (2008), below are some of the importance of higher education:

Assistance for growth and development of the students:

Generally, Higher Education can serve as an aid for the growth and the development of the students and a key for a better life. Higher education institutions can contribute to the creation of ideal citizens, who will in turn help in keeping the peace of the society. Higher education enables students to be independent, and thus, they learn how to be on their own once they have the right attitude. With the requisite books and other resources available and by attending the lectures given by the experts in the fields, they can increase their knowledge.

Wider job placement opportunities:

Higher education offers graduates wider job placement avenues. As a result therefore, they are usually able to get better jobs with more convenient opportunities. This is an advantage over those who don't pursue education beyond high school, and essentially this means graduates earn more than non-graduates.

Improvement of quality of life:

Higher education comes in its wake with opportunities to improve an individual's quality of life. Unlike high school graduates, college graduates have longer life spans, better access to health care, better dietary and health practices, greater economic stability and security.

Expansion of knowledge:

Theoretically, Higher education will enable individuals to expand their knowledge and skills, express their thoughts clearly in speech and in writing, grasp abstract concepts and theories, and increase their understanding of the world and their community. In all, the benefits of Higher Education are very clear and strong. However, they vary from course to course and between institutions in this regard. Admission into such courses and institutions have the potential to offer such students the opportunities for graduate recruitment into high demand professions and thereby improving their social mobility due to the prospective earnings associated with such profession. Hence, no one can down play the important role of admissions to applicants, parents, schools, colleges, universities, teaching and admissions staff.

The Concept of Admission

Admission as a concept is very crucial in the life of a college, school or university. It is the permission given or granted to an individual applicant to join the school, college or a university to study. Thus, all potential students wishing to study any course at any Higher Educational Institution apply for admission. Admission is the gateway to a school, college or university. Admission brings in the students. Admission can take the form of recruitment or selection. Recruitment takes place when there are sufficient places on a course such that all applicants with the required grades normally get a place. Selection also takes place when there are many more applicants than places available.

Admissions Policies and Procedures of Higher Educations

Higher Education Institution admissions policies and procedures differ depending on course and institution. Higher Education Institutions are autonomous institutions and hence, admissions processes are regulated by the sector according to the guidelines and code of practice on admissions by both National Accreditation Board and the National Council for Tertiary Education in Ghana. An admissions Policy summarizes the view an institution takes of admissions and the importance it attaches to it. It states what it is looking for in its students, how the process operates and where within the institution responsibility for admissions policy lies. Ideally, an institution's admission policy should be easy to find, transparent and up-to-date. Mullen (2011) opines that Admissions Procedures can involve the following:

Minimum Entry Requirement

Each Institution has its own minimum requirements that students need to meet before they can enter a higher education course. This is usually based on credit passes of at least grade C6 in West African Examinations Council Examination or D in Senior Secondary School Examinations results

(UEW Undergraduate Admissions Brochure, 2015). According to the National Accreditation Board Minimum Requirements for Admission to Tertiary Institutions in Ghana (2014) for any student to enter any Tertiary Institution in Ghana, the student should have credit in three core subjects including English, Mathematics, Integrated Science/ Social Studies and three credits in three electives. However, attaining the minimum entry requirement will not necessarily guarantee that a student can be offered a place. Majority of courses make offers at a higher level than the minimum requirements.

Cut-off Points and Quotas

Due to competition in placement, departments come out with cut-off points and quotas to facilitate selection of applicants into courses and programmes. Cut-off points are range of grade aggregates for entry into a programme or a course. Quotas are the maximum number of students a department is allowed to recruit within the academic year. This is done in respect of the available facilities and lecturers at a given time. Both the cut-off points and quotas are reviewed every academic year to reflect the current facility and staff capacity.

Undergraduate or Post Graduate Admissions Brochure/Prospectus

This is designed to inform students exactly what lecturers are looking for in terms of entry requirement for specific courses or programmes. SPA (2012) stipulates that details of what is required for entry, such as qualifications, grades of admissions tests, entrance examinations, interviews etc together with features about the course, details of the admissions process are vital for decision-making. The admissions brochure or requirement could also be produced in soft copy form on the website of the University concerned. For example, the undergraduate brochure of University of Education, Winneba contains general information on UEW's academic programmes.

Stages of Admissions Processes

The admissions processes go through various stages. According to Manual for Admissions Office, University Education, Winneba (2014), these stages are as follows:

Pre-application stage:

This stage involves the following activities:

- Revision of the previous Admissions Processes
- Revision of on-line application forms
- Revision of entry requirements of all programmes
- Revision of Admission Brochure for the admission year
- Mounting, testing and deployment of the Online Application Forms

Application Stage:

- At this stage, the following activities are undertaken
- Monitoring of on-line application sale
- Responding to Admissions Enquiries

54

- Communicating complaints identified with on-line application to the Software Developers for redress.

Pre-Selection Stage:

Activities expected to be undertaken in this stage include the following:

- Setting of Pre-requisites for the various academic programmes
- Grouping the applicants by gender, programmes, mode of entry and campus
- Evaluation of applicants: This activity involves looking for the academic records and date of birth for the mature applicants.
- Writing a letter to the Pro-Vice-Chancellor and Heads of Department reminding them to set questions for the Entrance Examinations.
- Communicating Entrance Examinations/Interviews Time Table to Heads of Department and the University Communities
- Inviting applicants to attend interview or write entrance examinations.
- Making available the list of qualified applicants billed to write entrance examination or attend selection interviews to departments.
- Entering of Examinations/Interview Scores electronically.
- Joint Admissions Board meets to consider the recommended list of qualified applicants from the various departments with their cut-off points and quotas.

Selection Stage:

This stage is reached after the Joint Admissions Board has met and approved the recommended list of qualified applicants from the departments. Activities undertaken at this stage include:

- Generating admission letters of successful applicants
- Displaying list of successful applicants on the University website.
- Posting of admission letters of successful applicants
- Monitoring registration of fresh admitted students.
- Arranging for medical examination for fresh admitted students.

How the Admissions Unit of University of Education, Winneba facilitates Academic Quality and Standards

Ensuring academic quality and standards has been the hallmark of the activities undertaken by admissions office. The University as part of the standing committees has Joint Admissions Board made up of Deans of Faculties. This is a subcommittee of the Academic Board chaired by the Pro-Vice- Chancellor. The committee's mandate is to ensure that only students who meet the minimum requirements of the various programmes are admitted into the University. The Committee meets regularly especially during the admission period to select qualified applicants and ensure that only qualified students are admitted into the University. Online software has been designed to set up the cut-off points for each programme which are usually determined by the Joint Admissions Board. The Division of Academic Affairs of the University of Education, Winneba organises entrance examinations to screen mature applicants before they are admitted into the University.

At the pre-application stage, the Admissions Unit in collaboration with academic departments reviews the entry requirements for the various programmes to suit the current demand. The approved entry requirements are advertised for prospective applicants to apply. In furtherance of this, the Admissions Unit reviews the Undergraduate and Postgraduate brochures for the year under review to reflect the current entry requirements for the programmes. The University of Education, Winneba admission brochure is produced both in print and online forms for the use of prospective applicants as well as serving as reference materials for the Admissions Unit. This helps the applicants to make an informed decision on what programme to apply for per their results. It also goes a long way to create a huge publicity for the university. Again, the Admissions Unit ensures that the cut-off points and quotas approved by the Joint Admissions Board are strictly adhered to in order to ensure fairness and equity. Furthermore, in order to ensure simplicity, security and administrative efficiency, complaints from prospective applicants are communicated to the IT Consortium for redress on timely manner. The Admissions Unit uses email, SMS facility and phone calls in communicating with applicants during the period of admissions. These means of communication make it possible for applicants to be updated on the status of applications promptly. Finally, Post admission audit is done to ensure that qualified students are those admitted for each programme.

Improving the Online Application Process

Online application has come to stay, so has competition for students. Most aggressive universities may have enrolled potential students before the least aggressive ones even made contacts. The need for a streamlined online application process has become more important than ever. Research reports that up to 31 percent of applicants do not complete an online application process after starting due to challenges associated with the filling of the online forms and technical problems associated with the website. The following strategies could be employed to enhance quality of the online application process:

- Simplicity
- Technical Flexibility
- Security
- Administrative efficiency

Simplicity

Complaints from prospective applicants have to do with the level of complexity in the application process. The complex nature of the process can force an applicant to abandon the filling of the forms due to the frustration an applicant encounters. Prospective applicants complain that the biggest challenge with most universities website was being able to navigate to find what they wanted at the site. For instance, the National Research Centre for Colleges and Universities Admissions (NRCCUA) in an annual survey of over 100,000 effectiveness of nearly 3,000 admissions website along seven functional areas. There are several important notes from their findings relevant to effective online application design.

- There should be a prominent link directly to admissions from the institution's homepage and the link should be in the top half of the page.
- Consistency within the website is important.

- Applicant's instruction should be simple and easy to follow
- Offering the ability to pay online is more convenient and can save money.
- Students expect to be able to apply online; the application should be easily downloadable or printable.
- It should be easy to find any information applicants might be looking for.
- It should be easy for applicants to contact admissions office by mail, phone, email and online.
- While it is important to make the application design as simple as possible so that applicants do not fail to complete the forms; it is important to allow applicants to save their application so that they can return to it later in case there are any changes or updates.

Technical Flexibility

Also, it is important that applicants be able to conveniently access application forms online as well as in mobile devices. Institutions should be strategizing and offering mobile compatible application forms for prospective applicants in the mobile age. Capability as well as access to data and application form via any browser, tablet or device could bring efficiency to software developers.

Security

Stakeholders continue to be worried that electronic submissions might not actually go through. That is why institutions request postage of printed copies of submissions. This is a duplicate process. Transmission failures have also been identified as a challenge to the admission process The institution could address the challenge by providing a confirmation page and email for submitted applications while notifying applicants of incomplete applications. In addition, confidential data on prospective applicants should be securely stored.

Administrative Efficiency

Effective data tracking by Admission Officers serves various purposes. The data tracking mechanism could allow the institution to contact applicants who have not submitted their applications and encourage them to do so. Tracking applications also alerts the software developer to potential problem points in the design. Furthermore, an efficient data tracking system enables quicker processing, cuts down cost, improves enrolment because student receive acceptance notifications, sooner, and often results in saving monetary cost related to time, labour and opportunity.

Conclusion/Recommendations

At the institutional level, one of the aspects of educational activities that need special analysis is students' admission. It is important to attract the right candidates and select the ones that can complete the academic training. If there is selection, the procedure and criteria are to be clear, adequate, transparent and timely. Minimum entry requirements and cut-off points must be religiously adhered to. In doing this, however, the identified challenges with the use of such system is that it overlooks the issue of access for the underprivileged, marginalized, persons living with disabilities and persons from less endowed schools. It is therefore necessary that the institution puts in place a concessionary quota system and admission cut-off points for such category of applicants. Measures must also be put in place to minimize bottlenecks to enable applicants apply for programmes of their choice online. In all, activities connected to admissions must aim at excellence.

References

Allen, H (2007). Why is Higher Education Important? Retrieved from http://www.crosswalk.com/family/homeschool/why-is-higher-education-important-1367463.html.

EUA Publications (2005). Developing an Internal Quality Culture in European Universities. Retrieved from http://www.eua.be/eua/jsp/en/upload/QC1_full.1111487662479.pdf.

EUA Publications (2007). Embedding Quality Culture in Higher Education. Retrieved from www.tempus-ib.org/sites/default/files/EUA_QA_Forum_publication.pdf.

European Commission's Training Manual on Quality Assurance in Higher Education - Basic Concepts (2007). Retrieved from http://www.tempuslb.org/sites/default/files/leaflet2_Quality_Assurance.pdf.

ESIB (2001). European Student Handbook on Quality Assurance in Higher Education. Retrieved from http://www3.uma.pt/jcmarques/docs/info/qaheducation.pdf.

Heather, A. (2007). Why is Higher Education Important? Retrieved from http://www.crosswalk.com/family/homeschool/why-is-higher-education-important-1367463.html.

Kezar,A., Frank V., Lester, J., & Yang, H. (2008). Why Education Important is for your future and how can Education IDAs helping you reach your Educational Goals? http://www.usc.edu/dept/chepa/IDApays/resources/education_important.pdf.

UNESCO World Declaration on Higher Education for the Twenty-First Century: Vision and Action, 1998. Retrieved from http://www.unesco.org/education/educprog/wche/declaration_eng.htm.

Immerwahr, J. (1998). The Price of Admissions: the Growing Importance of Higher Education. USA. Retrieved from http://www.highereducation.org/reports/price.pdf.

Manual for Admissions Office (2014).University of Education, Winneba, Academic Affairs.

Mullen, F. (2010). Barriers to Widening Access to Higher Education. Retrieved fromhttp://www.scottish.parliament.uk/Research%20briefings%20and%20fact%20sheets/SB_10-07.pdf.

National Accreditation Board (NAB) Minimum Requirements for Tertiary Education Institutions in Ghana (2014). Minimum Requirements for Admission to First Degree Programmes. GHANA GAZETTE,25TH JULY, 2014.

SPA (2012). Fair Admissions – What are the Current Issues in 2012? Retrieved from http://www.spa.ac.uk/documents/ContextualData/Full_SPA_Contextual_data_Research_Report-Feb2012.pdf.

SALT (2012). Module in the Framework of the Sub-Regional Training Programme for Senior Managers/Administrators of Higher Education, Ghana.

Schwartz, S (2012). Fair Admissions to Higher Education: Recommendations for Good Practice. Retrieved from http://www.admissions-review.org.uk/downloads/finalreport.pdf.

7

Evaluation of Teaching Practice Exercise in Nigeria

Joy-Telu Hamilton-Ekeke *Ph.D*

Abstract

*E*valuation is centrally concerned with the making of value judgments. In the school setting, evaluation underpins the teacher's development of curriculum activities, his/her selection of instructional objectives in his/her day-today lesson planning and choice of materials and methods by which to judge the progress of his/her students. Evaluation enables the teacher to make appropriate decisions about his/her on-going classroom activities and to plan future activities more purposefully and effectively in the light of his knowledge of the progress of his/her students. Appropriate decisions, however, depend upon correct judgments and these in turn can only be derived from adequate instruments and applications of knowledge glean as a result of training to become a teacher. This paper discussed the evaluation of student-teachers by supervisors who go to the practicing schools to supervise the would-be-teachers (student-teachers) in order to ascertain that the would-be-teachers are putting into practice the theories and methods learnt; as well as an examination process to assess teaching effectiveness to grade the student-teachers. It was recommended that the assessment of student-teachers should be done by both the cooperating teacher (mentor) from the practicing school as well as the visiting supervisor from the training institutions as this is not currently the case.*

Key Words: *Evaluation, Teaching Practice Exercise*

Introduction

Teaching practice is an exercise in which the student-teacher is guided to acquire practical skills and competences necessary for effective delivery (teaching) after training. This valuable experience and expertise are usually acquired by exposing student-teachers to environment (schools) similar to those in which they hope to work after graduation. The schools that absorbed the student-teachers are called 'cooperating schools'. In such cooperating school the apprentice teacher (student-teacher) is usually attached to a trained and professional teacher who guides and directs him / her.

This apprenticeship period is very important in the life of a trainee teacher as it should offer him/her the first hand experience in acquiring practical knowledge and skills of organizing learning. Teaching practice is therefore as important to a would-be teacher as industrial training is to a would-be engineer. Little wonder why Teachers Registration Council of Nigeria (TRCN) the regulatory body of teaching profession in Nigeria is advocating a one full year of teaching practice for would be teachers bringing the training period for a first degree teaching qualification to five years instead of the present four years.

The essence of teaching is to easily effect pre-determined behavioural change in the learner; and because teaching practice prepares the teacher for proper effect, its role in modeling the society can hardly be de-emphasized. But available evidence shows that this important function has not always been met.

Professional Expectations of Student-Teachers

The aim of the teaching practice exercise is to help the student-teacher to bridge the gap between theory and practice. It is assumed that by so doing the student-teacher will acquire the skills of diagnosis and analysis of the educational environment. Student practice teaching experience does provide a valuable means for guiding the student-teacher's growth through a carefully set out sequence of activities (which need to be adequately evaluated) which will eventually enable him/her to achieve the followings:

- Clarify student understanding of the purposes, developments, programmes and administrative organization of the education system of the country; widen his/her understanding of curriculum practices;
- Deepen student understanding of the principles of human growth, development and the learning process;
- Be sensitive to the social patterns of a school community and discover through first hand experiences ways of improving curriculum for pupils by effective use of community resources;
- Develop a positive professional attitudes towards other members of the teaching profession;
- Identify personal strengths and weaknesses in the spectrum of competences associated with effective teaching and learning;
- Becoming increasingly resourceful and creative in planning, developing and evaluating effective learning experiences with the pupils.

The above sequence of activities needs to be adequately evaluated as teaching can be considered to be good if all expectations are constantly realized.

Evaluation of Student-Teachers

It is a normal practice that lecturers of training institutions are posted to schools as supervisors to visit the student-teachers and observe the teachings to ascertain how they are practicalising the theories earlier assimilated in the course of their training in school. Supervisors employ a uniform rating scale for this purpose as handed over by the practice teaching co-coordinator. Since it is not convenient to visit the student-teachers regularly, it is then recommended that a three times visit for a particular subject area should be achieved by the supervisors. It is assumed that the first visit should come after one month of the exercise to allow the student-teachers settle into their assignment, the second visit is about the mid of the exercise and the third visit could be three weeks or thereabout before the conclusion of the exercise. The main aim of this supervision is to offer guidance and assessment in the development of knowledge and skills of teaching. It is usually not vindictive or vengeful. Eyike (1994) mentioned two major considerations of practice teaching supervision as:

- A teaching process that helps the student-teachers to practicalise the theories and methods learnt;
- An examination process to assess teaching effectiveness to grade the student-teachers.

The supervisors' emphasis according to Ekiye (*ibid*) should be on helping the student-teachers to function and capitalize on their strengths, by pointing out areas that require some improvement.

Since the student-teachers must attain certain reasonable competences to be accepted as trained teachers, their evaluation must border on aspects of responsibilities which Okorie (1979) [cited in Maduewesi and Azubike, 2011] mentioned as:

- Ability to plan for instruction;
- Competency in guiding the experiences of children;
- Class activity and evaluation techniques for participating in school activities.

Such unbiased guidelines can comfortably guide any supervisor in assessing the student-teachers including the rating scale designed by the training institution.

It must be admitted that there are some isolated cases of abuse of this supervisory process, where supervisors fail to visit some student-teachers even once, only to manufacture marks or grades, instead of on the spot assessment of the teaching behaviours of the student-teacher in the classroom. Also, most of the supervisors only manage to visit their scheduled student-teachers once and they are always quick to point accusing fingers on the schools management and population explosion of the student-teachers. There may be some truth in their assertions, but professionals must always be committed or dunces will take over the teaching profession in the nearest future, to teach or cheat our dear children. Some supervisors also go with a pre-determination to victimize or intimidate their student-teachers into amorous submissions or they may not make good grades while others unduly appease the student-teachers with undeserved grades, in order to gain cheap popularity among the student–teachers. All these isolated cases of abuse has not removed any shine from the practice teaching exercise, which has formed the bedrock of teacher training programmes, the world over.

Assessment of Teaching Practice Exercise: Quantification of Effective Teaching

Quantification of effective teaching has been made possible by National Commission for Colleges of Education (NCCE). NCCE (2005) came up with a unified assess format for the assessment of teaching practice exercise which is now popular in teacher training institutions in Nigeria. This has helped to erase the erroneous conception that teaching cannot be effectively evaluated because of its multifaceted dimensions (i.e. the occurrence of several activities at the same time in the classroom) as a result the exact weighting to attach to different activities and competences were not uniformed.

National Commission for Colleges of Education Teaching Practice Assessment Form

S/N	DESCRIPTION	MAX. SCORE	MARKS SCORE
1	LESSON PREPARATION		
	a. Statement of objectives	5	
	b. Content (i) Logical and Sequential	2	
	(ii) Adequacy	3	
2	PRESENTATION		
	a. Introduction	5	
	a. Development of lesson	5	
	b. Mastery of subject	10	
	c. Use of chalk board	5	
	d. Time management skills	5	
	e. Questioning technique	5	
	f. Effective use of instructional materials: relevance, adequacy and variety	5	
	g. Class participation	10	
	h. Summary and conclusion	5	
3	CLASS MANAGEMENT		
	a. Class control	5	
	b. Classroom arrangement	2	
	c. Reactions and reinforcement of pupils' responses	5	
4	COMMUNICATION SKILLS		
	a. Clarity of voice	2	
	b. Appropriate use of language	3	
5	EVALUATION		
	a. Suitability of assessment	5	
	b. Attainment of stated objectives	5	
6	TEACHER'S PERSONALITY		
	a. Neatness/Dressing	4	
	a. Comportment	4	
	TOTAL SCORE	100	

The behaviours and their effects on the learners are weighted according to the degree of relevance and effectiveness. For instance, mastery of the subject matter and competence in facilitating a lively class participation are the attributes with the highest weights (scores - 10) because the competent teacher must be a master in her field and the students must be seen to be actively collaborating, participating and enjoying the learning experiences or packages being exposed. Therefore, effective teaching can easily be quantified using the above format to determine the productive effects of teaching activities on the learners thus allaying the philosophical worries that effective teaching may not be quantifiable.

Supervision Techniques

We have examined how we can effectively evaluate/assess the teaching practice exercise, it will be beneficial to know the behaviour characteristics expected from any competent supervisor on arrival to practice school for teaching practice assessment. This is because these expected behaviours are already pre-coded under the clinical supervision (clinical supervision is defined as an important element of general supervision, focusing on helping the student-teacher improves on his/her performances through analyses and feedback of the observed elements in the classroom). Afe (1990) implies that clinical approach requires the supervisor to help the student-teachers analyse and understand observed behaviour that would help them change and improve when necessary. This ensures that a two-way communication to assessment is initiated and sustained while the supervision lasts.

As earlier mentioned, the ratio of supervision to assessment should be 3:1, which implies that more time and energy should be devoted to improving the teaching behaviours of the student-teachers than rushing to reduce their neophytes' (a beginner or novice at something) performances to numbers and grades. The pattern of clinical supervision is characterized by the following sub-headings:

- **Pre-Observation Conference:** as the name implies, it occurs before the assessment and is unavoidable between the assessor (supervisor) and the assessed (student-teacher) to ensure an establishment of rapport. Though the assessed should have known what is to be assessed through the orientation workshop; the supervisor and the assessed should use the opportunity to amplify those attributes being looked for. It is equally an opportunity to preview the student-teacher's plans for entering behaviours, specific objectives, actual instructions and evaluations as advanced by Robert Gagne's basic teaching model. The pre-observation conference takes the form of re-orientation, which will go a long way to relax the nerves and assessment pressures on the student-teachers, thereby promoting better teaching demonstrations.

- **Actual Classroom Observation:** this is probably the most important aspect of scientific clinical observation, where the supervisor is only concerned with the collection of data on the strengths and weaknesses of the student-teacher while in session. This data can only be collected through clinical observation of classroom performance without interrupting the acting teacher, or the flow of the educational activities going on, all through the duration of the lesson. This ensures that the student-teachers are not humiliated and dehumanized, especially in the presence of their students or learners and provide a conducive opportunity for modification of unacceptable behaviours and applications.

- **Analysis of the Teaching and the Strategies of Feedback:** the supervisor does this quickly on his own and alone, while standing out or seated, depending on the environment of practice school; without involving feedback from the competent supervisor. The supervisor now takes a second look at the observed grey areas and areas of success, before fashioning out a strategy to present a feedback to the student-teacher, without hurting his/her feelings or dampening the student's zeal to become a teacher; rather the approach should be seen to be corrective and diplomatic. Competent supervisor starts by commending the student-teacher on the little achievements observed in the student teaching, before gradually and tactically calling the student attention to the grey areas and what the student should have done under such situations, to ensure maximum pupil gains.

- **The Post-Observation Conference:** this marks the end of scientific clinical supervision, where the supervisor presents the student-teacher with a corrective feedback, while alone with the student-teacher and employing the strategy fashioned out in analysis and strategies phase, in order to ensure the steady growth and encouragement of the neophyte teacher. The post-observation conference should be a two-way communication process (supervisor-talk and student-teacher-talk) to ensure a participatory conference, not supervisors shocking it down the throat of the student-teachers.

Conclusion

Having professionally applied the scientific clinical supervision on the overall visit to the practice school, the student-teacher who must be elated to have learnt something from the supervisor to enable him/her improve on his/her teaching, now willingly escorts the supervisor to the school gate, before waving goodbye. This is exactly what teaching practice supervision should look like and anything in the contrary may be resisted, because it could be something else and not the normal scientific approach approved by training institutions world over.

One thing that is not acceptable to the teaching profession in this digital age is for non-professional teachers or lecturers to be supervising teaching practice under any guise whatsoever. This can only widen the educational tragedy being bemoaned by the concerned stakeholders in teacher education, where many dunces are already handling chalks in some classrooms, as cheaters and not teachers.

Recommendation

Currently, what is in practice in terms of assessment of student-teachers is the report and grading from the supervisors only. This practice is not comprehensive enough as the supervisor visit the student-teacher approximately three times in the six weeks period of the teaching practice. The supervisors' assessment only will not be adequate. It is therefore recommended that the cooperating teacher i.e. the subject teacher in the cooperating or practicising school who acts as a mentor to the student-teacher should also report and grade the student-teacher as he/she is in constant (everyday more or less) touch with the student-teacher. Both the cooperating teacher's grade and the supervisor's grade can be merged and the average taken as the grade for the student-teacher.

References

Afe, J. O. (1990). A System Approach to the Organization, Supervision and Evaluation of Teaching Practice. Benin City. An Unpublished Faculty of Education Seminar Series of Teaching Practice, University of Benin, Benin City.

Eyike, R. E. (1984). Teaching Practice: The Experience of the Headmasters Institute Benin City. In O. M. Onibokun (ed.) *The Organisation, Supervision and Evaluation of Practice Teaching.* Ibadan: Evans Brothers (Nig) Publishers Ltd.

Maduewesi, B. U. and Azubike, N. O. (2011). *Introduction to Practical Teaching,* Onitsha: West and Solomon Publishing Ltd.

Okorie, J. U. (1979). *Fundamentals of Teaching Practice.* Enugu: Fourth Dimension Publishers.

MANAGEMENT ISSUES

8

Role of Educational Leadership in the Transformation of Secondary Education in Rivers State

Ugochukwu K. Agi *Ph.D*

Abstract

*T*his paper considered the role of educational leadership in the transformation of secondary education in Rivers States. To achieve this, the concept of secondary education was defined. Against the backdrop of the goals of secondary education, review of literature showed that, it (secondary education) has not achieved its desired goals considerably. A number of factors were identified as militating against the achievement of goals of secondary education. However, the paper viewed that in the transformation of secondary education, the roles educational leadership has to play are fundamental and therefore outlined. The paper identified challenges which educational leadership is likely to face in the transformation of secondary education.

Key Words: *Role, educational Leadership, transformation, secondary education*

Introduction

In Nigeria and in many developing economies of the world, the role of education in national development has been heralded as inevitable and veritable. National Policy on Education identified education as the "instrument par excellent' for effecting national development (FBN, 2004) Thus for the fact that education has been adopted as the tool to address the myriad of development questions year in, year out, government at the various levels make substantial budgetary provisions to fund various programmes of education considered germane to the realization of national objectives. At the federal level e.g. total budgetary allocation to education from 1999-2013 was N3,128,156,428,420 representing 8.28% of the total budgets for those corresponding years. Between 1999-2013, 2006 education recorded the highest allocation to education at 10.48% of the total budget followed by the year 2013 in which education received 10.21%. The lowest was in the year 1999 when education was allocated 4.46% of annual total budget (Akpolu and Akpochato, 2009). Though a far cry from 26% of annual budget standard recommended by UNESCO and what is obtainable in some developing countries, it can be regarded as effort in gradual investment in education as an instrument for national development.

The role of education in the 21st century Nigeria has become more complex following challenges emanating from certain realities such as climate change, wars religious fundamentalism and extremism, terrorism, shrinking economies, unemployment, globalization, rights movements, HIV/AIDS pandemic, corruption, environmental issues and poor democratic culture, and leadership. Effective education is expected to address these challenges through equipping people with the right attitudes, skills and knowledge.

Given that every nation has its own unique way of addressing their challenges, the burden of addressing the plethora of problems identified demands that the Nigerian education requires to develop internal sensibilities, dynamics, continuous flexibility and responses which enable it to provide society with adaptability for sustenance in the face of desperate odds. All levels of education must be engaged to cause holistic adaptation along the problem continuum. Thus, the creative indulgence of Nigeria's education will be expected through its programs to commence addressing these challenges from the Early Childhood through the tertiary level education.

This paper has chosen to address the role of educational leadership in the transformation of secondary education as part of the effort in confronting the zero functionality of education in addressing fundamental structure issues in the Nigeria society.

However, the following questions need to be addressed first,:

- What is secondary education?
- What are the goals of secondary education?

Secondary Education

National Policy on Education describes secondary education as "the education children receive after primary education and before the tertiary stage" (FRN, 2004). A formal education given to children from age 11 – 13 and ending at age 15 -18; what is described as traditional and the norm enunciated by education policy and projections. Secondary education in Nigeria embodies a distinction that can be categorized into technical education, usually received in technical colleges and general education, which children receive in grammar schools, or secondary schools or comprehensive secondary schools. The structure of secondary education in Nigeria is similar to what is obtainable in France, Germany, the U.K., Russia and USA. In France, a distinction exists between the two Lycees. Lycee (A) is of general and technological education (Lycee d Enseignement Generale et Technologique or LEGT). Lycee (B) is focused on vocational education (Lycee d enseignment professional or LEP). This is concerned with vocational/technical studies and training. In German education system, the secondary education is structured into Gymnasium for general education and Hauptschule for technical/vocational studies and occupation. The British secondary education is similarly classified into general and vocational. Russia adopts the Polytechnical for general secondary education and technical schools (www.britannica.com,27/02/2016).

Technically, the similarities may be suggestive of the foundational importance of secondary education as 'window' to diverse society's initiatives for sustainability. A closer look into curriculum of secondary education of Nigeria reveals what secondary education aims to achieve. Divided into Junior and Senior Secondary Schools, general and vocational cores and electives, the curriculum is targeted at providing general, technical and vocational knowledge and skills necessary for the development of the country's agriculture, industry, commerce and economy as well as science and technology (FRN, 2004). This is besides being determinant for higher education.

Goals of Secondary Education in Nigeria

The broad goals of secondary education are identified as:

- Being a basis for useful life in the society, and
- Preparation for those seeking higher education

It is presumed that secondary education lays the foundation for a functional society. Beginning from education received from Junior Secondary, graduands who for any reasons, do not wish to continue would have learnt a craft or trade to enable them live meaningfully in their society. This, of course, contrasts and is completely at variance with the education bequeathed Nigeria after independence from Britain. At the Senior Secondary School, similar "curriculum of live support" is available (FRN, 2004). The curricula of both junior and senior secondary educations are both designed to address the issues of empowerment and employment which were both the bane of post independence era secondary education.

The Gap between the Potential Goals and Actual Goals of Secondary Education

This question is debatable. Broad Goal No. 1, of secondary education is to prepare individuals for useful living in the society. Are there indicators of useful living in Nigerian society owing to the secondary education received? There is no statistical information showing that those with useful living in Nigerian society are those with only secondary education. Though measuring quality of life, may vary from one nation to another, some common indicators are established as general and largely applicable. "Eurostat Statistics Explained" measured quality of life using the following dimensions:

- Material living conditions (income, consumption and material conditions)
- Productive or main activity
- Health
- Education
- Leisure and social interactions
- Economic and physical safety
- Governance and basic rights
- Natural and living environment
- Overall experience of life

It is pertinent to weigh the goal of useful living in society against the backdrop of the dimensions of quality life indicators. CIA World Factbook (2014) showed that population below poverty line in Nigeria is 70% by 2010. How much of secondary education graduands in this 70% of the population below poverty line is unknown owing to lack of statistics. A check on the sort of jobs school certificate holders are offered include clerical jobs, swimming pool guards, security guards, kitchen assistants, waiter/waitress, housekeepers, cooks, drivers, chauffeur, etc. Generally these are low income jobs and employments and doubts can be expressed if they could cause useful living in which people seek good education, affordable health, leisure and meaningful experience of life in Nigeria, what with given the down turn in the economy since the tail end of the last decade.

Further doubts are cast on the efficacy of the first goals of secondary education as Akande (2014)'s analysis of the state of the youth unemployment in Nigeria shows. From Akande's analysis, two-thirds of unemployed youth are between 15 and 24 years of age. The age bracket mentioned here is where most secondary education graduants fall. The analysis further shows that between 2010 and 2011, the rate of unemployed youth in rural areas stood at about 59.95%. Rural areas are where most secondary education are got since there are more community schools there. Many factors are usually held accountable for poor performance of graduands of secondary education, who, in turn hardly live meaningful lives (Adawo, 2010). Factors such as poorly equipped laboratories, technical workshops libraries, learning environment, uninspiring classrooms, poorly motivated teachers and visionless school leadership are usually held largely responsible for the production of well equipped students (Ololube, 2012; Hoy & Miskel, 2008; Agi & Adiele 2015; Hasley, Lauder, Brown & Stuart-Well; 2007; Adawo, 2010 & Akande, 2014).

Certainly, poorly performing schools are usually characterized by most of the factors mentioned above. However, more often, the essential ingredient of visionary and dedicated school leadership that is needed to identify and deal with such challenges, is also lacking (Ezuizo in Unachukwu & Okorji, 2014). School leadership is crucial even in putting the school in the part toward improvement (FRN, 2004; Nobile, London & El Baba, 2015 & Bell & Stevenbon, 2015).

Broad Goal 2 is to have secondary school education prepare individuals for higher education. The evidence of the accomplishment of broad goal 2 is readily seen in the insatiable demand for admission places in the universities. The other visible evidence is the proliferation of universities, colleges of education and polytechnics in the country which seems to be addressing shortage of access and provision (Akpolu and Akpochafo, 2009). These scenarios quickly point to success of secondary education in preparing people for higher education.

However, viewing the broad goal 2 against the backdrop of number of candidates that enter for the senior school certificate examinations and those adjudged qualified (5 credits with English & Mathematics) for admission into universities, may just reveal the true position of secondary education in preparing people for higher education. Analysis by Adawo (2010) shows that in the year 2000, 725,575 candidates sat for WAEC and out of these, only 58,864 passed at levels that could qualify them for higher education. Again in 2001, 1,099,296 took the same examination and only 178,281 qualified for admission to higher education. The analysis further revealed that in 2002 the number was 1,224,381 and those qualified were only 188,494. Again in 2005, 1,742,663 sat for WAEC and only 203,991 were deemed qualified, it could be deduced that secondary education needs reinvigoration in order to achieve its targets.

Taken together, secondary education which has those broad goals of preparing people for living well and higher education require appropriate attention and leadership to provide direction for the achievement of these goals given the revelation of its performance for useful living and higher education.

The question at this juncture is what could be factored into the seemingly inadequacy of secondary education in addressing the two broad goals identified in the National Policy on Education (FRN, 2004)? Akande (2014) has already identified deficient curricula, poor teacher training, deficient in infrastructure, teaching and teacher qualities as some of the factors contributing to "failure of educational institutions in providing adequate skills and preparation. However, there is strong indication that the factors mentioned above could only take on their full functionality under influential educational leadership like the principal who can initiate transformation in the system. This is due to the fact that school goals and directions are set by school leadership (Bierly, Doyle & Smith, 2016).

Assumption

The assumption in this paper is that broad goals of secondary education are not being effectively achieved as a result of a number of factors as adduced by Adawo (2010) and Akande (2014) but fundamentally because, probably the role of school leadership in the improvement of school students has lacked emphasis and attention. This paper therefore is focused on the role of school leadership in causing transformation in secondary education to bring about significant improvement in the achievement of the goals of secondary education in Nigeria.

The Questions

The questions are:

- What is transformation?
- What does transformation at the secondary education mean?
- What fundamental roles are expected of the school leadership in achieving transformation in secondary education?
- Are there challenges the school leadership stand to face in their task of transformation of secondary education?

Transformation

The term transformation is often confused with and sometimes used interchangeably with the term 'change'. Though the two signify departure from a given mode, each maintains separate and clear pattern and path that impact differently and with different consequences or results.

Transformation signifies a radical shift from the status quo or shift from an old way of doing things. In other words, the same thing would be done in an improved manner that brings better results, satisfaction or effect. Transformation involves doing an old thing with redefined values, purposes, attitude, beliefs and even norms that will raise the quality of what is being done (Ee Wan, 2013). The author further indicated that transformation may also see organization redefining its strategies, culture, and leadership with target at achieving efficiency.

Transformation is also thought of as complex and not straight forward. It could bring gains once the organization keys into its success motion or bring losses once there is attitudinal reversal backward in preference for status quo that had sustained inefficiency (Bierly, Doyle and Smith, 2016).

Transformation is not an external force. It is an internal force that fundamentally alters organization philosophy and operational methodology for the improvement of the organization (Ee Wan, 2013). Jean (2012) points to transformation as the redefinition of a whole field, paradigm or process... and quantum leap beyond what exists currently.

What Does Transformation of Secondary Education Mean?

Transformation of secondary education means improvement of the performance of secondary education for those who receive it either for useful living or higher education through the redefinition of attitudes, values, purpose, beliefs strategies, organizational culture and leadership thinking of school system elements and participants. It is systemic in that improvement of secondary education can be brought about if there is a paradigm shift (Ee Wan, 2013; Hoy & Miskel, 2008; Lunenburg & Ornstein 2008)

The transformation of secondary education ideally should target the following key areas in the secondary school, namely:

- Quality of curriculum content
- Quality of instructional delivery
- Quality of instructional methodologies
- Quality of entry process
- Quality of throughput process
- Quality of school learning community
- Development/Professional growth of teaching personnel
- Quality of relationship
- Community participation
- Facilities/infrastructure, provision, maintenance and utility
- Justice/equity system
- Rights and privileges
- Rate/quality of graduation
- Transparency
- Performance indicators of transformation process/feedback
- Effective transformation
- Quality of leadership processes
- Accountability
- Communication

For secondary school education to achieve its goals as listed in National Policy on Education (2004), the various dimensions of the issues raised above require rethinking, fresh approaches, new ways of being handled without distorting the curriculum. It means there is need for 'creative teaching' in secondary education.

As it is always the case in administration of schools, be it at any level, definition of the entire process, putting together the resources, programmes and plan to work remain a fundamental function for accomplishing school goals. This responsibility is the duty of the positional leader or head as it is today emphasized in leadership literature (Bierly, Doyle and Smith, 2016). Thus seeking effective secondary education transformation demands that school leadership plays a key role in the process (FRN, 2004; Hoy & Miskel, 2008; Boylan, 2016 and Keller, 2015).

Role of School Leadership in Transformation of Secondary Education

In Nigeria, the positional head of the secondary school is the principal. He is equally referred to as the school head or administrative head appointed by Schools Board for a given period of time to each school. In the traditional perspective, the tasks of his job have been defined and articulated by the Schools Board on appointment. Thus, year in year out, the principal maintains a routine that is easily predictable (Eziuzo, 2014). The author aptly describes the traditional principal responsibilities and tasks as comprising direct administration of:

- School community relations
- Curriculum and instruction
- Staff and Student personnel
- Physical facilities
- Finance and business management
- Sundry duties

No doubt these are defined line of responsibilities and many a principal faces those tasks on daily basis. However, there is the notion that effective schools with high achievement profile and non-effective schools with low achievement is already a phenomenon which defines education success. This notion in turn directs attention to the effectiveness and strength as well as the culture of a given school leadership. The split in the notion of effective school and school leadership and non-effective school and leadership is what marks the difference between traditionally prescription school leadership and situationally responsive school leadership, which is often represented or located in avalanche of modern literature of school leadership (Bierly, Doyle & Smith, 2016; Hoy & Miskel, 2008; Townsend, 2015; Torrence and Humes, 2015; Li, Hallinger & walker, 2016 and Shapira Lishchinsky, 2015).

The thrust of the other divide of school leadership is primarily on school improvement and student achievement. Therefore, school leadership exudes characteristics identified as promoting these nexuses of improvement and high achievement are prominently canvassed. Bierly, Doyle and Smith, (2016) indicated that "the most effective principals create vibrant learning communities whose faculty and staff collaborate to help every student fulfill his or her potential". They are the ones who make improvements that translate to transformation of a school to what parents, community, and society look forward to.

The Roles of School leadership in transforming secondary education, according to Ee Wan (2013), are:

- Managing Instrumental / technical aspect of school and
- People/emotional aspects of school.

In instrumental/technical aspect of school leadership, leadership is to address issues regarding effective systems, structures, technologies, processes that support and motivate those who work in this system for accomplishment of school goals. Thus, considered in parts, the role of the school leadership in the transformation of secondary education will include;

(a) **Definition of goal of school**
School leadership set to improve its school clearly sets its goals which now dictate how members of the school work. Effective school leadership not only sets goals, but also motivates staff and students and other stakeholders to clearly understand the direction the school is heading. Lack of clearly defined goals will have school members working at cross purposes

and setting their personal goals (Lunenberg & Orustein, 2004; and Dichter, Gagnon and Alexander (n.d.).

(b) **Developing professional learning communities**
School leadership set to have all members of school community participate in transforming school education considers the potentials, wellness of skills and knowledge of its staff. To fully tap into and exploit the potentials of staff for attitudinal change, value reorientation and belief and trust in bringing about new thinking, school leadership needs to mount platform for teacher collaboration, work coordination and learning of best practices germane to curriculum execution and students' achievement. Together, teachers learn better form one another on improving their practices (Bierly, Doyle and Smith, 2016). Teachers can now account for their practices and results as they meet to assess their performance and device ways to improve on their lapses.

(c) **Redesigning school internally**
Transformation of school requires that the technical/instrumental aspects of school receive cultural shift. Duties and responsibilities can further be reduced, reassigned or redesignated to create channels for smaller and quicker accountability. Technically, many teachers in the same subject area can take up aspects or be made to model to achieve a given target (Ee' Wan, 2013). Administratively, many driver groups targeting specific achievements can emerge.

(d) **Definition of performance objective**
School leadership seeking transformation of secondary education requires stating clearly the performance objectives of school in collaboration with staff members. This can be made possible when staff members as earlier stated, are knowledgeable of schools and school vision of transformation (Cook and Hunsaker, 2001; Moorhead and Griffin, 1995; Robbins, 2004). Thus, the performed objective needs to specify what overall school achievement is expected to be as well as at unit and sub work levels. This largely involves target setting and accountability.

(e) **School culture is to be understood**
In transforming secondary education, school leadership has a role in setting tone for the school. Members of school require to understand what their roles are in the process of transformation. School culture that emphasize trust, commitment, confidence, initiative, leadership, shared vision, respect for authority and knowledge, research, collaboration, participation, freedom, human rights creates a path toward school where achievement and performance is valued (Hoy & Miskel, 2008 and Beirly, Doyle and Smith, 2016).

(f) **Staff development/motivation**
Emphasis should be on staff development and motivation in sustaining transformation effort in secondary education. Developing staff capacities is to enhance their opportunities to assume higher responsibilities and to grow them in preparation to assume leadership roles. This adds momentum to sustainable transformation and sharpens school vision for greater achievement (Cheung, 2015; Li, Hallinger and Walker, 2016, Bierly, Doyle and Smith, 2016).

(g) **Learning leadership structure**

Leadership literature is agog with discussion of different leadership behaviours. Probably, this is a new concept. However, what it means is merely providing avenue for teachers and others to share, participate and learn from school leadership and the school leadership in turn grows in knowledge and practice with sharing with professional colleagues (Cuttrell & James, 2016 and Boylan, 2016). The concepts of situation and distributive leadership support this organic platform of school leadership development and improvement (Hoy & Miskel, 2008).

(h) **External collaboration and synergy**

School leadership knows that schools are in the neighbourhood and generally are seen as part of society. It is therefore necessary for school leadership to note that no school is an island. Transformation of a given school therefore needs to take into consideration parallel developments around for the purposing of comparing notes and making better decisions and choices (Halseey, Lauder, Brown and Stuartswell, 2007).

(i) **Accountability process**

When school leadership sets goals and targets and clearly defines vision and programme to achieve same, accountability process is necessary to evaluate the level of transformation and make further decision (Dichter, Gagnon Alexander, n.d.).

What are the Challenges School Leadership are Likely to Face in Transforming Schools?

- Constraints due to government interference.
- Financial constraints in internal physical adjustments to facilities to suit emerging ideas of transformation.
- Resistance from staff who may not have capacities and potentials.
- Government transfer policy in moving principal periodically. Principals are often moved about at short intervals for reasons ranging from political, age, competence.
- Principals' competence in clearly conceptualizing and explaining school mission.
- Misunderstanding of leadership's intention by community, parents and even Board members.
- Political and economic situations can hamper transformation effort of school leadership. Dull political and economic climates can affect leadership morale.

Suggestions

- Regular exposure of school leaders to international comparative best practices.
- Regular training in school leadership practices.
- Need for Schools Board to permit school leadership to lead school for 6 years on the minimum to enable them have programs.
- Schools board should be encouraged to take interest in initiatives of school leadership.
- Granting extensive freedom to school leadership to innovate and then brief schools.

- Formation of Board of Governors in schools to whittle down the overbearing influence of Schools Board.
- Having school leadership set-standards for themselves.

Conclusion

Secondary education is an important educational component of the educational system such that it is the window to higher literacy. Its impact has always been marginal due to the overbearing influence of tertiary education. Designed to be a sufficient end for those choosing not to go beyond that point, it has not been seen as achieving that goal of providing adequate livelihood nor for the other purposes. However, it has been noted that a lot of factors are responsible for the inadequacies of secondary education including school leadership. As a way out, its transformation is suggested with the school leadership playing prominent role.

References

Agi, U. K. & Adiele E. E. (2015). *Educational Management and Administration*. Port Harcourt: Harey Publication Coy.

Akpolu, N. E. & Akpochato, B. C. (2009). "An analysis of factors influencing the upsurge of private universities in Nigeria". (www.krepublishers.com/02-journals/jss/jss 4/03/2016).

Bierly, C., Doyle, B. & Smith, A. (2016). "Transforming schools: How distributed leadership can create more high performing schools". (www.socininpactatbain.com/patner-for-transformingschoolsapex. 27/02/2016).

Boylan, M. (2016). "Deeping system leadership: Teachers leading from below" *Journal of Educational Management, Administration & Leadership, 44(1):51-72*.

Cuttrell, M. & James, C. (2016). Theorizing head teacher socialization from a role boundary perspective. *Journal of Educational Management, Administration & Leadership*, 44(1): 1 -19.

Dichter, S. F., Gagnon, C., & Alexander, A. (n.d.). Leading organizational transformations" (www. mckinsey.com/... 28/02/2016.

Ee Wan, K. (2013). *The role of leadership in organizational transformation*. (www.cscollege.gov.sg/knowledge/pages/The-Roles-of-leadership-in-orgnaizational -Transformation.aspx. 29/02/2016).

Eziuzo, G. O. (2014). Secondary School Administration and Supervision. In G. O. Unachukwu, & P. N. Okorji, *Educational Management: A Skill Building Approach*. Nimo-Anambra State: Rex Charles & Patrick Limited.

Harsey, A. H., Lauder, H., Brown, P. & Stuart-Wells, E. (eds.) (2007). *Education: Culture, Economy Society*. New York: Oxford University Press.

Hoy, W. K. & Miskel, C. G. (2008). *Educational Administration: Theory & Research and Practices*. Australia: Wadsworth Cengage Learning.

Lai, E. & Cheung, D. (2015). Enacting teacher leadership: The role of teachers in bring about change. *Journal of Educational Management, Administration & Leadership, 43(5): 673 – 692*.

Li, L., Hallinger, P. & Walker, A. (2016). Exploring the medicating effects of trust on principal leadership and teacher professional learning in Hong Kong primary school. *Journal of Educational Management, Administration & Leadership*, 44 (1) 20-42.

Moorhead, G. & Griffin, R. N. (1995). *Organizational Behaviour: Managing people and Organizations*. Boston: Houghton Mifflin Company.

Robbins, S. P. (2004). *Organizational Behaviour* (10th ed.). Delhi: Pearson Education.

Townsend, A. (2015). Hybrid leadership in action? *Journal of Educational Management, Administration & Leadership*, 43 (5) 719 – 738.

9
Nexus between Education and Security in Nigeria

Jurji N. Gomos & Felix D. Tappi

Abstract

The educational backwardness in northern part of Nigeria was/is artificially created by the members of the ruling class. This political gimmick was started by the colonial administration of Sir Lord Luggard under the pretext of his policy of non-interference with the Islamic culture of the core north. This policy continued even after flag independence when successive indigenous governments have seen the obvious advantage of Western education against other forms of education. In trying to be pretentious, majority of the people were further thrown into the abysses of darkness, ignorance, abject poverty, unemployment, hence, not accessing the weapon of rational thinking which have direct or indirect connection with their lives. Under this situation, gullible religious preachers and unpatriotic politicians survive by manipulating the people to their advantages. The preachers pitched them against their brothers/ sisters through hate teachings and indoctrinated them with the fallacy that they can live a life of their prophet or savior. Can anybody in this world live the life of a prophet or that of God? This paper argued that the reluctant attitude of the government in providing western education in the core north like other parts of the country makes condition for peace difficult to be achieved. Because allowing people to live in darkness is a paradox to peace. The paper observed that lack of western education in northern part of the country creates a conducive atmosphere for the survival of evil forces and a breeding ground for terror to thrive.

Key Words: *Manipulation, education, security*

Introduction

Western education, like traditional education and Islamic education, apart from moulding the characters of people and acquiring the necessary skills and knowledge, has the power and potentials of widening our horizon of knowledge, understanding global issues, making comparison with what is happing in our societies and other societies. It also affords us the opportunity to ask questions, seek explanations and develop our minds independently on issues, events and phenomenon's happening in and outside our societies. These capabilities and impacts make western education stand tall and very distinct from other forms of education where people assimilate values, norms and goals without being allowed to ask questions or seek further classifications and explanations about issues or events which they do not comprehend. The traditional and Islamic educations are acquired through memorization and imitations.

It therefore means that societies which make western education accessible, affordable and properly acceptable among its citizens are ready to move out of darkness, superstition, ignorance, fanaticism and hostility. They are prepared to move into light, freedom and security because with proper exposure of their citizens on issues and events around them, they are less likely to be manipulated by unsuspected gullible and unpatriotic elements of the societies. To avoid this darkness and insecurity, leaders with clear foresights make deliberate and conscious efforts to increase the penetration of western education to every nook and cranny of their societies. This is achieved through the investment of billions of naira in the building of more primary, secondary and tertiary institutions in order to educate their populace. As noted by Jonathan (2015), during an interview in Geneva, "I always believe if we do not spend billions educating our youths today, we will spend it fighting insecurity tomorrow." The leadership also engages in the training of qualified teachers, providing conducive school learning environment and teaching equipments as well as making education accessible and affordable to their citizens. The provision of western education to any society is not a luxury but necessity in the spirit of eliminating darkness, illiteracy, ignorance, unemployment, hostility, suspicion, hatred and making the condition difficult for terrorists or hooligans to thrive. Thus, as observed by Jouve (2005), knowledge is a natural right of every human being which nobody has the right to deprive him of under any pretext except in a case where a person himself does something which deprives him of that right. The above observation is in consonance with the spirit and philosophy of the Nigerian constitution which is stipulated in Chapter 11, Section 18, Subsection 2 a, b, c that says,

Government shall strive to eradicate illiteracy, and to this end, Government shall as and when practicable provide free, compulsory and universal primary education, free, university education and free adult literacy programme.

Beautiful as this injunction is, the government has failed woefully by not carrying out practically what the constitution is saying throughout the nook and cranny of the country. The substantive issue in the constitution is that government must struggle to eliminate this canker worm called "illiteracy" from our society. This is so because it is a serious disease associated with darkness, poverty, bitterness, hostility, suspicion, hatred, ignorance, unemployment and underdevelopment. Other characteristics of illiterate persons are that they are highly temperamental, very emotional, and sentimental, they can be easily manipulated for they lack the mechanism of self-assessment and ultimately self-control. Equally, in this paper it is argued that societies that are biased toward western education and hostile to freedom tend to promote ignorance, distorted religious teachings, civilization, hatred, hostility and suspicion in the minds of its citizens as well as between and among its members. According to Fanon (1985), Africa is a continent riddled with superstitions and fanaticism and Boer (1994) describes African people as ignorant and those who wander in moral twilight because they do not know what they are doing.

In view of the important role played by western education in degrading and decimating illiteracy in different societies of the world, thereby keeping it safe for peace to reign, it is the candid view of this paper that if peace is to be obtained in the core northern part of the country, especially the north-east, which is today a breeding ground for terrorism, government and non-governmental organizations must make deliberate and conscious efforts in providing western education in this part of the country.

Lackadaisical Attitude of the Government

Africa is not a fortune continent. It is a continent that all her resources were stolen out to foreign countries by people who once ruled over her either by the colonial masters or by her sons and daughters. It seems there was an agreement between the foreign masters and their indigenous African colleagues who took over from them. This conspiracy against Africa and her resources was/ is very devastating. It leads to the spillage of her natural wealth to foreign banks with far outrageous consequences of impoverishing the large majority of her citizens. It culminated to lack of creation or establishment of industries, schools, health care facilities, roads, railways, houses and food which can chase away famine, hunger, diseases, ignorance, illiteracy and unemployment. The lackadaisical attitude of the members of the ruling class was based on two theories, theory of racism adopted by the colonial masters and the theory of class segregation by the Nigerian indigenous ruling elites who took over the reins of government from the colonial masters. The colonial masters did not want to introduce western education in Nigeria because of their strong believe that Nigerians were inferior as such would not be allowed to rub shoulders with the whites. Since, they are inferior; they are not worthy to eat or receive the same training that can enable them to be at par with the whites. The racist theory upgraded the Europeans and downgraded the Africans. Hence, the Africans do not need western education so as to make them remain perpetual slaves that would be respecting, honouring and venerating the Europeans who were then seen as semi-gods.

To the Nigerian ruling elites who took over the reign of government from their western collaborators, they looked down upon their fellow Nigerians who entrusted them with the mantle of leadership. As noted by Feinstein (1987), very few people went through the schooling process in northern Nigeria in the 1930s. Such education was generally restricted to the children of royalty and occasionally extended to those of the aristocracy and the related Mallam class. It is on record that the first school in northern Nigeria was started in 1922 and was set up for the training of young princes similar to that built by the British in India. Many of the people who graduated from this school later became who is who in northern Nigeria and occupied sensitive positions in Nigeria. These groups of leaders adopted the gullible and crude materialistic style of leadership through the ruthless plundering and stealing of the Nigerian wealth to starch it away in foreign banks and buying of properties in Europe to the detriment of building schools and other necessary infrastructures in their home country. According to Wilmot (2007), before the arrest of the Bayelsa State governor, his counterparts used to collect their Federal allocation, head for the nearest bureau de change, change Naira into hard currency, and head for their mansions in Europe. They would stay there until the next allocation was due; enjoying the health, education, housing and facilities they denied their impoverished citizens at home. It is difficult to imagine people more heartless, who view the suffering of the people who elected them with such supreme indifference.

The plundering and stealing of the wealth of the Nigerian people by both the European and Nigerian members of the ruling class has brought about untold hardships, pains, suffering, poverty, illiteracy, ignorance, unemployment, diseases, bitterness and darkness among vast majority of the people in Nigeria. The plundering situation makes it difficult for members of the ruling classes to provide western education which can bring light, freedom and liberation to the vast majority of the downtrodden masses in the country. According to Jonathan, this situation is worse when we take into account the states affected by the Boko Haram insurgence. For example, 83.3 percent of male population in Yobe state has no formal western education and in Borno state it is 63.6 percent (cited in Anaba, 2016).

The Unscrupulous, Unpatriotic Religious Leaders

These groups of people always rid on the back of people who are poor, illiterate, ignorant, unemployed, inflicted with diseases and bitterness. The conditions started above afford the teachers/preachers easy opportunity to play on the intelligence of the people through the process of manipulating their minds for them to achieve their set agendas/goals. This is evident in the theology used by the preachers/teachers when using the religious books either the Bible or the Quran as the case may be. By the use of the theology, they can plant either the seed of hatred or bitterness or love or cooperation in the minds of their adherence. As observed by Yusufu (2014), manipulation means, essentially, controlling the action of a person or group without that person or group knowing the goals, purpose and method of that control and without them being aware that a form of control is being exercised on them at all.

This manipulative tendency is often demonstrated by fanning the ember of hatred and bitterness among the followers of a particular religious group against another, or within the same religious group, that is one denomination against the other denomination that is either Catholics against Protestants or the Muslim Shiite against the Sunni group. In effect, it can be inter-religious group conflict or intra-religious group conflict. According to Gabriel (2006), remembering his past life when he was a little child as a Muslim, his religious training planted seeds of hatred in his mind against non-Muslims. In his words, his religious teacher told him, "Christians hate you. They want to wipe Islam off the face of the earth. The Quran tells us exactly that they will never be our friends unless we convert to Christianity."

This teaching invariably created in the minds of the young ones spirit of vengeance, defense, attack and hatred, in-spite of the fact that they have no concrete evidence to support what their teachers/preachers alleged against the Christian group. As children, they could not ask questions such as why would the Christians want to wipe out Islam? Is it possible for the Christians to achieve this? Hence, they began to attack the Christians without any form of provocation. If the children were educated, they would have raised questions on why their religious teachers were fanning such ember of hatred in their minds against the non-Muslims.

On the level of intra- religious manipulation, the Christian Protestant Church of Christ in Nation would want to separate or disassociate their members from becoming members of the Catholic faith or the other way round; they will tell their members that it is only their denomination that teaches the correct word of God hence, moving into other denomination would mean following the wrong way and one would miss seeing God. They argued that other churches do not have good doctrines. In the spirit of competition, they totally discouraged their members from joining other Christian religious denominations or fellowships despite the fact that they preached about the same Jesus Christ. Each of the denominations would want to discredit the other and maintain supremacy. The implication is very clear; each of the Church denomination is struggling to get more converts and maintain their existing members. More followers mean more political power, better economy and more social prestige. The more a church has large membership, the more money it will collect each Sunday. In some Churches, special days are carved out for the collection of special offerings like Reverend farm's day, RCC farm's day and sowing seeds. By these collections, the Reverends or Pastors live comfortable, better and affluence lives as opposed to the lives of their members who are financially drained each Sunday. In other words, they are exploiting their members and throwing them into a state of poverty. Because they cannot save, they cannot invest and cannot generate profits as each time they are in a deficit. The manipulation is done deliberately to prevent the innocent people from knowing the real intension or reasons why the religious teachers would not want to lead them off the hook and to know who really they are. Hence, religion becomes the opium of the masses as propounded by an Anglican priest.

What is Education?

Education in everyday's life experience connotes the art which concerns itself with the processes of acquiring information, knowledge, skills and techniques of survival as a member of a particular social group. In other words, it is concerned with the concepts of initiation, transmission, socialization and equipping young members of the society with worthwhile values, goals, customs and cultures of a specific society into which an individual is born into as a member of the group. For us to do justice to this concept called education, it is necessary for the paper to consider some definitions given by other scholars and authoritative sources. In light of the above, Scott and Marshall (2005) observed that education is a philosophical as well as a sociological concept, denoting ideologies, curricula, and pedagogical techniques of the inculcation and management of knowledge and the social reproduction of personalities and cultures. This definition is essential because for the society to continue, it must device means on how it will transmit its basic ideals to sustain peace, harmony, love, cooperation and integrate its members. These ideals are systematically and comprehensively put into a particular package as a guideline to the teacher on what is essential for the new member to learn and acquire, for him/her to be accepted and given certain positions of respect, honour and responsibilities in the society.

While Otite and Ogionwo (2006) noted that education refers to the acquisition of knowledge and skills required to adapt to and exploit the social and physical environments in the process of development. It is the process of training and bringing up the young and also the old members of a society, morally, spiritually, and intellectually. The important points raised in this definition have to do with equipping or updating the young and old members of the society with information, technical know-how that will enable the members of the society to survive or get fitted into their environment. This is vital because there is need for mutual social relationships between members of the society and their environment. Without education, members of the society become misfits because they are not properly guided on what is right or wrong. Through education the people are equipped with the ingredients on how to protect themselves and the society against perceived and actual enemies. They are also guided on how not to be manipulating by unpatriotic elements of the society who will hide under smoke screen to unleash terror in the society in order to achieve their selfish interests. Educated minds recognize changing world, changing society, changing values and an ever-growing world of knowledge which from time to time can help one with information that can affect his/her opinion or world view in a positive way. According to Ilori (2013), "to be locked in one's point of view is to lock out opportunity for intellectual growth. A willingness to change one's thinking, one's prejudices, as new information comes to light is a mark of the educated person."

Educated people tend to be more tolerant in accepting other people points of view which, even though biased, might have some iota of truth that can bring about intellectual growth. Also, the mind of the educated is flexible to changes which advance humankind through reason than violence. The educated people are guided by the need for progress and logic than by sentimental judgment and sheer emotion. As noted by Socrates (469-399BC), the essence of education is to dispel error and to discover truth and to Aristotle (384-322BC), the aim of education is for the attainment of happiness through perfect virtue [cited in Ilori (2013)].

What is Security?

According to Oxford Advanced Learner's Dictionary, security refers to "the activities involved in protecting a country, building or person against attack, danger etc.", whereas, Encyclopedia Britannica (1982) defines security as the means and devices designed to guard persons and property against crime, accidents, disasters, fire, espionage, sabotage, subversion and attack. Analysing the two definitions, one issue is very clear and is re- echoed consistently in the definitions which has to do with safeguarding the life of a person, sovereignty of a group or society against any real or perceived danger. The danger could imply someone trying to take your life, destroying your property or any valuable which you have sacrificed time and money in obtaining. It also includes protecting the land which you have tiredly acquired or inherited from your ancestors. Not wanting to lose something valuable and precious in your side. In effect, it involves taking critical and necessary actions, inactions and thoughts that can make you avoid taking risks and confrontations which can be detrimental to one's life and property or the society in general. For example, the annulment of the popular June 12 election was based on the background of personal security of Babangida and his immediate family. As argued by Agbese (2013), Babangida was worried that if he does not annul Abiola's election something terrible or sinister would affect his life and that of the members of his family. According to Omoruyi, Babangida was quoted as telling him in the heat of the crisis that;

> They will kill me; they will kill the president elect, chief MKO Abiola, if I went ahead with the election and announced the winner… which we all know to be Bashorun MKO Abiola. I know so, I am not daft. He won; he tried; I feel bad about the whole matter [Cited in Agbese 2013)]

Why was he able to take this critical and in-depth analysis of the situation surrounding him as of that period? The answer was obviously because of the level of his education which makes him conscious of the implication in insisting to give the election to his bosom friend Abiola. The condition as of that time was not palatable because many interest groups who did not want Abiola to be the president of Nigeria came up. It was alleged that these groups were both within and outside the military circle and among the politicians too. The action of Babangida did not only safeguard his personal life and that of his immediate family members, but the crisis which could have rocked or engulfed the entire country.

Connection between Education and Security

The absence of western education in any given society brings insecurity to that society. This is so because people in such societies live in darkness, ignorance, illiteracy, poverty, unemployment, superstition, fanaticism, fear and isolation from other societies. The climate is easily exploited and manipulated by the few privileged members of the ruling class in the society to their advantages. To always keep themselves above the other underprivileged group of people in the society; they exploit sentiments based on religious differences, ethnic issues, sectionalism, nepotism, the question of the son of the soil and favouritism.

Knowing fully that the people are incapacitated to ask questions or seek further explanations on any agenda brought before them or critically analyse and understand the situation under discussion, members of the ruling class seize that advantage to pitch them against each other or one society against the other. This creates tension, animosity, fear, conflict, hatred and bitterness among the large majority of the masses in the society. The masses living under these conditions do not see the value of life; they have nothing, hence, would not fear losing anything as such they are prepared to lay down their lives at any given time. To them dying is even better than being alive. This explains why terrorism like Boko Haram and other forms of insurgency thrives under such conditions in north eastern part of the country. To stop that ugly situation, the government and non-governmental organisations must make a conscious and deliberate effort to increase the penetration of western education to those areas.

When education is provided, made affordable and accessible to the people, they will use it to assess, analyse, evaluate, understand and appreciate each discussion and action that may be taken in view of the security implications to the life and property of the individuals, the society and the country in general. Education generally deals with the issue of seeking the truth, taking action that will bring happiness, cooperation, love, peace, understanding and protecting one or the society against mischievous and unscrupulous people in the society. Education makes people to have knowledge, skills and information that can enable them to survive in the fast changing world. With the skills and knowledge, they can initiate and create entrepreneurial opportunities which can make them self-reliant, self-independent and economically buoyant. Education makes people to be tolerant of others, enable the individuals to share opinions with those they disagree with and accept each other's point of view when necessary even though they may have their differences. This is as a result of the flexibility of minds in them. They are always interested in moving forward as well as making comparison with people in other societies. The educated can differentiate between those traditional values which are important and can add value to the changing world and those that are bad could be discarded. Even the borrowed cultural values are properly scrutinized to find those that can help our traditional societies to move forward and throw away the unprogressive values. Education is the only instrument that one can use to sieve the condition or situation of life and not illiteracy. When there is self-contentment, self-independent, self- reliant, self-comfort and self-esteem, no individual no matter his/her status and power can manipulate anybody and by implication the security of the society can be guaranteed.

Conclusion

In view of the importance of education to the question of peace and security in all known human society, it is pertinent that the government must make conscious and deliberate effort in providing western education to all its citizens no matter their social, physical status and place of location in the country. When a large number of youths are left uneducated and uncared for, they become a problem to themselves and constitute a great threat/danger to such a society and can snowball into the tsunami of insecurity as is the case in north eastern part of Nigeria. Any society that refuses to educate its citizens with western education should be prepared to spend billions of naira in fighting insecurity tomorrow. But societies that spend billions in educating their citizens today will not waste its scare resources in fighting insecurity tomorrow because the societies are already secured. In effect, there is a strong bond of relationship between education and security.

Recommendations

- The Government and the private sectors should invest more in building schools beginning from primary, secondary and tertiary institutions in all the nooks and cranny of the country. For example, all the thirty six states in the Federation should have Federal Polytechnic, Federal College of Education, and Federal Unity Schools in each of the three Senatorial districts in the states.

- Education should be made free, compulsory, accessible and affordable to all the citizens of the country no matter their social status, physical ability, ethnic nationalities, political affiliation, social class interest and religious inclinations. For example, the issue of using computers to write Joint Admission and Matriculation Examination is class biased policy aimed at knocking out the children who come from poor families from passing such examinations, how many students in the rural areas can access computer training? How many computer literate teachers do we have in our secondary schools in the country? How many schools in the rural areas can afford electricity light power? How many can afford buying a generator and equally continue to fuel it?

- The idea of imposing unnecessary charges such as development levies, Parent Teacher Association charges, examination fees, supervision fees, Post-University Matriculation Examination fees (the post-University Matriculation Examination is an unconstitutional issue), computer/laptop fees, high acceptance fees, departmental fees, dressing fees and other charges should be discouraged by the Government as these are deliberate attempts to frustrate the desire and ambition of people who come from poor families to access education.

- Teachers should be properly trained and motivated to enable the system attract the best brains into the educational industry. Lack of motivation and morale booster has made the system to miss qualified manpower to other sectors of the economy under the guise of seeking greener pastures. This leads to the development of a phenomenon called "brain drain." The much needed equipments and learning facilities should be provided as no worker can put in his/her best in a system where there are no working tools or instruments.

- The Government should set up many adult education/literacy centres where public enlightenment can be given to the masses that could access the regular and formal system of schooling due to financial and other factors. Public enlightenment helps to build and safeguard the security and the philosophy upheld by the government of such a country.

References

Ajayi, J. F. A. & Webster, J. B. (1977). *The emergence of a new elite in Africa.* In, J. C. Anene & G. N. Brown, *Africa in the Nineteenth and Twentieth Centuries: A Handbook for Teachers and Students.* Ibadan: University Press.

Agbese, D. (2013). *Ibrahim Babangida the Military, Politics and Power in Nigeria.* Abuja: Published by Adonis & Abbey Publishing Company.

Anaba, E. (2016). *$2.1b Arms Deal, others: why I won't speak on probes now-Jonathan.* Vanguard Thursday January 28.

Boer, J. H. (1994). *Mission: Heralds of Capitalism or Christ?* Ibadan: Daystar.

Fanon, F. (1985). *The Wretched of the Earth*. England: Penguin Books.

Feinstein, A. (1987). *African Revolutionary: The Life and Times of Nigeria's Aminu Kano*. Enugu: Fourth Dimension Press.

Gabriel, M. A. (2006). *Journey into the Mind of an Islamic Terrorist, Why they hate Us And How We Can Change Their Minds*. Florida: Frontline.

Ilori, J. A. (2013). *Philosophy of Christian Education: an African Perspective*. Bukuru: African Christian Textbooks.

Jouve, E. (2005). *My Vision Muammar Gaddafi with Edmond Jouve. He is a Prophet and Revolutionary. A seer and a fighter. This is the Authentic Voice of the world's most controversial leader*. London: John Bake Publishing Ltd.

Oxford Advanced Learner's Dictionary International Student's Edition

Scott, J. & Marshall, G. (2005). *Oxford Dictionary of Sociology*. Oxford University Press.

Usman, Y. B. (2014). *The Manipulation of Religion in Nigeria 1977-1987*. Zaria: Centre for Democratic Development Research and Training.

Wilmot, P. (2007). *Selected Lectures*. Sociology Department, University of Jos.

1999 *Constitution of the Federal Republic of Nigeria* with amendments 2011.

BUSINESS ISSUES

10

Social and Economic Transformations and Its Implications on the School Environment: A Focus on Educational Strategic Policies

Boateng & Ohene B. Apea *Ph.D*

Abstract

is a natural phenomenon and it affects every nation. When this happens, research is utilized to identify the factors of observed change, and policies are made to address the factors which affect national development. New education policies must be made and adopted periodically by nations to cope with socio-economic issues. Ghana has seen such times and has come out with policies to address the observed challenges. This paper attempted to indicate that the time has come for some important factors to be considered in the drafting of education strategic policy. The study was able to divulge that the school environment and the curriculum are vital for achieving the mission of the ministry. Consequently, broader consultations and extensive research on the dynamics and factors of change are vital for the drafting of policies.

Key Words: *Social, Economic, Transformation, School Environment, Strategic Policies*

Introduction

Socio-economic issues are dynamic, and the factors responsible for the observed change at any point in time vary from country to country. Issues, problems and challenges are simply the product of a reaction. So the state in which we find ourselves was arrived at after our country went through the socio-economic change. Lack of critical analysis of these factors influencing the economy, and refusal to put measures in place to annul their effect on our economy, makes us responsible for the situation.

Education in Ghana has gone through many reforms, and several policies have been made. Albeit, the quality of our products has dropped significantly. The truth is failure to be either observant or frank about issues (Hayford, 2012). The best way to describe the observed undeniable drop in the quality of graduates, or the glaring fear that grip many about the future of the country in respect of the crop of graduates and youth in the society, is that, there is a watering of the leaves of education not the roots! The authors are of the view that, one of the solutions to the socioeconomic challenges lies in the school environment. And the only way to attend to that is by finding out what is being done right but not important to the cause.

Development of the Educational System in Ghana

Below is a summary of the transformations the educational system in Ghana has gone through. These are summarized from UEW (2015), who in a very simple way, talked about the evolution of education in Ghana:

- History tells us that education in Ghana started in the castles by European merchants and was ultimately taken over by Christian missionaries.

- Then in the nineteenth century, education came into the hands of the British administrators. Dr. Kwame Nkrumah, who became the Leader of Government Business, then took over in 1951. The first step Dr Nkurmah took was to introduce a policy called Accelerated Development Plan.

  "It brought a rapid increase in enrollment in primary schools; emergency teacher training was introduced, and a large number of pupil teachers were appointed. Facilities for middle, secondary and technical schools were greatly increased. Parents were asked to buy only textbooks and stop paying school fees. Such educational provisions continued until Ghana achieved independence in 1957. This means that prior to independence, a strong foundation had been laid for education. During this period, about half a million children were attending primary school. The number of primary schools rose from 3,571 in 1957 to 3,713 and middle schools from 1,311 to 1,394 in 1959" (UEW, 2015).

- This was followed by the introduction of the Education Act of 1961.

  This Act *"made primary and middle schools free and compulsory for all children. The government decided to provide and pay teachers and asked the local authorities to provide school buildings. In line with this policy, the Minister of Education stated that any parent who failed to send his/ her child to school would be fined. This new directive meant that all children of school-going age should be found places in school. The system therefore introduced some decentralization in the provision of education"* (UEW, 2015).

- As a result of the apparent challenges due to facilities, resources, manpower etc., required to promote the compulsory education law, the government, in 1963, paid more attention to the provision of educational facilities and resources. Attention was however paid to the quality of education.

  "As a result the government began to supply free textbooks not only to primary and middle schools, but also to all assisted secondary schools" (UEW, 2015).

- This free textbook supply continued until 1966 when the government invited parents to make some contribution to the cost of textbooks and stationery.

- According to UEW (2015), pre-primary education was introduced in 1964 to predispose young children to early childhood education. Provision was made for 4-6 year old children by setting up nursery and kindergarten schools.

- Continuation school system was introduced in 1968 to make the elementary school system practical-oriented.
  "This system was an attempt to provide practical job training to school leavers to provide employment for the youth. It was also aimed at eliminating the rush for white-collar jobs which were becoming scarcer in the country. Basic education during this period consisted of six-year primary and four-year middle programs after which the middle school leaving certificate examination was taken. The continuation school system, although was laudable, did not last for long mainly because the government could not mobilize adequate resources to sustain it" (UEW, 2015).

- The introduction and expansion of 6th form education as a path to university education took place in the early 1960s. By the year 1966, 6th form courses with a student population of about 2,000 students were observed for 20 secondary schools.

- It was not until 1974 that the nine-year basic education (six-year primary and three-year junior secondary school) was introduced.
  "From the late 1970s, however, the quality of basic education which had been high in the previous years, began to deteriorate as a result of poor national economy which led to thousands of Ghanaian teachers leaving for Nigeria. Poor supervision and ineffective management of schools also led to further deterioration in the quality of education" (UEW, 2015).

- The free and compulsory education was later stressed in the 1992 Constitution of Ghana. It was targeted that by 2005, all Ghanaians of school going age should be in school. This has been difficult to actualize, there have been efforts made by successive governments to make provision for its implementation.
  "The Ministry of Education, however, continues to explore avenues that will expand access to basic education. For example, the Ministry introduced a capitation grant in 2005, which is gradually expanding access to basic education. Expansion of basic education also necessitated that certain measures were taken to provide teachers. The training of teachers which had begun in the early 1940s received expansion. A two-year Certificate B Teacher Training was then introduced in the 1950s followed by the Certificate A Training. The National Teacher Training Council was set up in 1958 to look after the interest of teachers. The four-year training program was re-introduced for middle school leavers in 1962. Currently, there are 38 teacher training colleges training teachers for basic schools" (UEW, 2015).

- To cater for the obvious need for more facilities to cope with the large population required to be enrolled in schools, the government established the Ghana Education Trust (GET) to take charge of secondary schools.
  "...there was a need to expand secondary education to absorb the large number of junior secondary school leavers. Shortly after independence, the government required about 4 percent of each

generation to be in secondary school. Pupils in secondary schools were about 2,500 in 1958. This number increased to 6,000 in 1964. The number of secondary schools also increased from 38 in 1957 to 59 in 1960" (UEW, 2015).

- Technical and vocational institutes and polytechnics have been established over the years to provide practical skills' subjects to students. In addition, the sector has witnessed increased number of public and private Universities.
  "The University came about as a result of agitation by educated Africans on the British Government In the process of expansion, Kwame Nkrumah University of Science and Technology, which used to be Kumasi College of Technology, was established in 1961. As time went on, the Government established a third university, the University College of Cape Coast, in 1962 to train teachers. Since that time, university education has continued to expand with the introduction of the University of Development Studies and University of Education, both in 1992 and the University of Mines and Technology in 2005" (UEW, 2015).

Observations

The historical development of education in Ghana revealed that after independence, government was faced with the need to educate Ghanaians (UEW, 2015). Over the years, that initial need created the problem of cost-both to parents and to the Government. But the benefits of education are invaluable so the expenditure on education was justified, albeit that challenge still faces the nation even now.

Alongside the finances was also the need to maintain standards and make provision for advanced education at the University level. With the rising number of diploma awarding institutions, polytechnics, teacher training colleges, nursing training colleges, public and private universities, there is hope for the aspiring youth. The future of the country is bright. However, the question as to whether the philosophy of education in Ghana is being actualized still remains to be answered (Hanson, 2015; Hayford, 2012; Kweitsu, 2016; Owusu-Mensah, 2016).

Reforms and policies, facilities and resources, however important they are, the curriculum, school environment, and the quality of teachers are crucial for the attainment of the philosophy of education in Ghana.

In support of this, UEW(2015) noted that, although, successive governments in Ghana have recognized the indispensable role which education plays in the country's socio-economic development... adequate human and material resources will be mobilized to provide wholesome education toward total development of Ghana.

Philosophy of Education and Strategic Policy

The mission of the Ministry of Education is "...to provide relevant education to all Ghanaians at all levels to enable them to acquire skills that will assist them to develop their potential, to be productive, to facilitate poverty reduction and to promote socio-economic growth and national development" (MoE, 2003).

Goals for the Education Sector

In fulfilment of the Education Mission, the Ministry of Education will provide the following:

- Facilities to ensure that all citizens, irrespective of age, gender, tribe, religion and political affiliation, are functionally literate and self-reliant.
- Basic education for all
- Opportunities for open education for all
- Education and training for skill development with emphasis on science, technology and creativity
- Higher education for the development of middle and top-level manpower requirements.

In providing these services, we will be guided by the following values:
- Quality education,
- Efficient management of resources,
- Accountability and transparency,
- Equity.

Education Strategic Plans (ESPs)

The current Education Strategic Plan (ESP) 2010 – 2020, spells out the strategies of the government for the education sector over the next decade. The plan builds upon its four predecessors and upon earlier visionary strategies. Below are the previous and the current ESPs.

ESP 2003-2015 Goals:

Throughout the ESP, these are generally re-ordered and grouped within four areas of focus:

1. Equitable Access to Education
   - Pre-school education
   - Access and participation in education and training
   - Girls access to education

2. Quality of Education
   - Quality of teaching and learning for enhanced pupil/student achievement
   - Academic and research programmes
   - Health and environment in schools and institutions
   - Prevention and management of HIV/AIDS

3. Educational Management
   - Educational planning and management

4. Science, Technology and TVET
   - Technical and vocational education and training
   - Science and technology education and training

From: (MoE, 2003, 2010a, 2010b)

The ESP, therefore, presents a synopsis of government intentions and conditions that address the following policy goals for education:

- Increase access to and participation in education and training
- Improve the quality of teaching and learning for enhanced pupil/student achievement
- Improve and extend technical/vocational education and training
- Promote and inculcate the values of good health and environmental sanitation in schools and institutions of higher learning and in their personal lives
- Strengthen and improve educational planning and management
- Promote and extend the provision of mathematics, science and technology education and training
- Improve the quality and relevance of academic and research programmes
- Promote and extend pre-school education
- Identify and promote education programmes that will assist in the prevention and management of HIV/AIDS
- Provide girls with equal opportunities to access the full cycle of education

ESP 2010-2020

Mission Statement: To provide relevant education with emphasis on science, information, communication and technology to equip individuals for self-actualisation, peaceful coexistence as well as skills for the workplace for national development.

Summary of Policy Drivers for ESP 2010 – 2020

The chapter has provided an overview of the policy basis for the strategic plan. Further insights into current policies may be obtained by referring to the various source documents produced by the relevant bodies. In summary, the policy basis of the ESP 2010 2020 is as follows:

- To put into effect the key provisions of the 2008 Education Act that relate to access, decentralisation, inclusion, quality, and system monitoring,
- To implement the Science, Technology and Mathematics Education (STME), Information and Communication Technology (ICT), Technical and Vocational Education and Training (TVET), Special Education Division (SpED), Tertiary Education, Teacher Education policies as they relate to enrichment of education provision, improvement in quality, and personal and national development,
- Following enactment of the appropriate laws and measures, to implement the Government commitment to fee abolition and other poverty alleviation measures, and the provision of teaching incentives, and increased study opportunities at secondary and tertiary levels.
- To continue to subscribe and commit to the principles that relate to Education for All and the Millennium Development Goals (MDGs) 2, 3, 6 and 7.

Focus and Limitations of the Policies

The ESPs give attention to ensuring increased access to education, free education for all, promoting information technology, vocational skills training, and effective management of the sector and provision of resources and good remuneration for teachers. The policies sought to attend to the goals in order to reduce poverty and achieve the MDGs. The policies sought to put to effect education acts and provide facilities and resources and increase access. It was to implement policies of old which do not take into consideration the current challenges that the nation faces. Curriculum was not considered for modification to ensure not only quality but the needed skills and knowledge necessary for this time. In addition, the school environment, particularly impartation of knowledge and skills to students, was not considered even for the teacher training schools. Whether we need to change our ways of teaching, what additional knowledge or skills are required, what should the child know and be able to do upon graduation, and what are the current trends and needs that are necessary for our students to compete internationally? These are issues and questions that were necessary to be considered. And it is apparent that what we want the education to do and how it is to be done were completely ignored in the policies. Hayford (2012) describes the observation different by stating that, education and employment play a key role in the political economy of nations, contributing to the unprecedented sense of economic and social progress. He added that, the unbreakable linkage between education, employment, economy and society is often lost on these analysts, not least politicians.

What the policies considered are good and vital but there were important factors which were ruminated on. And these are that the one in our view, are equally crucial for the future of the nation. A survey was carried out to sample ideas on the policies by explaining the goals of the policies to participant and allowing them to indicate their views on the limitations of the policy. The outcome is as shown in the table below.

Table 1: Policy Analysis by Participants

PARTICIPANT OBSERVATIONS	RESPONSE (%)	
	Agree	Disagree
The policies focused on ensuring that the educational system functions properly but did not redesign it	43	57
The policies did not consider current classroom challenges	60	40
The policies paid attention to maintain standards using bodies but did not specify the exact school environment challenges which it wants to address	61	39
The policies as standards are comprehensive and address the major factors affecting education	50	50
The policy did not consider modification of educational curriculum to tackle issues of unemployment	57	43
Modification of educational goals to reflect the requirements of the nation in terms of advancement in technology etc	57	43
The policy does not consider provision of educational facilities apart from physical infrastructure at all levels	66	34
The policies did not spell out the specific measure to ensure that ICT and vocational training yield the expected result at all levels	86	14

As hinted earlier, the participants (43%) agree with the obvious fact that curriculum review was not considered in relation to observed challenges in society. And 61% of the participants were of the view that the policies paid attention to maintain standards using bodies such as accreditation board etc. but did not specify the exact school environment challenges which the bodies ought to address. It is, thus, apparent that there are specific needs that the people would have loved to be addressed, and that the actual drivers of change were not all considered in the drafting of the policy. It appears the goals set for education many years ago which do not completely provide the solution to the current national issues, are the ones the new policy is focusing on.

The Real Situation

Globalization, modernization and the advent of information technology have significantly impacted national development. The positive change cannot be over emphasized, however, alongside the benefits are undesirable changes. Successive governments have done extremely well in mitigating the undesirable outcomes of sociopolitical and socioeconomic changes. In spite of the efforts, identification of factors and the effects of the change is necessary for policy developments and governance. It is worth stating therefore, that the needs and aspirations of Ghanaians have changed. Many years ago, extended families took care of their own. Now people are more focused on the nuclear family and this change has been promoted by laws (which supports the nuclear family to inherit the wealth of the family head), so in recent times, there is a norm in Ghana which says, let those who inherit bear the cost of burial. People spend more time out working to make ends meet, and in the process, what we witness are children (house helps) taking care of children! Parents now leave home early to get to work, and children of primary school age leave home at about 3.00 am to go to school and return as late as 8.00 pm. The life in some homes is now different from what we are familiar with. The youth have adopted new culture and values. Their mode of dressing, manner of speech, attitudes and behaviors has changed. They no longer know the importance of simple social values such as greetings. A child will help you with your luggage only when they will benefit from it. People have gradually forgotten the games and stories which taught us moral values, changing the adage 'charity begins at home' to 'charity begins on the streets'.

The quest for wealth and a better life has made some corrupt. Some people have become so materialistic to the neglect of duty. A teacher is in a hurry to leave the class so that he can go and drive his taxi to make ends meet. Lecturers are equally influenced, and researches are considered by some as only a necessity for promotion. Politics is now a tool for enrichment, even the youth now work hard on campus to prepare the grounds for a political career, because as a politician, your class and financial status will change. 'Sakakwa' (money ritual) is now wasting away our youth. Distrust and dishonesty are no longer shameful acts as long as you get 'your cut' (share). This is the situation, not only in Ghana, but other developing countries around the globe.

The moral fabric of society has broken down. Ironically, this is also the time when many religious bodies have sprung up. In almost every town, there is a 'prophet'. Ritual murder, armed robbery, etc. are increasingly observed in the once safe country. It is no longer shameful for a lady to move in with a man. Having a girlfriend is now admirable. What used to be difficult to discuss, and do in public is no longer shameful and forbidden, because values and sense of pride have been lost to modernization. These are paving way for policy and constitutional amendments in a subtle manner. Sometime ago, a national debate on homosexuality and the right to grow and use cannabis (Indian hemp or 'wee') would not have been possible. We valued good behavior. Broken homes, divorce, and 'streetism' are on the increase leading to a corresponding increase in immorality.

Surprisingly, the modern age of information technology which brought huge promises for national development is corrupting our youth through the media. The new social value, 'money', is the reason why the youth use their rare skills of computer programming to 'dupe' and defraud people of their hard earned cash. The nation has forgotten its values and norms, coveting what destroys. Why would the younger generation not be more interested in that? Now we hear students say, 'sir I just want the degree to show that I also have one...', the essence of education is lost.

In the midst of this chaos, many are making money, and do not care what becomes of the future of the country. The mistakes (spelling and grammar) evident in the print and visual media, and inability to write good reports, are all indications of the failing educational system and shortcomings of the policies. The Ghana Education System is living on past glories. This is what Hanson (2015) has to say,

> *"There are general concerns people have raised in the past in line with formal education in Ghana. Is formal education making any significant impact on this nation? Are students in Ghana merely passing through our educational institutions? How are they impacting our society? Several people have received all forms of formal education, but how educated are they? Their general attitudes and behaviours speak otherwise. Clearly, people are going to school but not showing any visible signs of that? For some, it is just a fashion; everyone is receiving some form of formal training! What impact has formal education had on your life, if any? It is common to hear a seemingly uneducated or less-educated or learned person make remarks of how they expect more from the so-called formally educated person. That is a common utterance since in some cases, the behavior of some educated people leaves more to be desired. It is usually questionable! If you are educated, how educated are you?"*

Such stories abound and even though the commentators do not realize where the actual problem spring forth from, they are in their own way pointing out the limitations of the educational curricula. Hence, this indicates that the educational strategies are not comprehensive and representative. It apparently did not give attention to some important factors!

In summary, our nation has undergone drastic and major changes socioeconomically. Consequently, the factors of change are what ought to be targeted at when drafting policies. The foregoing discussion and the opinions sampled from fellow citizens in a survey (mainly by interview) revealed that the factors responsible for these observations include:

- Globalization
- Misuse of information technology
- Loss of nationalism
- Ostensibly altered social values and ideals
- Policies that are not comprehensive
- Political neglect of obvious facts
- Improper education of the masses on new factor influencing their lives
- Increasing unemployment situation

Educational policies which give attention to the school environment and curriculum modification to cater for national aspirations in the wake of globalization are thus crucial for ensuring the future of the nation. The country's future lies in the youth. Therefore, well-educated, skilled and healthy youths are essential in spite of the external influence. Whatever the situation or factors influencing socioeconomic developments, the nation must not lose sight of the youth. The solution lies in the classroom.

This study identified during the survey that, the modernization (85.71%), agents of cultural transformation (71.43%), and the school environment (93.23%) are among the factors responsible for affecting the quality of education in Ghana.

Table 2: Factors Identified by Participants as Affecting Quality Education

Factors Affecting Quality Education	Respondents (%)
Standard of living	85.71
Factors affecting social change	100.00
Modernization	85.71
Economic growth	100
Agents of cultural transformation	71.43
Monitoring and evaluation of teacher performance	71.43
Assessment of the productivity of students after graduation	71.43
School environment	93.23
Involvement of industrial sector	85.72
Characteristic of the industrial sector and its effect on employment	57.14
National development needs	100.00
Definition of clear-cut goals for education at all levels	57.14

When the participants were asked to assess the inclusion of the identified factors on a scale of 1-5, the data in the table below was obtained. It was observed that approximately 85.7% of the respondents placed social and economic factors, review of curriculum and disparity in social class on a scale greater than or equal to three. This indicates the relevance of these factors in the discussion on socio-economic development and most importantly, their inclusion in the educational policy.

TABLE 3: FACTOR FOR INCLUSION IN POLICY

ITEM	SCALE*				
	1	2	3	4	5
Social factors influencing education			100		
Economic factors influencing education		14.29	28.57	28.57	28.57
Disparity in social class		14.29	42.86	42.86	
Loss of culture and tradition		28.57	71.43		

Effect of external culture through media	28.57	14.29	28.57		28.57
Standard of living		14.29	3	42.86	
Curriculum review			14.29	28.57	57.14
Link industrial activities with training					100

NB: The responses under the scales are in % of participants.

The country requires graduates who have the abilities that will enable them provide meaningful service to the nation. The following are to be expected of graduates at the respective levels of education:

University Graduates

- Communicate ideas effectively
- Design and develop products of commercial value
- Write a meaningful technical report
- Propose sound solutions to problem
- Plan and execute projects at least on a smaller scale but follow protocol
- Be very observant and critical in their analysis
- A conscientious researcher with an eye for details
- Ardor to keep schedules
- Very good report writing skills
- Knows and understands their professional rights
- Innovative and creative at all times, for example, they should be able work with limited resources and still provide adequate results).
- A good data analyst
- Good at data base design and management, as well as basic programming
- Have a legal knowledge of business and industry
- Ability to convert ideas to commercially viable products
- Have a sound knowledge of the current trends in their fields and issues in the country relating to their field which requires attention
- Indicate originality and independent mind by finding solution to a chosen problem with little supervision and share the findings with experts

HIGHER INSTITUTION

Innovative, creative, excellent communicator, application of knowledge to solve problems, and boldness to take initiative.

Secondary Certificate and Diploma Graduates

- Meticulous in Following laid down procedures
- Have very good writing skills
- Use simple computer software that are useful for providing service and managing business (e.g. like Microsoft access, excel and publisher, CorelDraw, adobe premiere and Photoshop, and others for special jobs depending on the professional course being studied)

SECONDARY AND DIPLOMA
Skills, vocation, and extensive knowledge relevant for development of the individual and the nation

- Good understanding of what they read
- Ability to summarize written information
- Simple computing
- Design and fabrication of simple useful objects
- History of Ghana and systems of government
- Extensive literature knowledge on areas and subject matters (fiction and biography) determined as necessary for the times
- Fundamental human rights
- Moral and life education (sex, religion, culture and tradition)
- Ability to engage in a formal debate in a professional manner

Basic School Leavers

- Read and write very well
- Speak English and another Ghanaian language other than the mother tongue with relative ease
- Use computer to type and search for information (use of Microsoft word and encyclopedia Encarta
- Draw and sketch ideas
- Do little projects with supervision
- Be able to make a list of items in an organized manner
- Know and be able to recite the national pledge and anthem
- Ability to memorize and reproduce
- Activated creative instincts (computer games, outdoor games, and building projects)
- Passion for knowledge and skill (competition and reward)

BASIC EDUCATION

Literacy and knowledge

There is no graduate with these qualities who will not be productive. If the policy sets goals for each level of education (as shown above) based on national development plans and come out with methods to measure them quantitatively before they graduate, for example, a professional assessment which must be passed before degree is awarded), then we will be certain of a brighter future for the nation. Students' performance has to be measured based on the goals for that level of education. The policies and government must introduce radical methods that will redirect the cause of national development. The school environment and revised curriculum will be major variables crucial in the redirection agenda.

Conclusion

It is evident that injecting so much money and time in the educational sector without deliberate attempt to focus on those factors which significantly affect national development and social change, will be like watering the leaves of a sick plant instead of the leaves. The focus should be to ensure that the educational system gives so much attention to the 'production process' and features of the product. Effective monitoring and evaluation, as well as quality assurance to maintain product quality. Consequently product quality in terms of predefined attributes based on national developmental plans is very essential for the way forward. Broader consultations and extensive research on the dynamics and factors of change are vital for the drafting of education policies.

Recommendations

In respect of the analyses and findings, the following are recommended:

- Complete overhauling of the educational strategic policy.
- Educational strategic policy makers should include experts from various sectors when considering curriculum review.
- New policies need to consider revising the social emotional school environment.
- Before considering an ESP, extensive research must be carried out to determine the factors affecting education in the country.
- A national policy on national goals drafted by involving all stake holders and political parties, in consonant with the positive features of globalization, industrialization, technology, and socioeconomic dynamics.
- The current education curriculum must be reviewed in line with national goals developed to tackle current and future needs.
- Extensive research on the dynamics and factors of change must be carried out.

References

Hanson, A. E. (2015). Formal Education in Ghana- A Story of Disappoinment. Retrieved March 27, 2016, from https://www.modernghana.com/news/407516/1/formal-education-in-ghana-a-story-of-disappoinment.html

Hayford, K. A. K. (2012). The Cost of Poor Educational Policies in Ghana - Ghanaian Chronicle. Retrieved March 27, 2016, from http://thechronicle.com.gh/the-cost-of-poor-educational-policies-in-ghana/

Kweitsu, R. (2016). Ghana's Education Sector: Key Challenges Hindering the Effective Delivery of Education and the Way Forward. Retrieved March 27, 2016, from https://www.modernghana.com/news/579629/ghanas-education-sector-key-challenges-hindering-the-effec.html

MoE, G. (2003). Government of Ghana 2003 to 2015, Volume 1 Policies, Targets and Strategies, *1*(May 2003).

MoE, G. (2010a). Government of Ghana 2010 to 2020 Volume 1, Policies, Strategies, Delivery, Finance. Ministry of Education.

MoE, G. (2010b). Government of Ghana Education Strategic Plan 2010 - 2020 ESP Volume 2 – Strategies and Work Programme. Ministry of Education.

Owusu-Mensah, K. (2016). Education Reforms, Fallen Standards and ..... Retrieved March 27, 2016, from https://www.modernghana.com/news/92533/1/education-reforms-fallen-standards-and-.html

UEW (2015). Evolution of Educ 2. University of Education Wineba, Ghana. Retrieved from http://ccs.infospace.com/ClickHandler.ashx?ld=20160327&app=1&c=deal wifi4&s=dealwifi&rc=DealWifi4&dc=&euip=41.66.194.166&pvaid=694e56 66a42c47d68ffca2eb9d157e46&dt=Desktop&fct.uid=8189b0e58cd5492eaee15e439538c408 &en=+I14PArAkOd/YoTSlJUp1WCzxFUeCLg/AMu

11

Trainee Teachers' Perception of Entrepreneurship Education as a Strategy for Job Creation: Counselling Implications

Chiaka P. Denwigwe *Ph.D*

Abstract

Through a descriptive survey, this study investigated the perception of Nigerian trainee teachers on the use of entrepreneurship education to create employment opportunities. The Colleges of Education in the North Central Geopolitical Zone formed the population while six hundred trainee teachers (300 males and 300 females) selected through multi-stage sampling from three Colleges of Education in the zone formed the sample. Relevant data were collected using a questionnaire designed by the researchers and validated by experts. One research question namely, 'what do trainee teachers perceive as the factors that will encourage entrepreneurship education?' was asked to guide this study. Three hypotheses were formulated to guide this study; they include Trainee teachers' perception of the use of entrepreneurship education to promote job creation is not significantly high, Trainee teachers' perception of the use of entrepreneurship education to impart self-reliance skills leading to job creation is not significantly high. A pilot testing with 30 respondents gave a reliability coefficient of 0.85 which was significant at 0.05 significant level. Data analysis was done using descriptive statistics. Based on the findings, some useful recommendations were stated such as embracing current best practices in entrepreneurship education as a way of orienting the youths towards self-reliance. Such best practices include the institution of business clusters where people will exchange ideas and come up with paradigm shifts that will create jobs. Adults who were not opportune when young to receive business education would have a second chance as they interact with graduates with the creative mentality in the cluster zones. Other recommendations were to strengthen the infusion of aspects of entrepreneurship education into the curriculum at all levels of education and the introduction of entrepreneurship clubs at all levels of education. The counselling implication is that counselling for entrepreneurship is needful since Entrepreneurship Education is significant in overcoming the massive unemployment rate in Nigeria.

Key Words: *Perception, Entrepreneurship, Education, Strategy, Job creation.*

Introduction

Nigerians are becoming increasingly aware of the significance of education in human capital development. This increase in the degree of knowledge has translated to a very high demand for education. Unfortunately, the available vacancies in the job market are not commensurate with the huge number of graduates coming out yearly from our educational institutions. The rate of unemployment in our nation is increasing at a geometrical rate considering the number of students turned out annually from universities and other higher institutions (Okoh, 2014). To worsen this is the fact that the education provided for our teeming youths is somewhat deficient in that it lacks the ability to equip the younger ones with the skills that will make them employable or even the employers of labour. Some graduates are not only unemployed but unemployable due to poor academic quality (Okoh, 2014). Poor academic quality naturally stems from education that is not functional or entrepreneurial. Ijaiya (2007) noted that many school leavers in Nigeria lack the requisite skills for gainful employment. Henderson and Robertson (2007) observed that the entrepreneurial spirit remains tenuous (weak) in an ageing society where the working environment in time to come will depend heavily on the creativity and individuality of the young. It simply means that in the present dispensation, mere paper qualification hardly can put food on one's table neither can absolute dependence on national oil wells make for sustainable development. Many natural resources are wasting away in Nigeria while the youths who lack the wherewithal to harness them roam the streets in pursuit of white collar jobs from an already saturated job market. What is needed is the type of education that will inculcate self-reliance in learners.

In spite of efforts by successful Nigerian entrepreneurs such as Aliko Dangote, Mike Adenuga, Femi Otedola and others, in showcasing the role of entrepreneurship to national development through entrepreneurial efforts, the rate at which youths, especially the trainee teachers imbibe long-term entrepreneurship ideas is relatively minimal. This low level of buying into the entrepreneurship ideas is against the global shift into entrepreneurship with less emphasis on white collar jobs. The statements that the idle mind is the devil's workshop and that the hungry man is an angry man suggest that youths who are not gainfully employed will become cheap instruments for destabilizing the nation. The reason is that they will be lured easily into crimes like robbery, kidnapping, insurgency, militancy and rigging of elections, etc. To gainfully employ the teeming youth population and divert their attention from crimes, entrepreneurship education must be encouraged. Since trainee teachers are the would-be primary drivers of education, their perceptions about entrepreneurship as a means of job creation are very necessary and can significantly promote or discourage entrepreneurship education. It is against this backdrop that this study investigated the trainee teachers' perception of entrepreneurship education as a means of creating employment opportunities.

The Concept of Entrepreneurship Education

Different people have defined entrepreneurship education in a variety of ways. Entrepreneurship education enables students to have knowledge; skills and motivation which will help them develop entrepreneurial progress in different areas. Okoro and Afunobi (2010) described entrepreneurship education as that which makes for the acquisition of occupational valuable skills and production of artisans. Omolayo (2006) viewed entrepreneurship education as an act of starting a company and arranging for business deals which involve taking risks to be able to gain some profit using educational skills acquired. Nwangwu (2007) commented that entrepreneurship education seeks to combine the factors of production. These factors of production include land, labour and capital to provide a product or service for consumption by the public. Berchard and Toulose (1998) defined it as a collection of formalized teaching which enlightens, directs, and equips whoever is interested in a business creation or small business development. Entrepreneurship education makes room for innovation, creation of job opportunities and promotes economic growth. It is an employment strategy that can lead to economic self-sufficiency. To make Nigeria a united, strong and self-reliant nation with a great and dynamic economy and a land of bright and full opportunities for all citizens as enshrined in the national development plan of 1970 to 1974 will remain a Herculean task unless we rise to the demand for entrepreneurship education. It is because the benefit of entrepreneurship education is immense.

Entrepreneurship education promotes a culture of enterprise which impacts on national development. It helps to develop business skills especially among the younger generation and also helps in the inclusion of marketable skills in teacher training programmes. It contributes to providing courses and support for graduates who wish to start their own business and also promotes the type of teaching that is relevant to students' job opportunities. Entrepreneurship education prepares youths to be responsible and enterprising individuals by exposing them to opportunities of acquiring actual life learning experiences where they can bear risks, manage the knowledge and learn from the outcomes. Through this process, they become entrepreneurs or develop entrepreneurship attitudes. They imbibe organizational skills, such as management of time, leadership qualities, interpersonal skills and team spirit which will enable them to be good employers or employees. Entrepreneurship Education, if well delivered, can lead to improved academic performance, improved attendance to school, increased problem-solving and decision-making abilities. It imparts financial management skills, public speaking skills and makes for enhanced social and psychological development.

Given the need for adequate preparation for employment among school leavers and graduates, it becomes highly necessary to embrace entrepreneurship education. However, entrepreneurship education is faced with distinct challenges which hamper its progress. These include lack of identifiable role models, inadequate media coverage of entrepreneurship activities, poor social regard for entrepreneurs and their activities, lack of encouragement from teachers, career guidance counsellors and significant orders on the issue of choosing entrepreneurship as a career, and so on. There is indeed need to provide an enabling environment that will trigger the entrepreneurship spirit among Nigerian trainee teachers.

Purpose of Study

This study was designed to investigate the trainee teachers' perception of entrepreneurship education as a strategy for job creation, and to examine gender differences in such perceptions.

Significance of the study

Findings from this study will be significant in that it will help better planning of entrepreneurship education. It will create greater awareness of parents, educational administrators, government and other stakeholders on the importance of entrepreneurship education as a means of job creation.

Research Question

What do trainee teachers perceive as the factors that encourage entrepreneurship education?

Hypotheses

The following three hypotheses were put forward and tested in this study:

- Trainee teachers' perception of the use of entrepreneurship education to promote job creation is not significantly high.
- Trainee teachers' perception of the use of entrepreneurship education to impart self-reliance skills leading to job creation is not significantly high.
- There is no significant gender difference in trainee teachers' perception of the use of entrepreneurship education to promote job creation.

Method

The study was a descriptive survey. The study population consisted of all the trainee teachers in the Colleges of Education in the North Central Geopolitical Zone. Through multi-stage sampling, three colleges of education were selected from three of the states in the zone. 200 trainee teachers (100 males and 100 females) were selected from each of the three colleges of education in the three sampled states for the study. In all, 600 trainee teachers were the sample with 300 being males and 300 females.

Instrument for Data Collection

Trainee Teachers Perception of the use of Entrepreneurship Education for Job Opportunities Questionnaire (TPEJOQ) designed by the researcher was the instrument for data collection. TPEJOQ comprised four sections A B, C and D. Section A of this tool was used to gather demographic information while sections B, C and D contained 20 items which gathered information on the respondents' perception of the use of entrepreneurship education. A four-point Likert-type of scale with the responses 'strongly agree', 'agree', 'disagree' and 'strongly disagree', was used to measure the responses.

Validity and Reliability of the Instrument

Some experts in Measurement and Evaluation and Guidance and Counselling validated the instrument. After scrutiny, they came up with suggestions that led to the addition and deletion of some items in the questionnaire. A pilot testing carried out on 30 respondents found to be similar in characteristics to the respondents of the study population yielded the reliability of the instrument. A reliability coefficient of 0.85 was obtained using the Pearson Product Moment Correlation Coefficient and was deemed significant at 0.05 significant level. Therefore, the instrument was considered reliable.

Analysis of Data

The data collected by the TPEJOQ was analyzed using simple percentage and chi-square as the statistical instruments.

Presentation of Results
Research Question 1

What do trainee teachers perceive as the factors that encourage entrepreneurship education?

The simple percentage analysis which gave the answer to research question 1 is presented in table 1 below.

Table 1: Percentage Analysis of the Responses of Subjects on the Factors that Encourage Entrepreneurship Education

S/N	Statements	SA	A	D	SD	TOTAL
1	Funding by Government and provision of current learning materials are necessary to encourage entrepreneurship education.	295= 49.2%	200= 33.3%	85= 14.2%	20= 3.3%	100%
2	Better media coverage of entrepreneurship activities will promote entrepreneurship education.	300= 50%	220= 36.7%	45= 14.2%	35= 5.8%	100%
3	Without the use of role models, competitions, sensitization campaigns and awards people will not be sufficiently aware of entrepreneurship education.	250= 41.7%	280= 46.7%	50= 8.3%	20= 3.3%	100%
4	Counselling for parents to support children who want to embrace entrepreneurship is needful.	330= 55%	230= 38.3%	30= 5%	10= 1.7%	100%
5	Discrimination by members of the society against people who choose entrepreneurship as a career is appalling and should be stopped.	280= 46.7	200= 33.3%	60= 10%	60= 10%	100%
6	Misconceptions about entrepreneurship must be corrected	355= 59.12%	180= 30%	40= 6.7%	25= 4.2%	100%

Table 1 above shows that in all the cases, those who responded in the affirmative (i.e. strongly agreed and agreed) put together scored over 80% while those who disagreed scored 20% or below. Specifically 82.5% of the trainee teachers agreed that Government funding and provision of current learning materials are necessary to encourage entrepreneurship education while 17.5% disagreed. 86.7% agreed that better media coverage is necessary for improved entrepreneurship education while 13.3% disagreed. 88.4% agreed that without the use of role models, competitions, sensitization campaigns and awards, people will not be sufficiently aware of the importance of entrepreneurship education while 11.6% disagreed and so on. Therefore, the trainee teachers perceive the factors in table one above as the things that encourage entrepreneurship education.

Hypothesis 1

Trainee teachers' perception of the use of entrepreneurship education to promote job creation is not significantly high.

The Chi-test analysis of the data with which this hypothesis was tested is presented in table 2 below.

106

Table 2: Chi-test Analysis of Trainee Teachers' Perception of the Use of Entrepreneurship Education to Promote Job Creation

S/N	Statements	SA	A	D	SD	TOTAL	X2(Cal.)
1	Equips one with skills to be an employer of labour/employable	200	180	120	100	600	844.5
2	Equips one to identify new business opportunities	300	120	95	85	600	
3	Equips one to respect the dignity of labour and to fend for himself/herself	160	170	120	150	600	
4	Provides one with skills and support necessary for career in small scale business	300	200	70	30	600	
5	Creates more job opportunities than education for white collar jobs	250	150	100	100	600	
6	Helps one to aspire to achievement and self-improvement both at school and in later life	190	200	120	90	600	
7	Provides good experience and opportunity to have higher quality education and future employment, so it is alright to introduce it into the curriculum at all levels	270	180	100	50	600	
8	It gives an improved status and prestige as it helps create good employment	200	186	114	100	600	
TOTAL	Observed Frequencies Expected Frequencies	1870 (233.8)	1386 (173.3)	839 (104.9)	705 (88.1)	4800	

Degree of Freedom (Df) =(c-1)(r-1)=(4-1)(8-1)=21

Critical value at .05 significant level and at 21 d.f= 32.67. Since the x^2 (calculated) value of 8445.4 is greater than the critical value of 32.67 at .05 significant level and at 21 d.f, hypothesis 1 which states that the Trainee teachers' perception of the use of entrepreneurship education to promote job creation is not significantly high is rejected while the alternative is accepted.

Hypothesis 2

Trainee teachers' perception of the use of entrepreneurship education to impart self-reliance skills leading to job creation is not significantly high. The Chi-test analysis of the data with which this hypothesis was tested is presented in table 3 below.

Table 3: Chi-test Analysis of Subjects' Perception of the Use of Entrepreneurship Education to Impart Self-Reliance Skills Leading To Job Creation

S/N	Statements	SA	A	D	SD	TOTAL	x^2 (cal)
1	Gives one confidence in his/her skills and experience	250	200	90	60	600	4703.4
2	Provides one opportunity to develop psychomotor skills greatly needed for job creation	250	180	90	80	600	
3	Provides meaningful training for self-reliance	300	120	80	100	600	
4	Helps one to engage in tasks that yield profit and make one independent	200	200	120	80	600	
5	It is a step in the right direction for graduating students who are equipped with creative and innovative skills and experience	350	100	75	75	600	
6	In addition to the main course of study, it is needful for all students as a career option in future since it equips one with needed skills	280	130	90	100	600	
TOTAL	Observed frequencies Expected frequencies	1630 (271.7)	930 (155)	545 (90.8)	495 (82.5)	3600	

$Df = (c-1)(r-1) = (4-1)(6-1) = 15$

Critical value at .05 significant level and at 15 d.f= 24.99. Since the x^2 (calculated) value of 4703.4 is greater than the critical value of 24.99 at .05 significant level and at 15 d.f, the hypothesis two which states that Trainee teachers' perception of the use of entrepreneurship education to impart self-reliance skills leading to job creation is not significantly high is rejected while the alternative is accepted.

Hypothesis 3

There is no significant gender difference in trainee teachers' perception of the use of entrepreneurship education to promote job creation.

The x^2-test analysis of the data with which this hypothesis was tested is presented in table 4 below.

Table 4: x^2-test Analysis of Perceptions of Trainee Teachers Based on Gender

Variable	SA	A	D	SD	Total	Df	• -calculated	Critical	Decision rule
Males Females	150 900	80 100	40 50	30 60	300 300		88.5	7.8	Reject null hypothesis
Total (observed frequencies) Expected Frequencies	240 120	180 90	90 45	90 45					

Df=(c-1)(r-1) =3

Table 4 shows a calculated x^2 value of 88.5 which is less than the critical value of 7.8 at 0.05 significant level at 3 degrees of freedom. Therefore the null hypothesis 3 which states that there is no significant gender difference in trainee teachers' perception of the use of entrepreneurship education to promote job opportunities is rejected and the alternative is accepted.

Summary of Findings

- Trainee teachers perceive the following as the factors that encourage entrepreneurship education: funding by government and provision of current learning materials, better media coverage of entrepreneurship activities, the use of role models, competitions, sensitization campaigns and awards to create awareness, counselling parents to support children who want to embrace entrepreneurship. Also, they perceive discouraging discrimination by members of the society against people who choose entrepreneurship as a career, and corrections of misconceptions about entrepreneurship as factors that promote entrepreneurship.
- Trainee teachers' perception of the use of entrepreneurship education to promote job creation is significantly high
- Trainee teachers' perception of the use of entrepreneurship education to impart self-reliance skills leading to job creation is significantly high.
- There is a significant gender difference in trainee teachers' perception of the use of entrepreneurship education to promote job creation.

Discussion of Findings

The factors perceived by trainee teachers to encourage entrepreneurship education are in line with the work of some other researchers. For instance, Gabadeen and Raim (2012) reported that poor funding of higher learning in Nigeria has terribly affected the implementation of entrepreneurship education curriculum. They also reported a deficiency in the current learning materials made available to students offering entrepreneurship education in Nigerian tertiary institutions and that this hinders the actualization of the goals of entrepreneurship education as stated in the higher education curriculum. It then means that funding and provision of current learning materials by

Government will encourage entrepreneurship education. According to Ifedili and Ofoegbu (2011), students perceive entrepreneurship education as one of the additional courses imposed on them by the school authorities to fulfil graduation requirements and so exhibit poor participation in all entrepreneurship activities on campus. It is a misconception and buttresses the finding of the present study that correction of misconceptions is necessary to encourage entrepreneurship.

The results show a favourable disposition of trainee teachers towards entrepreneurship education as a means of creating job opportunities and are in line with the view of Obioma (2012) that the Nigerian youths have an inherent potential to be enterprising and only need a little push to spark off this enterprising spirit. The result shown in Table 2 and Table 3 that the trainee teachers' perception of the use of Entrepreneurship Education to promote job creation and impact self-reliance skills leading to job creation is significantly high agrees with the finding by Ejiofor (2009). The average undergraduate has an excellent entrepreneurship perception irrespective of his course of study. No doubt, many, especially trainee teachers, have come to the realisation of the need for the teeming job-seekers to be gainfully employed. They view entrepreneurship education as a right option through which they can channel their energy, creativity, and potentials into innovations and problem-solving ventures that will eventually yield high dividends. The finding in Table 4 that there is a significant gender difference in trainee teachers' perception towards the use of entrepreneurship education for job opportunities are in line with the finding by Nwoye (2007), which discovered that female entrepreneurship skills lag behind and are influenced by different social, psychological and cultural factors. It also agrees with the finding by Reynolds, Bygrave, Autio and Hay (2002) that men are more likely to be involved in entrepreneurship than women in a ratio of 2: 1. However, it is evident nowadays that women are taking giant strides into particular entrepreneurship endeavours which men formerly dominated such as generator repairs, electrical repairs and maintenance, carpentry and so on. This will help to close up the gap in perception between males and females.

Counselling Implications

Counselling as a helping profession should put programmes in place to encourage trainee teachers to embrace entrepreneurship education as a means of promoting job opportunities. The Counsellor should help the trainee teachers to make wise, intelligent choices and decisions that will assist them to become employable and employers of labour. Parents should be counselled to support children to embrace entrepreneurship. Counsellors should be at the vanguard of campaigns to enlighten people on the need to embrace entrepreneurship, encourage the establishment of cluster zones with interplay of human and material resources for the purpose of introducing paradigm shifts for job creation, discourage any discrimination against entrepreneurship as well as correct misconceptions about entrepreneurship.

Conclusion

The investigations showed trainee teachers to be favourably disposed towards using entrepreneurship education as a strategy for job creation. An enlightened perception towards entrepreneurship education is paramount in a society in which technology is gradually taking over and is encouraging downsizing and out-sourcing. There is the need to embrace warmly entrepreneurship education which provides the needed survival skills by way of flexibility and creativity. Self-confidence, discipline and perseverance are keys to success in entrepreneurship and should be promoted through public enlightenment. It is a significant challenge for educationists and policy-makers to see that courses and support especially funding are provided to promote entrepreneurship education.

Recommendations

The Study has made the following recommendations:

- The institution of programmes (trainings) for the small business start-ups highlighting issues like raising funds, primary accounts, employment issues and marketing, etc and aimed at people who want to be self- employed/encouraging wealthy and philanthropic individuals to invest into our economy so as to stem the tide of unemployment.
- Current best practices in entrepreneurship education such as the institution of business clusters where people will exchange ideas and come up with paradigm shifts that will create jobs should be embraced as a way of orienting the youths towards self-reliance. Adults who were not opportune when young to receive business education would have a second chance as they interact with graduates with the creative mentality in the cluster zones.
- There should be strengthening of the infusion of aspects of entrepreneurship education into the curriculum at all levels of education.
- The introduction of entrepreneurship clubs at all levels of education.
- Operations of Nigeria Directorate of Employment (NDE), Small and Medium Enterprise Development Agency (SMEDA), National Poverty Eradication Programme (NAPEP), Industrial training Fund (ITF) and other agencies relevant to job creation and youth employment should be reactivated and made more responsive to the issue of employment.

References

Berchard, J. P. & Toulose, J. M. (1998). Validation of a Didactic Model for the Analysis of Training Objectives in Entrepreneurship. *Journal of Business Ventures.* 13(4). In econpapers.repec.org/ RePEc:eee:jbvent:v…(2013). Retrieved, 5th July, 2014.

Ejimofor, V. I. (2009). Refining the University Entrepreneurship Courses: A Case Study of the University of Abuja. *Journal of Social and Policy Issues, 6(3),* 45-49.

Gabadeen, W. O. & Raim, L. (2012). Management of Entrepreneurship Education in Nigerian Higher Institutions: Issues, Challenges and Way Forward. *Abuja International Journal of Education and Management Sciences, 1 (2),* 246.

Henderson, R. & Robertson, M. (2007). Who wants to be an Entrepreneur? Young Adults' Attitude to Entrepreneurship as a Career. *Career Development Int.* 5 (6), 279-287.

Ifedili, C. & Ofoegbu, F. (2011). Managing Entrepreneurship Education in Nigerian Universities. *European Journal of Educational Studies 3(1)* ISSN 1946-6331.

Ijaiya, B. S. (2007). Addressing Youth Unemployment through Entrepreneurship Education. *llorin Journal of Education*, Vol. 27.

National Development Plan 1970-1974. *www.ascleiden.nl/…/development-plans-..*Retrieved 10th July, 2014.

Nwoye, M. (2007). Gender Responsive Entrepreneurial Economy of Nigeria: Enabling Women in a Disabling Environment. *Journal of International Women,* 9 (1).

Nwangwu, I. G. (2007). *Higher Education of Self-reliance: An Imperative for the Nigerian Economy.* NEAP Publication.1-8.

Obioma, G. (2012). Entrepreneurship Education: Curriculum Content and its Imperative for National Development. *Abuja International Journal of Education and Management Sciences,* 1 (2), 2012. P.48.

Okoh, N. D. (2014). *Presidential Address (Bishop's Charge).* Presented at the First Session of the Ninth Synod of the Church of Nigeria (Anglican *Communion*) of the Diocese of Abuja

Okoro, I. F. & Afunobi, A. O. (2010). The Need for Entrepreneurship Education: A Case of Home Economics. *Issues on Contemporary Education Book of Readings.* Department of Educational Foundations and Administration, Imo State University Owerri. 154-160.

Omolayo, B. (2006). Entrepreneurship in Theory and Practice. In F. Omotosho, Aluko, T.K.O, Ware, O.I,& Adaramola, G. (Eds.). *Introduction to Entrepreneurship in Nigeria.* Ado-Ekiti: UNAD Press.

Renolds, P. D., Bygrave, W. D., Autio, E., & Hay, M. (2002). Global Entrepreneurship Monitor: 2012 *Summary Report.*

12

Briefs and Benefits of the Ghana Universities Staff Superannuation Scheme

Alhassan Iddrisu

Abstract

*T*his article seeks to provide relevant information on the origin of the Ghana University Staff Superannuation Scheme (GUSSS), its benefits and to aid members on how to calculate these benefits for effective retirement planning. The article benefits from existing literature on GUSSS and other privately managed pension schemes. It also makes use of interviews gathered from beneficiaries of the pension schemes as a way to compare feedback on relative satisfaction of the GUSSS. Simplified information has been used to illustrate computations of benefits for all categories of staff. The paper enables self-assessment as a guide to effective retirement planning. This is intended to establish a case for the scheme and to attract new members in order to boost the liquidity of GUSSS.

Key Words: *Superannuation, Social Security, Pension Scheme, Ghana Universities*

Introduction

The issue of retirement and the quality of social security for retired workers is a source of concern to both employers and employees. In Ghana, retired workers depend on pension for their sustenance (Gockel and Kumado, 2003). Pension is a monthly income paid from a defined scheme to retired workers who, during their working life, contributed to such a scheme for their social security during their retirement life. Contribution to pension funds is a legal requirement in Ghana (Natioal Pension Act, 2008). Workers are expected to contribute 5.5% of their basic salary to be supplemented by 13% of same basic by the employer. The total contribution of 18.5% of the workers' basic salary must be paid to the pension fund manager within two weeks after the deduction (ibid). There are several pension fund managers in Ghana. The Social security and National Insurance Trust (SSNIT) is the recognized government social security fund manager. There are other private social security fund managers, and the Ghana Universities Staff Superannuation Scheme (GUSSS) is the most prominent.

Recent developments in the labour front on the management of workers' pension have triggered certain actions by government, which in itself is a source of concern for the management of the GUSSS. Government has cancelled the payment of pension to retired members of the GUSSS and by default, requiring the various GUSSS Management Boards to absorb such pension payments. There is also the call from government for the Universities to join the SSNIT Pension scheme. This call was premised on the allegation that the various schemes in the Universities are not sustainable and could possibly create pension problems in the future. On the other hand, the Boards of the GUSSS in the various Universities are working assiduously, to prove that the schemes are not only sustainable, but also that they can provide a better pension life than any other scheme manager. Actions taken so far include the enhanced contribution scheme and moves towards unification of all the GUSSS in the public universities.

History of Pension in Ghana

Formal pension scheme in Ghana has gone through various phases since its introduction in 1950. The CAP 30 Pension Scheme was introduced in 1950 to remedy the discriminatory pension benefits which characterise the colonial pension regime. In 1961, the Compulsory Savings Act (Act 70) was also introduced. The Social Security Act (Act 279) then followed in 1965. Today, the National Pension Act (Act 766), which came into force in 1990, provided for pension reforms in the country by the introduction of a three-tier contributory pension scheme. As part of the researcher's examination, the three-tier scheme will be expanded later in the article.

The CAP 30

Before 1950 and the introduction of Cap 30 pension scheme, there existed a Pension Ordinance for British Officers in the Gold Coast. This was a non-contributory reward scheme for civil servants, which was intended to eliminate an earlier discriminatory pension scheme, the 1946 Pension Ordinance. Due to flaws in this Pension Ordinance, the British Administration had to replace and unify pension of European Officers and that of the Non-European Officers. This led to the creation of a single non-discriminatory pension scheme that gave equal benefits to both local and expatriate workers in the country at that time. The new pension scheme, known as CAP 30, and which derived from chapter 30 of the Pension Ordinance of 1946, was a non-contributory reward scheme for civil servants. For members to benefit from the CAP 30 scheme, they should have worked for 10 years. The scheme provided for a voluntary retirement age of 45 years and a compulsory retirement age of 50 years (Gockel and Kumado, 2003). The CAP 30 scheme targeted at boosting efficiency and loyalty of civil servants especially, coming at a period where the Gold Cost was experiencing a transition from an expatriate dominated civil service to an indigenous one (Amartey, 2015). However, member's non-contribution to the scheme challenged its sustainability.

Meanwhile, End of Service Benefits (ESB) scheme, a non-contributory scheme, which existed before CAP 30 could not be sustained on economic grounds and was, therefore, terminated in 1990.

Compulsory Savings Act (Act 70) - 1961

There emerged impetus to create a social security scheme with national coverage, following the challenges CAP 30 faced. In 1961, an attempt at developing a Social Security Scheme with national coverage was made, leading to the enactment by Parliament of the Compulsory Savings Act of 1961 (Act 70) NPRA, 2015. The Compulsory Savings Act (Act 70) was thus initiated to promote national savings and to provide social security on a national scale (ibid). Act 70 was replaced in 1965 by a Parliamentary Act on Social Security, (Act 279) which extended coverage to all establishments with employees of up to five (5) or more with the exception of employees already covered by the CAP 30 Pension scheme. These exceptions covered:

- Members of the Armed Forces
- Officers and men of the Police Service
- Staff of the Prison Service
- Foreigners in the diplomatic missions
- Senior members of the universities and Research Institutions (Nii Amarteifio, 2011)

The focus for the payment of retirement contribution therefore moved from being a reward for loyalty to one that was based on the right of all individual workers in Ghana (from both formal and informal sectors) (Kpessa 2010).

Provident Fund (Act 279) - 1965

A Provident Fund Scheme was later introduced by the 1965 Act of Parliament, Act 279. This fund, which would later be converted to a pension scheme in 1970, was jointly administered by the Department of Pensions of the Ministry of Finance and the State Insurance Corporation (Nii Amarteifio, 2011). Unlike the CAP 30 scheme, this provident fund scheme was contributory. Funding of defined contributions was based on contributions made by both employees and employers (usually on behalf of the employees). These contributions were then invested and when the employees reached retirement, became permanently incapacitated or died prior to retirement; the total contributions as well as the returns from the investments were paid as lump sum to the individual or his/her dependents.

The reason for this one off payments was due to its simplicity and ease of operation even to illiterate or poorly educated contributors. The Provident Fund scheme was regarded as a post independence initiative that would assist Ghana generate the needed pool of financial resources to fund developmental projects such as the construction of roads, health facilities, schools and provision of amenities such as electricity and good drinking water (Kpessa, 2010).

SSNIT (PNDCL 247) - 1990

In the early 1990s, the Provident fund scheme or provident funds as they came to be called was converted to social insurance by the government at that time, the Provisional National Defense Council (PNDC). The Administration of this new scheme was entrusted in the hands of an independent corporate body, the Social Security and National Insurance Trust (SSNIT). The main difference between this new scheme and the previous one was the shift from a lump-sum payment to a monthly payment of retirement benefits. The contributions made by both employers and their employees under the old scheme were however maintained. Under the new scheme, participants must have contributed for at least 240 months (20 years) to the scheme to qualify for retirement benefits. The scheme was designed for three main contingencies namely; old age/retirement, invalidity/disability and the dependents/survival's benefits (Kpessa, 2010).

The Three Tier Pension Model (Act 766) – 2008

The new pension Act (Act 766) came into force in 2008 seeking to reengineer the entire pension system in the country. The act introduced a three-tier pension scheme and brought into being the National Pension Regulatory Authority (NPRA). Under the act, the NPRA will regulate the administration and management of all registered pension schemes in the country. The act also calls for the re-establishment of SSNIT to administer the first tier of the new pension model and also to provide for other related pension matters in the country.

The first tier is a mandatory *Defined Benefit Scheme* which will be managed by SSNIT. Out of the 18.8% monthly SSF contribution, the first tier takes 13.5%. The remaining 5% is invested under the second tier. The second tier is also mandatory, but managed as a *Define Contribution Scheme* which, according to Act 766. Funds designated for this tier shall be managed by an approved Trustee licensed by the National Pension Regulatory Authority (NPRA). The 3rd tier is a voluntary fully funded provident fund to be managed by private fund managers approved by the NPRA.

Benefit under the first tier is in the form of monthly income as well as death and invalidity should a contributor die before retirement. SSNIT will not pay one-off lump sum benefit at retirement. However, under the tier two, employees are entitled to a lump sum payment which is expected to be higher than the present SSNIT and CAP 30 Schemes. Note that both tier two and tier three are defined contribution schemes and therefore the level of benefit is a function of both contribution and returns on investment. Meanwhile some categories of workers, especially senior members of Ghana's public universities and research institutions, were still left out of the three tier schemes.

Pension Schemes before SSNIT

Four Pension schemes preceded SSNIT, which was established in 1972, by the Social Security Decree (NRCD 127). Before this, there existed four pension schemes, which had close resemblance to the CAP 30 Scheme. These schemes include the following:

- The Teachers Pensions Ordinance (1955) for Teachers
- The Ghana Universities Staff Superannuation Scheme (1976)
- The CRIG Pension Scheme for Research & Senior Staff of the Ghana Cocoa Research Institute who joined before 1984
- The Ghana Armed Forces Pension Scheme of 1962

GUSSS - 1976

The exemption of senior members of public Universities and Research Institutions by the Social Security Act of 1965 (Act 279) created an impetus for the creation of the Ghana Universities Staff Superannuation Scheme (GUSSS) on 1st January 1976. The scheme was intended to be operated by all Public Universities in Ghana. The membership to the scheme covered the following category of staff of the universities.

- All existing members of the GUSSS as at 1st January 1976
- University Teachers and Research Fellows
- University Administrative, Library, and Professional Staff of the status comparable to that of University Teachers

Individual universities have, since the inception of the scheme, operated and managed the schemes independently. At the individual level, universities have established Boards of trustees, known as GUSSS Management Board (GMB), charged with the responsibility of managing the schemes sustainably. Membership to the GMB is made up of the following:

- A Chairman appointed by the Vice-Chancellor.
- One members appointed by Council.
- One member elected by Convocation
- Two members elected by the Academic Board
- One member elected by the Ghana Association of University Administrators.
- One member elected by Fund Managers
- Registrar
- Director of Finance (as the Fund manager)
  (University of Ghana Amended Regulations on the GUSSS)

Membership to GUSSS

Membership of GUSSS is automatic for the category of staff described under membership. In some universities, however, any staff who wants to join the scheme do so in writing to the Registrar. However, upon attaining membership, members must complete a nomination form. The nomination form is a declaration that the nominated person(s) will receive the benefit of the staff in the event of death. The name(s), date of birth, relationship and percentage nominee(s) will receive must be indicated in the form. The form should be witnessed by a responsible officer. The nomination form can be changed at any time by the member.

Funding

The GUSSS is funded from the mandatory Social Security Fund (SSF) contribution, from which is deducted monthly from payroll. The SSF contribution is made up of contribution by employer, in this case Government, and the employee, which are both drawn from the consolidated fund (Adjei, 1999).

At the University of Ghana, contribution to the scheme is compulsory for all newly appointed staff in the eligible category. Different Universities may have different arrangements. In any case, admitted staff and those who are already contributing to the scheme cannot opt out while they are still employed by the University. This is to avoid jeopardising the solvency of the scheme. However, as the scheme is intended to motivate staff to stay and work in the universities, members who are on leave without pay losses their membership. This means that working in the university is a condition precedent for membership.

As staff whose salaries are funded by government, GUSSS members' contributions should have been 5.5% from the employee's salary and 13% from the employer making 18.5% of members' basic salary. However, this currently stands at 25% from employee and 13 from employer, translating to a total of 38% of the basic salary as shown in Table 1.

Table 1: GUSSS Contributions - Statutory and Enhanced

Contributor	National Pension Act (Act 766)	GUSSS	Difference
	% of Basic	% of Basic	% of Basic
Employer	13	13	0
Employee	5.5	10	4.5
Enhanced[1]	0	15	15
Total	18.5	38	19.5

Source: Extracted from Data from the Payroll Office, UDS, 2015

Enhanced GUSSS

As a Management Board, the GMB, in the Public Universities are concerned for the good pension welfare and good pension life for members. To achieve and sustain its objectives, the GMBs in the public Universities convinced members to strengthen the financial muscle of their respective schemes. Consequently, members' contribution has been increased over the years. In March 2000, members' monthly contribution was increased from 5% to 7.5%. This was, further, increased to 10% in March 2001. The 10% contribution continued to September 2011 when the enhanced contribution was introduced. The first enhanced contribution was agreed at 40% of members' basic. However, upon the implementation of the new salary regime, known as the Single Spine Salary Structure in 2010, payment of which was effected in October 2011, the monthly contributions was restructured: 10% as normal contribution, and 15% as enhanced contribution. This brought the employees' contribution to 25%. Consequently, the total members' monthly contribution to the scheme currently stands at 38% (25% basic by the employee and 13% by employer) of members basic salaries[2]. Members accepted these new arrangements because, aside enhancing the liquidity and solvency of their respective schemes, there were tax benefit for members. The current Tax allowance available to members as a result of this compromise is 4.5% of their basic salary (i.e. 10%-5.5%).Members' contribution is a direct deduction from their monthly salaries and paid into the bank account of the Scheme.

Qualification under the GUSSS Scheme

Under normal circumstance, benefits under the scheme are available to members only on retirement. There are two types of retirements recognized by the scheme. These are compulsory retirement, which is at age 60 and voluntary retirement, which is before age 60 but not before age 55. In addition to the two qualifying conditions (i.e. compulsory retirement and voluntary retirement) a member should have contributed to the scheme for a minimum period of (15) fifteen years. In situations where a member cannot qualify for the benefits under the scheme because he could not attain the minimum pensionable age or serve the minimum contribution period, he shall be paid his total contribution (both employers and personal) plus interest at a rate equivalent to 91-day Government of Ghana Treasury Bill (University of Ghana Amended Regulations on the GUSSS). Advance Gratuity

---

[1] Enhanced Employee GUSSS contribution

[2] The numerical history and trend of the enhanced GUSSS contributions was obtained from the GUSSS Office at the University for Development Studies

Advance payment of gratuity is available for a member who attains age 58. A member interested in this facility must apply to the GUSSS Management Board. The member may be granted up to 40% of his gratuity to enable him prepare for retirement subject to the payment of interest to be determined by the Board. This amount plus the interest shall be recovered from the total gratuity due him on retirement.

Benefits

In pension management, pension benefits can be determined using two different models, namely defined benefit scheme (DBS) and defined contribution scheme (DCS). The DBS model guarantees benefits to be paid on retirement. The guaranteed benefit is usually expressed as a function of a known formula, the salary of the employee and period of contribution (Davies, 1993). On the other hand, scheme managers using the DCS model; maintain separate and identifiable accounts for individual members. Members' contributions are credited to their individual accounts. These contributions are then invested in high yielding instruments the returns of which are credited to respective members' accounts. The amount in members accounts on retirement stands for the members' benefit (Mosinyi, 2008).

The GUSSS is a defined benefit scheme (DBS) model; as such benefits can be predetermined because they based on certain known factors. The factors used to determine the benefit of members include the following:

1. *The number years of contribution:* The minimum number years to contribute to the scheme in order to qualify for benefit, is 15. This means the maximum number of years to join the scheme is 45. As a contribution scheme, a year is absolute and not rounded. That is 1 year 11 cannot be rounded to 2 years. Similarly a month is a period in which the full salary is earned.

2. *The terminal salary:* This refers to the salary a member is entitled to take at the date of retirement. If a member serves a lecturer but promoted to associate professor in the last month to his retirement, his terminal salary will be the associate professor's salary.

3. *The $\left(\frac{1}{40}\right)$ factor:* It is assumed that the maximum number of years member can contribute to the scheme is 40. So multiplying this factor by the actual number of contribution, gives us the fraction of the standard number years expected. The implication is that the more years a member contributes, the higher this fraction, consequently, the higher the benefit. It seems to the present researcher that the $\left(\frac{1}{40}\right)$ factor is out of date, because circumstances at the entry point have changed. The minimum qualifying certificate for entry to the senior member level is MPhil, which takes more than 20 year to obtain.

4. *The enhanced GUSSS multiplier, which is 1.5:* This is a pension booster as a result of the enhanced contribution.

The GUSSS scheme offers two options for staff on retirement. These are *Full Pension* and *Residual Pension Plus Gratuity*. These options are available for staff going on compulsory retirement and those going on voluntary retirement. This can result in retirees taking either full pension or a reduced pension. This is different from the SSNIT scheme. The SSNIT scheme has two types of retirement benefits namely: old age *retirement Pension* and old age *retirement Lump Sum*. However, the amount to be taken is a function of whether the staff on *compulsory* or *voluntary* retirement. Full pension is available only for staff on compulsory retirement (i.e. those who attain age 60). Reduced pension is paid to staff on voluntary retirement (i.e. between 55 and 59).

Computation of Benefits under GUSSS
Option 1: Full Pension

Under the Full pension option, pension is calculated at the rate of one fortieth $\left(\frac{1}{40}\right)$ part of terminal salary for each completed year of contribution, subject to a maximum of 40 years. There is no lump sum payment under this option. Pension is thus calculated as follows:

$Pension = \frac{1}{40} \times ts \times n$
Where:
ts is Terminal Salary
n is the Number of years contribution

For example, if Alhassan retires on an annual salary of GHC28,815.50 after contributing to the scheme for 39 years, his pension under this option will be calculated as follows:

$Pension = \frac{1}{40} \times 28,815.50 \times 39$
$Pension = GH¢28,095.11$

This will result in a monthly pension of GH¢2,341.26

Option 2: Residual Pension Plus Gratuity
Under this option, the retirement benefits of retiring staff are paid as follows:

1. A lump sum gratuity is paid. This is calculated as one quarter $\left(\frac{1}{40}\right)$ of full pension (as in option 1) multiplied by a factor of twenty. In the above example, gratuity payable to Alhassan will be:
   $Gratuity = \frac{1}{4} \times 28,095.11 \times 20$
   $Gratuity = GH¢140,475.55$

2. The remaining three quarters $\left(\frac{3}{4}\right)$ of the full pension shall be paid as residual pension. In this case Alhassan's pension will be calculated as *Residual Pension* $\frac{3}{4} \times 28,095.11$ which is GH¢21,071.33 per annum. The monthly pension can thus be derived by dividing this by 12 (i.e. 12 months). Alhassan's pension will thus become GH¢1,755.95.

Full Pension and Gratuity under the Enhanced GUSSS
Benefits under the enhanced GUSSS scheme is calculated in the same way as discussed earlier but with a multiplier of 1.5 as illustrated below:

Option 1: Full Pension under Enhanced GUSSS

$$Full\ Pension = \frac{1}{40} \times ts \times n \times 1.5$$

Where:
ts is Terminal Salary
n is the Number of years contribution

Using the example on Alhassan, full pension under the enhanced GUSSS can be calculated as follows:

$$Full\ Pension = \frac{1}{40} \times 28,815.50 \times 39 \times 1.5$$
$$Full\ Pension = GH¢42,142.67$$

This will result in a monthly pension of GH¢3,511.89.

Option 2: Residual Pension Plus Gratuity Under Enhanced GUSSS

$$Gratuity = \frac{1}{4} \times 42,142.67 \times 20$$
$$Gratuity = GH¢210,713.35$$

Residual Pension $\frac{3}{4} \times 42,142.67$, which is GH¢31,607.00 per annum.

Monthly pension = GH¢2,633.92.

Payment of pension shall be on monthly or quarterly basis and shall be guaranteed for a period of twenty years. However, if a pensioner lives beyond the guaranteed period, pension shall continue till death. Amount of pensions shall be indexed to prevailing salaries (i.e. Amount of pensions shall increase when salaries are increased).

Self-Assessment

The following section is meant to guide members (who are in or nearing retirement age) to reasonably calculate their benefits for effective retirement planning. The five categories of members are used in the process. Note that the computations are applicable the respective equivalencies. They are:

- Full professor
- Associate professor
- Senior lecturer
- Lecturer
- Assistant lecturer

The assumption is that all of them have worked for 15 years and have contributed to the scheme and have met all the requirements of the scheme. I have further assumed that all of them have reached the last step in their respective levels of the single spine salary scale.

Table 2 shows the benefits due to the staff from the GUSSS.

Table 2: Computation of Benefits under the GUSSS Enhanced Scheme

Staff Category	Parameters				Benefits			
	1/40 Factor	Terminal Salary	Number of Years Served	Enhanced GUSSS Multiplier (1.5)	Option 1 Full Pension		Option 2 Residual Pension Plus Gratuity	
					Full Pension (annual)	Monthly Pension (Option 1)	Gratuity (Lump Sum)	Monthly Pension (Option 2)
	a	b	c	d	e = (a*b*c*d)	f = (e/12)	g = (e*0.25*20)	h = (0.75*e)/12
Professor - Full	0.025	44,854.16	15	1.5	25,230.47	2,102.54	126,152.33	1,576.90
Professor - Associate	0.025	41,929.43	15	1.5	23,585.30	1,965.44	117,926.52	1,474.08
Lecturer - Senior	0.025	34,250.55	15	1.5	19,265.93	1,605.49	96,329.67	1,204.12
Lecturer	0.025	32,017.22	15	1.5	18,009.69	1,500.81	90,048.43	1,125.61
Lecturer - Assistant	0.025	27,977.96	15	1.5	15,737.60	1,311.47	78,688.01	983.60

Source: Author's computations from the Single Spine Salary Structure

For those who will take option two, i.e. *reduced pension plus gratuity,* their respective gratuities are shown in figure 1. As noted earlier, the reduced pension plus gratuity option afford the staff to take a lump sum made up of 25% of 20 years full pension. In addition the remaining 75% of the full pension is paid to the staff on monthly bases till natures call. The monthly pensions under the two options are shown in figure 2.

Figure 1: Gratuity for Staff after 15 Years of Contribution to the GUSSS

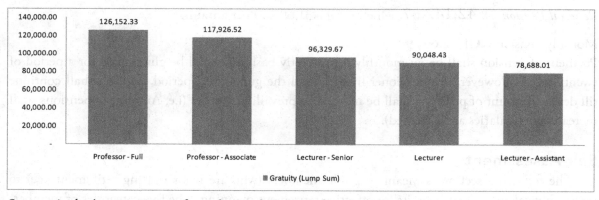

Source: Author's computations from the Single Spine Salary Structure

It is obvious that monthly take-home pension under the Full Pension option is higher than that of Reduced Pension. This is evidenced in figure 2. This notwithstanding, members (from records available at the GUSSS Office) prefer the Reduced Pension option because of the lump sum available from the option.

Figure 2: Monthly Pension under Full and Reduced Pension Options

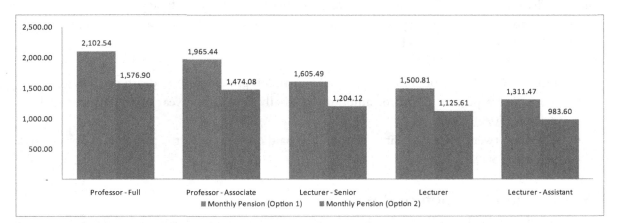

Source: Author's computations from the Single Spine Salary Structure

GUSSS Conditionality
Currency

All payments into and from the scheme shall be in currency recognized in Ghana as legal tender. For expatriate staffs who have contributed to the scheme, they shall be considered as having been employed in Ghana with payment of benefits under the scheme. Amount of pensions shall be indexed to prevailing salaries (i.e. Amount of pension shall increase when salaries are increased).

Short in Minimum Pensionable Age

Where a member cannot qualify for the benefits under the scheme because he could not attain the minimum pensionable age or serve the minimum contribution period, he shall be paid his total contribution (both employees and personal) plus interest at a rate to be determined by the Management Board. Currently the Board pays a compounding interest of 13%.

Pension Period

Payment of Pension shall be on monthly or quarterly bases and shall be guaranteed for a period or twenty (20) years. However, if a pensioner lives beyond the guaranteed period, payment of pension shall continue till death.

Death of a Member

In the event of death of a pensioner before the guaranteed period of twenty (20) years, balance of pension shall be paid as follows:

- To the beneficiaries named in the nomination form deposited by the member with the Finance Officer.
- Where no nomination form was deposited with the Finance Officer, the balance of pension shall be paid under a will made by the said member and admitted to probate.
- Where the two exist and there is conflict the nomination shall take precedence
- In any other case, in accordance with the rules of intestacy.

In the event of the death of member while in the service of the University and qualifying for benefit under the scheme as provided under Rules 6, Death Gratuity shall be paid.

In the event of the death of a member in service or pensioner before the guaranteed pension period, lump sums accruing shall be paid as follows:

- Fifty percent (50%) of amount due shall be paid on presentation to death certificate.
- Twenty five percent (25%) of amount due shall be paid one year after payment of fifty percent (50%).
- The final twenty five percent (25%) shall be paid one year after the payment of seventy-five percent (75%).

Dismissal and Vacation of Post

If a member is dismissed for a criminal offence, he shall, in respect of the total years of service, be entitled only to such portions of the benefit payable, as may be attributable to his own contribution, except that the Council, after due consideration of all the circumstances and on the advice of the Management Board, especially as effecting the member's wife, children and or other known dependents, may grant the member whatever proportion of the remaining benefits attributable to the University's contribution which is not granted by the Council to the member, shall be retained and applied towards future premiums and expenses under the scheme (UDS, GUSSS Revised, p 10).

If a member is dismissed on grounds other than a criminal offence and qualify for benefits under the Scheme he shall, in respect of the last two years of his service, be entitled only to such portion of the benefits payable as may be attributable to his own contribution but in respect of previous years, if any, to the full benefits, except the Council on the advice of the Management Board may grant the member whatever proportion of the benefits they consider fit (UDS, GUSSS Revised, pp 10 & 11).

Any portion of a benefit attributable to the University's contribution which is not granted by the Council to the member shall be retained and applied towards future premiums and expense under the scheme.

- If a member vacates his post with the University, he shall forfeit the benefits under his scheme. However, he shall be paid his own contribution plus interest as determined by the Management Board.
- If a member's appointment is terminated, he shall be entitled to full benefits.

Inputs from Beneficiaries

One basic objective, which permeates the various siloes of GUSSS schemes in the public universities, is to achieve good pension life for members. The introduction of the enhanced contributions epitomizes this objective. Management of the various schemes has been urged by stakeholder of the scheme to work hard not only to achieve this overriding objective, but sustain their respective scheme. Some retired members contacted have lauded the scheme, citing the following benefits.

- The gestation period of 15 years is good and can widen the net for more beneficiaries. People can join the scheme at age 45 and can still qualify.

- The formula used to calculate the pension uses realistic terminal salaries. It does not use averages as in the case of SSNIT pension calculations.
- There is an improvement in the gratuity due to the implementation of the 1.5 pension booster. The 1.5 factor was incorporated into the pension calculation to compensate members accepting the enhanced contribution.
- There is an opportunity for members to borrow from the scheme to support them purchase vehicles or build houses. This gives members the opportunity to own vehicles or own houses before retirement.
- Member constituencies have representations on the management Board of the scheme, enabling them to have better input and control over their pension benefits and management.
- The advance gratuity of 40% can support members to effectively plan and prepare for retirement.
- Members have easy access to the GUSSS offices, which are located on the premises of the various universities.
- Various schemes have invested into hostels. This goes to support government objective of making university education accessible to all. The management of hostels has created jobs for the unemployed in the country.

Meanwhile, interactions with members reviled that management of the GUSSS need to review the formula for pension calculation. The $\left(\frac{1}{40}\right)$ factor in particular needs adjustment. That factor was used on the assumption that, members will join University service at least, at age 20 and can work and contribute to the scheme for at most 40 years. However, current entry requirements have been strengthened. One needs at least a minimum of MPhil to join the senior member level in the university. This can take not less than 25 to attain, and render service to the university for at most render 35 year. Given this, the $\left(\frac{1}{40}\right)$ should be reviewed to $\left(\frac{1}{35}\right)$.

Conclusion

From the above examination, it becomes obvious to conclude that the GUSSS is an attractive pension scheme for academia in Ghana. It is easy to join and become a member. The scheme has only 15 years gestation period after which members qualify to draw the full benefit of the scheme. Members have easy access to the managers of the scheme and can thus make meaningful input to its management. Access to information on members' contributions is fast and can be obtained from the GUSSS Office, which is locally based in the University. The scheme offers attractive lump sum gratuity payment, with monthly pension ranging between GH¢1,500 for full professor and GH¢900 for assistant lecturer who have contributed to the scheme for the minimum 15 years. The scheme offers an advance payment of up to 40% of gratuity when a member attains 58 years. There is no red tape in the processing and payment of members' benefits as all procedures for processing these benefits are confined to the GUSSS Office, which is locally based in the University.

In all, the GUSSS has the potential of providing academia with attractive social security after retirement. The pension package is capable of offloading worries of the academia over their lives after retirement. This offers them the opportunity concentrate on lecture delivery as well as on research and publications.

Recommendations

- The GUSSS may be the only investment available for the future of members: the future which is desired by all members; the future where salaries, allowances and other pegs will no longer flow, thereby reducing members' income to the level of pension only.
- Further, the age beyond retirement is characterized by significant waning of the physical strength of the retired, so much so that, the health of the retired is significantly challenged. The GUSSS in my view will tremendously be the source of support when the main stream salary and allowances stop to flow.
- All members must therefore take kin interest in the management of the scheme in order not to jeopardize it sustainability.
- Management of the respective schemes should work at investing in high yielding instruments in order to strengthen the future liquidity of the schemes.
- The current wave of investment into hostel projects should be encouraged.
- Furthermore, the moves towards unification of the schemes should be expedited in order to form a formidable scheme for the provision of excellent social security for members' retirement life.

References

Adjei, E. N. A. (1999). Pension Scheme in Africa: The National Experience of Ghana. *Social Security Documentations, Africa Series No. 21, International Social Security Association.*

Amarteifio, B. A. (2011). The Problem of the CAP 30 Pension Scheme in Ghana. *Thesis, KNUST, Kumasi.*

Amartey-Vondee, E. (2015). The Regulatory Framework for Occupational Pension and Other Private Pension Scheme – the Experience of Ghana. *FANAF Symposium on Social Security in Africa, Abidjan.*

Davies, B. (1993). Better Pension for all. *London: Institute for Public Policy Research.*

Kpessa, M. (2010). The Politics of Retirement Income Security Policy in Ghana: Historical Trajectories and Transformative Capabilities. *African Journal of Political Science and International Relations, Vol. 5, pp 92-102.*

Kumado, K. and Gockel, F. (2003). A Study on Social Security, Retrieved from library.fes.de/pdf-files/bueros/ghana/50022.pdf (Accessed on September 12th, 2012).

Mosinyi, W. (2008). Pension Funds have a Massive Development Role, Mmegionline, accessed on Wednesday June 10, 2015

National Pension Regulatory Authority (n.d.), National Pension Act (Act 766), (pdf), Available at http//www.npra.gov.gh/pdf/NPRA 2008 Act 766.pdf (accessed on 18th August, 2015).

SSNIT pension House (n.d.). Old Age Retirement Benefit, (pdf) Available at www.ssnit.org.gh/news.php (Accessed May 26th, 2015).

University for Development Studies, GUSSS Revised, Derisco Co. Ltd, unpublished.

University of Ghana, Amended Regulations on the GUSSS, unpublished.

13

Types of Fraud and Their Impacts on the Financial Information Presented

Joan I. Egwuasi *CNA*, Rita N. Udoye *Ph.D* & Chioma l. Ikeanyionwu

Abstract

*T*he issue of corruption as a determining force in the actualization of organisational goal attainment cannot be understated. Hence, this paper examined fraud as an aspect of corruption with its prevailing negative impacts on financial information presented. To carry out this task, the paper looked at the meaning and the various types of fraud and their impacts on the financial information presented. The paper concluded that the practice of fraud will destroy and mar the realisation of the objectives of establishing business organisations. From the findings of the study, the paper recommended, among other things, that there should be regular checks of financial information before presentation to the public and the internal control units of organisations should be sound.

Key Words: *Fraud, Impact, Financial Statement, Crime*

Introduction

The sole objective for the establishment of any business organisation is profit making. However, there are several issues, constraints and activities that can mar the processes towards the realisation of this objective. According to Urhoghide and Yakubu (2014), the true and fair view opinion on the financial statement of business organisations by the statutory auditors is designed to give credibility to such financial reports. This, in turn, is expected to induce confidence in the users of financial statements that wish to make an investment decision, thereby leading to the achievement of the objective of such an organisation.

Regrettably, today, this picture is fast fading away due to organised financial crimes such as embezzlement, bribery, bankruptcy and fraud, among others. In total affirmation, Ibeaja (2009) posited that white collar crime (such as mentioned above) is rampant and has been for sometimes in the business community of the Nigerian economy. Furthermore, Amara, Ben-Amar and Jarboui (2013) were of the view that nowadays, the global economy considers a series of economic and financial crises, which have caused a distrust of marketers, investors and public opinion vis-à-vis the company accounts. They also argued that financial scandals are not the sole causes of the crises of confidence prevailing in the business world but the real scourge that affects the economy is undoubted "fraud".

The Concept of Fraud

Fraud as a concept has several definitions. Ibeaja (2009) views fraud as a dishonesty in the form of an intentional deception or a willful misrepresentation of a material fact, lying, the willful telling of an untruth, cheating, the gaining of an unfair or unjust advantage over another. From the corporate viewpoint, fraud can be developed in a meaningful framework for fraud auditing. Hence, corporate fraud can be classified into two broad categories of:

- Frauds directed against the company; and
- Frauds that benefit the company.

While the former is intended to benefit only the perpetrators, as in the case of theft of corporate assets or embezzlement, the latter is committed to enhancing the financial position or condition of the company by such ploys as overstating income, sales or assets, or by understating expenses and liabilities. This is often referred to as the misappropriation of assets. These may also include vendors, suppliers, contractors and competitors bribing employees.

According to Dummies.com (2016), there are basically four types of financial frauds. These are:

- Embezzlement
- Internal theft
- Payoffs and kickbacks
- Skimming

Embezzlement, also known as larceny, is the illegal use of funds by a person who controls those funds. This might be seen when such a person uses the company's funds for personal needs. Internal theft, on the other hand, is the stealing of company assets by employees, such as taking office supplies or products the company sells without paying for them. This is usually the culprit behind inventory shrinkage. Payoffs and kickbacks are situations in which employees accept cash or other benefits in exchange for access to the company's business, often creating a scenario where the company that the employee works for, pays more for the goods or products than necessary. The extra money finds its way into the employee's pocket who helped facilitate the access. Skimming, on the other hand, occurs when employees take money from receipts and do not record the revenue in the books.

In a closer related situation, Quffa (2016) sees financial statement fraud as the deliberate misstatements or omissions of amounts or disclosures of financial statements to deceive financial statements users, particularly investors and creditors. Quffa further stated that fraud can be committed by senior management, mid and lower-level employees and organised criminals. Ibeaja (2009) also posits that the various methods of financial statement fraud include:

- Fictitious revenues
- Timing differences
- Improper asset valuation
- Concealed liabilities and expenses
- Improper disclosures

In his explanation, Ibeaja (2009) asserts that fictitious revenues are created simply by recording sales that never occurred. They can involve real or fake customers. The end result is an increase in revenues and profits, and usually assets (the other side of the fictitious accounting entry). The red flag associated with this include unusual increase in assets, customers with missing data (especially with physical addresses and phone numbers), and unexplained charges in certain relationships or ratio trends, where revenues grow but accounts receivable does not.

Timing difference, also known as the improper treatment of sales, is perpetrated in several ways. This is to exaggerate revenues for the current fiscal period. One way is to push excess inventory to sales people or consignment whereupon the inventory is treated as a sale, knowing fully that much of it will be returned – but in the subsequent period. This method is known as channel stuffing. Sales also can be booked for other violations of Generally Accepted Accounting Principles (GAAP), for instance, a three-year contract to provide services across the period can all be booked as revenue in the current year to inflate profits for the next set of financials, at the expense of future financials and obviously not in compliance with GAAP and the matching principle. The red flag for these centres around the ways such improper transactions would be perpetrated. If the sale is a legitimate one but posted too early, channel stuffing red flags include excessive returns of merchandise, accompanied with sales credits. Improper asset valuation happens when an increase can be the result of adding values to the original costs or by decreasing the contra accounts that go with a depreciable asset. By inflating the amounts of assets (commonly receivables, inventory and long-lived assets), capitalising expenses, or deflating contra accounts (allowance for doubtful debts, depreciation, amortisation, etc.), the financials will show a higher than truthful equity and profit. The red flags include:

Unusual or unexplained increase in book value of assets; unusual trends in ratios or relationship of assets to other parts of the financial report, for instance, consistent increase in number of days on receivables ratio, changes in the ratio at receivable to revenues; violation of GAAP in recording expenses as assets.

For the concealed liabilities, one way to perpetrate this fraud is simply to postpone the recording of liabilities in the 12th month of the fiscal year so that the current year will have fewer expenses and record that liabilities in the first month of the fiscal year. It is due to this type of fraud that financial auditors perform subsequent period substantive tests – looking for invoices that are dated the year under audit but posted in the first month of the subsequent year. The red flags associated with this include:

Excessive transfer from one entry to a related entry; employment of different audit firms for different subsidiaries or related business entities; vendor invoices and other liability transactions that are not recorded in the books.

Ibeaja (2009) describes improper disclosures as a clandestine act. This is the covering up of frauds in the books. This can be a way to hide evidence of a fraud. The red flags here include:

- Disclosure notes that are so obfuscated, i.e. difficult to determine the true nature of the event or transaction;
- Discovery of undisclosed legal contingencies or any other significant event;
- Discovery of undisclosed fraud.

Impacts of Fraud on Financial Information Presented

Fraud has several negative impacts on business organisations. According to Quffa (2016), the effects of financial statement fraud include the following:

- It undermines the reliability, quality, transparency and integrity of the financial reporting process;
- It jeopardises the integrity and objectivity of the auditing profession, especially auditors and auditing firms;
- It diminishes the confidence on the capital market, as well as market participants, in the reliability of financial information;
- It makes the capital market less efficient;
- It adversely affects the nation's economic growth and prosperity;
- It results in huge litigation costs;
- It destroys careers of individuals involved in financial statement fraud;
- It causes bankruptcy or substantial economic loss by the company engaged in financial statement fraud;
- It causes devastation in the normal operations and performance of alleged companies;
- It raises serious doubts about the efficacy of financial statements audit; and
- It erodes the public confidence and trust in the accounting and auditing profession.

Adeniji (2012) also presented some effects of fraud on financial information of a company to include:

- Fraud will lead to the non-compliance of the requirements of statutes;
- Fraud will lead to the non-compliance of accounting standards and applicability;
- Fraud will lead to the non-acceptance of industry accounting principles where there are no accounting standards;
- Fraud will lead to incomplete, inaccurate and invalid transactions and balance in the financial information presented;
- The transactions and balances will not be properly classified and presented;
- Material items will not be adequately disclosed.

Conclusion

The effects of financial fraud are enormous. Cotton (2003) attributes the collapse of Enron, World.com, Tyco, Adelphia and others, to corporate fraud where over billions of naira was said to have been lost. In Nigeria, Cadbury Nigeria Plc, whose books were criminally manipulated by management, was said to have lost over $15 million. Also, the case of the nine commercial banks was fraudulent and constituted financial crimes in Nigeria, about one trillion naira was reported to have been lost through different means.

It is clear from the foregoing, therefore, that the practice of fraud will destroy and mar the realisation of the objectives of establishing business organisations.

Recommendations

Based on the findings of this paper, the following recommendations become necessary. These are:

- There should be regular checks of financial information;
- The internal control unit of business organisations should be sound;
- Companies should avoid setting unachievable goals;
- Companies should avoid applying excessive pressures on employees to achieve goals; and
- There should be an established clear and uniform accounting procedure with no exception clause.

References

Adeniji, A. A. (2012). Auditing and Assurance Services. Lagos: Value Analysis Consult.

Amara, L., Ben-Amar, A., & Jarboui, A. (2013). Detection of Fraud in Financial Statements: French Companies as a case study. International Journal of Academic Research in Accounting, Finance and Management Sciences. 3(3), 40-51.

Cotton, M. P. (2003). Corporate Fraud Prevention, Detection and Investigation: A practical Guide to Dealing with Corporate Fraud. Australia: Price Waterhouse Coopers.

Dummies.com (2016). Basic Types of Financial Fraud in Businesses. http://www.dummies.com/how-to/content.basic-types-of-financia-fraud-in-business.html. Retrieved on March 24, 2016.

Ibeaja, U. (2009). Fraud Risk Assessment and Accounting Information towards Corporate Growth. Business Search, 1st Annual Conference Journal of School of Business and Management Technology. 1(1), 30-40.

Quffa, H. C. (2016). Financial Statement Fraud. www.google.com. Retrieved on March 20, 2016.

Urhodhide, R. & Yakubu, F. A. (2014). Forensic Accounting and Forensic Fraud in Nigeria: An Empirical Approach. The Certified National Accountant, a Bi-monthly Journal of the Association of National Accountants of Nigeria. July – August, pp 21-26

LIBRARY AND INFORMATION TECHNOLOGY ISSUES

14

Integrating Educational Technology in the Philippine Contemporary Classroom Environment

Jake M. Laguador *Ph.D*

Abstract

*T*his literature review explores the extent of integrating educational technology in the Philippine contemporary classroom environment. It describes the profile of the Philippines compared to other ASEAN member states in terms of the total population, gross national income (GNI), literacy rating and ICT development index (IDI) as well as the educational technology integration in principle and practice; determining the barrier for its integration. Results showed that some of the identified probable causes of educational technology integration in the Philippines are: inadequate financial support and infrastructure, human capital, management support, as well as behavioural and environmental aspects. Gross National income is considered a factor that can directly or indirectly influence the Literacy rating and ICT Development Index value of the country while the total population based on ranking of countries has nothing to do with the ranking of GNI, Literacy Rating and IDI value of each country.

Key Words: *Educational Technology, Basic Education, ASEAN, ICT Development Index*

Introduction

Information is power and has its own strength to diversify into different forms and actions that can either build or destroy a nation. Education is the grass root of information that grows or dies naturally if it will not be nurtured according to the needs and demands of the changing environment. Technology has brought numerous transformations and innovations in the way society manages and deals with business, politics, religion, economy, education and many others. In all aspects of life, it directly affects negatively and positively the development of the fast changing condition of the society. The benefits of such advancement in computer technology had tremendously succeeded its objectives of providing convenience in the way people learn and communicate from receiving, sending and processing information makes everything moves faster than ever.

People learn from formal or informal schooling which describes education based on experience from the environment where technology plays an important part of learning process to make the transfer of knowledge more consistent, reliable and effective. This is where educational technology comes in the likeness of a perfect illustration of teachers and students having fruitful discussion and sharing of knowledge and values through the use of appropriate modern-day instructional materials.

The word *Educational Technology* first appeared as published research article in the database of Sage Journal in the article of Davis (1944) entitled "Adolescence and the social structure" in which the author envisaged that:

> *"There are three directions in which this obstacle may be overcome: first, the invention of new educational technology; second, the elimination of irrelevances from the curriculum; and third, the overhauling of the incentive mechanism"*

The author used the concept of educational technology to improve the reading habit among adolescents as well as the revision of irrelevant curriculum. The obstacle being pointed out by the author is the problem in the connection or relationship between the functions of adolescents in the real world situation and their school life.

On one hand, Stecchini wrote an article in 1964 entitled "Prospects in Retrospect: On Educational Technology" where the author mentioned that "teacher is a prisoner of the technology of education." This implies that it has been a long journey for educational technology among teachers to deeply appreciate, embrace and apply innovations on their traditional way of delivering instruction through lecture method using printed textbooks. Findings of the study of Sprague and Dahl (2009) validate technology as a valuable methodology to facilitate learning with students who typically do not enjoy more traditional methods inherent in a university learning environment. Stecchini called this technology in the article as *teaching machine* used primarily for positive reinforcement in language teaching when during that time, there was a dominance in the used of textbooks.

It is hard to believe that since the beginning of educational technology until its proliferation in the contemporary classroom environments, there are still some teachers who resist and refuse to accept the role of technology in the development of learners' ability and there are those who would never be given an opportunity to experience the benefit it would bring due to lack of resources (Belawati, 2003). This is where creativity of teachers brings out the instructional materials coming from being resourceful. The image of classroom environments in the Third World countries like the Philippines is a mixture of faded black and white with a brighter sense of hope from teachers that through their efforts, there will be colorful lives among the pupils that will stand out in the crowded pigments of the future. Latchem (2013) noted that after four decades of digital experiments in classrooms and the expenditure of billions, it really should not be so difficult to find strong evidence of significant overall improvement in educational outcomes

This study is guided by the Diffusion of Innovation (DOI) Theory, developed by E.M. Rogers in 1962, which is one of the oldest social science theories. It originated in communication to explain how, over time, an idea or product gains momentum and diffuses (or spreads) through a specific population or social system. The end result of this diffusion is that people, as part of a social system, adopt a new idea, behavior, or product. Adoption means that a person does something differently than what they had previously (i.e., purchase or use a new product, acquire and perform a new behavior, etc.). The key to adoption is that the person must perceive the idea, behavior, or product as new or innovative. It is through this that diffusion is possible.

As part of the Third World countries, Philippine Government is facing major concerns in the basic education like inadequate classrooms, chairs, textbooks and laboratories due to the excessive number of students enrolled in public schools. Therefore, the need for classroom buildings is being prioritized than putting up ICT infrastructure which is quite expensive to obtain and maintain.

The integration of technology in the delivery of instruction is considered vital in the implementation of student-centered approach of teaching method in the Philippines. But due to inadequate financial resources (PREL, 2003) of third world countries, the government could hardly provide enough support for basic education to sustain quality teaching and learning process. Aside from financial resources, it is the task of this study to review the status and other barriers against the integration of educational technology in the contemporary classroom environment in the Philippines compared to other ASEAN member states. There is great faith that these technologies will improve teaching and learning, and consequently afford these countries a greater stake in today's knowledge society (Rodrigo, 2001). The findings of the study may serve as substantial input to the policymakers who are considered to be in a unique position to bring about change (Wallet, 2014).

Objectives of the Study

This literature review explores the extent of integrating educational technology in contemporary classroom environment in the Philippines compared to other ASEAN Member States. Specifically, this study aims to describe the profile of the countries under study in terms of the total population, gross national income (GNI), literacy rating and ICT development index (IDI); educational technology integration in principle and practice as well as the barrier for its integration.

Methods

This study utilized qualitative analysis using Literature Research Methodology which is to classify information contained in literatures, to select typical examples to re-organize and come to conclusion on the basis of qualitative description. The qualitative analysis of literatures has special values in distinguishing the past trends and forecasting future models (Lin, 2009). This study also applied inferential statistics to test correlation among the profile variable of the countries.

This literature review is an exploration of findings from research articles and previous studies conducted from January 2000 to April 2015 from the database of Sage Journals, Directory of Open Access Journal and Google Scholar using the following keywords as filters: Educational technology 'and' Interactive Classroom; and Classroom Environment.

Local literatures on the status of integration of technology in the Philippines were also reviewed and investigated. Three papers from the report published by the UNESCO Institute for Statistics were reviewed and served as secondary source of data and information.

Results and Discussion

Technology has a great deal in doing business and community development ranging from small and large scales. It directs people from leaving old means of performing tasks or improving the things that had been part of everyday routine. Education has a huge contribution in the economic development of a nation, therefore it should not be left behind the latest trends in technology. Educational technology refers to a variety of technology-based programs or applications that help deliver learning materials and support learning in the classrooms to improve academic learning goals

(Cheung, 2013). Technology in education is not just an add-on but is literally reshaping teaching/learning paradigms. It modifies pedagogy and pedagogy dictates requirements to technology (Di Blas, Fiore, Mainetti, Vergallo & Paolini, 2014). The introduction of technology in the classroom may eventually, however, facilitate a level playing field by empowering all students to use computers (Clay-Warner & Marsh, 2000). Online instruction has been demonstrated to increase the academic achievement for post-secondary students (Smith (2012) and the use of technology seems to have had a positive impact on test scores, which always pleases the instructor and the students (Ueltschy, 2001).

Asia-Pacific countries have recognized the importance of ICT in education. They have responded to this challenge by formulating policies and developing strategies in different ways (DepED ICT4E Strategic Plan).

In addition to the instruction of basic computer skills or computing, ICT is used to teach other subjects to enhance or expand student learning opportunities (Wallet, 2014). Learners today expect to access information from anytime and from anywhere (Dale & Pymm, 2009). Use of interactive technology leads to an increase in student participation and discussion, student enjoyment of the learning process, and generally higher test scores on material presented (Ueltschy, 2001). With the proliferation of entertainment games, supported by heavy investment in the underlying technologies, educators are now examining the educational values of gaming and attempting to incorporate games into their teaching. In Singapore, the game sector is worth many million Singapore dollars (SGDs), and gaming is an engaging activity of the young (Koh, 2012). Perceived usefulness has been defined as an indicator of the extent to which a person believes that using a particular technology will enhance their performance, and therefore represents an indicator of an individual's extrinsic motivation to use a technology (Arbaugh, 2000).

UNESCO Institute for Statistics data may be used to inform policymakers to formulate decisions related to: national capacity and/or infrastructure levels (e.g. electricity, Internet, broadband) for integrating new ICT tools in schools; the types of ICT currently being neglected and/or emphasized in relation to concerns of usability and affordability (e.g. radio- versus computer-assisted instruction); whether ICT-assisted strategies are evenly distributed nationwide; whether girls and boys have equal access; the types of support mechanisms currently in place or the lack thereof; and the relative level of teacher training provided in relation to the demands placed on them to teach and/or use ICT in the classroom (Wallet, 2014).

Policymakers widely accept that access to information and communication technology (ICT) in education can help individuals to compete in a global economy by creating a skilled work force and facilitating social mobility (Wallet, 2014). As one's willingness to use a particular technology is likely to influence the extent to which one takes advantage of it (Clay-Warner & Marsh, 2000).

Within the framework of formal commitments, national plans to implement ICT objectives in education take on many forms including strategy papers, investment programs, decrees and regulations that establish programmes with short- to medium-term targets (i.e. usually 5- to 10-year plans) aligned with longer-term goals and objectives. Moreover, countries vary in terms of how explicitly they formalize their plans. For example, formal, stand-alone plans on ICT in education, which may or may not be sector-wide, could be perceived as relatively transparent compared to National ICT Master Plans that include components on education or National Education Plans that include an ICT component (Wallet, 2014).

Profile of the Philippines compared to other ASEAN Member States

The profile describes the total population, gross national income (GNI), literacy rating and ICT development index (IDI) of developing countries among ASEAN Member States. These are considered some contributing factors in achieving the mission of quality education through integration of educational technology in contemporary classrooms in ASEAN community.

Table 1: Country Classification

Country	Classification
Myanmar (Burma)	Undeveloped Economy
Laos	Semi-Developing Economy
Cambodia	Semi-Developing Economy
Thailand	Developing Economy
Vietnam	Developing Economy
Malaysia	Developing Economy
Indonesia	Developing Economy
Philippines	Developing Economy
Brunei	Graduating to Developed Economy
Singapore	Advanced / Developed Economy

There are 70 percent of the ASEAN member-states considered developing countries and 1 percent which is Myanmar belongs to undeveloped while Brunei is graduating to developed economy while Singapore belongs to advanced/ developed economy based on the Gross National Income per capita of World Bank national accounts data

Table 2: Total Population of ASEAN Member States

World Rank	Country	Population Estimates (2016)	World Share
4	Indonesia	260,581,100	3.5
12	Philippines	102,250,133	1.4
14	Viet Nam	94,444,200	1.3
20	Thailand	68,146,609	0.9
26	Myanmar	54,363,426	0.7
44	Malaysia	30,751,602	0.4
71	Cambodia	15,827,241	0.2
105	Laos	6,918,367	0.1
113	Singapore	5,696,506	0.1
174	Brunei	428,874	<0.1

Source: Countries in the world by population (2016). This list includes both countries and dependent territories. Data based on the latest United Nations Population Division estimates. http://www. worldometers.info/world-population/population-by-country/

Indonesia has the highest total population among the ten ASEAN member states with 3.5 percent of world share followed by the Philippines and Viet Nam while Singapore and Brunei Darussalam obtained the least total populations which are considered developed countries among the member states. There is no reviewed literature that tells population of the country has significant contribution in the integration of ICT in education. But when two samples compared between one group with large population and the other one with small population, it is more manageable to provide instruction to smaller population and the attention to be given to each individual is higher than in a group with large population.

Table 3: Gross National Income per capita of ASEAN Member States (in US$)

Country	2011	2012	2013	2014
Cambodia	810	880	960	1,020
Myanmar				1,270
Lao PDR	1,120	1,300	1,490	1,660
Vietnam	1,390	1,560	1,740	1,890
Philippines	2,640	3,000	3,340	3,500
Indonesia	3,010	3,580	3,740	3,630
Thailand	5,000	5,610	5,840	5,780
Malaysia	9,080	10,200	10,850	11,120
Brunei Darussalam		37,320		
Singapore	48,330	51,390	54,580	55,150

World Bank National Accounts Data, and OECD National Accounts data files.
Source: http://data.worldbank.org/indicator/NY.GNP.PCAP.CD

Table 3 presents the Gross National Income per capita of ASEAN Member States (in US$). Gross National Income per Capita is also presented in the study to determine how countries performed over the other that could provide baseline information and insight as to reasons for the barriers of technology integration in education. Among the developing countries, Malaysia has the highest Gross National Income per capita based on 2011 to 2014 World Bank national accounts data while Cambodia, Lao PDR, Myanmar and Vietnam obtained the least.

Table 4: Literary Rating among ASEAN Member States

Country	Male	Female	Total Population
Cambodia	84.0	70.5	77.2
Laos	87.1	72.8	79.9
Myanmar	95.2	91.2	93.1
Indonesia	96.3	91.5	93.9
Vietnam	96.3	92.8	94.5
Malaysia	96.2	93.2	94.6

Brunei	97.5	94.5	96.0
Philippines	95.8	96.8	96.3
Thailand	96.6	96.7	96.7
Singapore	98.6	95.0	96.8

Source: https://www.cia.gov/library/publications/the-world-factbook/fields/print_2103.html

This entry includes a *definition* of literacy and census bureau percentages for the *total population*, *males*, and *females*. Low levels of literacy, and education in general, can impede the economic development of a country in the current rapidly changing, technology-driven world. The given data were taken from the population age 15 and above who can read and write (www.cia.gov). Cambodia and Laos obtained the least literacy rating with 77.2 percent and 79.9 percent respectively, while Philippines, Thailand and Singapore obtained the highest rating greater than 96 percent.

ICT Development Index 2015

The ICT Development Index (IDI), which has been published annually since 2009, is a composite index that combines 11 indicators into one benchmark measure. It is used to monitor and compare developments in information and communication technology (ICT) between countries and over time.

Table 5: ICT Development Index 2015

IDI 2015 Rank	Economy	IDI 2015 Value	IDI 2010 Rank	IDI 2010 Value
19	Singapore	8.08	11	7.62
64	Malaysia	5.90	61	4.85
71	Brunei Darussalam	5.53	53	5.05
74	Thailand	5.36	92	3.62
98	Philippines	4.57	105	3.16
102	Viet Nam	4.28	94	3.61
108	Indonesia	3.94	109	3.11
130	Cambodia	2.74	131	1.98
138	Lao P.D.R.	2.45	135	1.92
142	Myanmar	2.27	150	1.58

The main objectives of the IDI are to measure the level and evolution over time of ICT developments within countries and the experience of those countries relative to others; progress in ICT development in both developed and developing countries; the digital divide, i.e. differences between countries in terms of their levels of ICT development; and the development potential of ICTs and the extent to which countries can make use of them to enhance growth and development in the context of available capabilities and skills.

The Index is designed to be global and reflect changes taking place in countries at different levels of ICT development. It therefore relies on a limited set of data which can be established with reasonable confidence in countries at all levels of development.

Table 5 shows the ICT Development Index for 2015 of ASEAN Member States. Singapore, Malaysia and Brunei are the top 3 with the highest IDI value in 2015 while Cambodia, Laos and Myanmar obtained the least values. The rank of Singapore in the world rank drops from 11 in 2010 to 19 in 2015 as well as Brunei Darussalam from 53 in 2010 to 71 in 2015 while Thailand and the Philippines climb 18 and 7 spots, respectively for five years. There is so much to do for the Philippines in terms of IT infrastructure, fast access to information and human capital to let the country consider self-sufficient in dealing with technology.

Educational Technology Integration in Principle and Practice

Moving forward to the main objectives of technology integration in contemporary classrooms defines the future of education more interactive, engaging and challenging. To discover in what ways students use and enjoy using a particular technology, as no tool is helpful unless it is utilized (Clay-Warner & Marsh, 2000). The success it could bring to the achievements of learners and ease in the transfer and delivery of instruction for teachers is considered beneficial for all stakeholders. The use of technology in relation to education certainly will change (Ridener, 1999) the way learning takes place in the classrooms. Technology is transforming how businesses operate, how educators teach, and how students learn (McCorkle, Alexander, and Reardon 2001). Teachers make pedagogical decisions in their planning and use of technologies in the classroom (Murcia, 2014). Educators both train students in how to use technology and use technology to teach discipline-specific courses. Some strategies for using technology in teaching specific subjects can be generalized and adapted to teaching many different subjects (Ball & Eckel, 2004).

The Philippine Government through its Department of Education (DepED) has envisioned "21st Century Education For All Filipinos, Anytime, Anywhere. This means an ICT-enabled education system that transforms students into dynamic life-long learners and values-centered, productive and responsible citizens. In order to achieve this vision within the next five years, they aim to: completely integrate ICT into the curriculum, which includes the development of multimedia instructional materials, and ICT enabled assessment; intensify competency based professional development programs; establish the necessary ICT infrastructure and applications; and develop processes and systems that ensure efficient, transparent and effective governance (DepED ICT4E Strategic Plan).

The integration of technology and the classroom provides for a constructivist orientation to education that actively involves students and teachers in interaction and reflection both individually and as a group (Shotsberger, 1996; Ridener, 1999). More intensive and interactive classroom-based educational sessions are more effective than other approaches (Hughes, Roche, Bywood & Trifonoff, 2013). Latchem (2013) explores the reasons for educational technology principles and practices not being more widely accepted and successfully applied in everyday teaching and learning. Technology use is often premised with the notion that technology is widely available, both inside and outside the classroom, and the availability of ICT plays an indispensable role in its implementation or lack thereof (Elwood & MacLean, 2009).

Technology reaches both ends of the world to make things done uncomplicated. Like computer mediated communication (CMC) which is an exciting tool that has great potential to enhance learning (Clay-Warner & Marsh, 2000) through virtual learning community perspective (Peltier, Drago & Schibrowsky, 2003) as well as the use of interactive whiteboard technology (Murcia, 2014; Nichols, 2015). It is not at all problematic for students to use; indeed, they find it a friendly and familiar way to communicate with each other and the instructor (Ball & Eckel, 2004). Technology Acceptance Model (TAM) seems particularly helpful for predicting whether and why learning takes place in Internet-based courses (Arbaugh, 2000).

There is a need for the country to adapt the following technology in order to sustain delivery of instruction like new software application. One of the many advantages of social software is that it creates the potential to build shared environments for active learning that are available anywhere and anytime, provided that the user has access to the appropriate technology (Miles & Rainbird, 2014). Software design for a hand-held technology (Rhodes, 2010) helps teachers in the delivery of instruction with ease. Learners can access online multimedia instruction from networked classrooms (Smith, 2012). Teaching and learning materials can be enhanced by a mixture of innovative teaching methods, software, and information available through the Internet and digital libraries (Moussa & Somjai, 2015).

Shifting to online administrations allows test makers to use the myriad capacities of technology (Thurlow & Kopriva, 2015). Since much of the graduate education experience deals with interacting with teachers and other students to build communities of learning, the online education experience needed to make sure that *virtual* communities of learning were present. It is important to note that online educational formats are not identical across all universities that use the Internet to deliver all or portions of a particular class Peltier, Drago & Schibrowsky, 2003).

With the recent proliferation of multimedia devices and broadband networks within K-12 facilities, online multimedia instruction is now viable for the classroom setting. Ueltschy (2001) noted that traditional lecture-based teaching has been criticized as a passive knowledge delivery process with much room for improvement. Many secondary schools have begun to augment traditional teaching practices by incorporating online instruction for recovery purposes, remote learning, and teaching alternative curriculums (Smith, 2012).

With the growing influence of social media on contemporary society, educators have to adapt to new ways of engaging students in the learning process. The use of iPod technologies, as part of this new breed of social media and associated gadgetry, offers fresh opportunities to enhance the student learning experience (Dale & Pymm, 2009). When posting comments to the network, students have more time to reflect upon their readings and to consider previous comments than they may have in the more immediately interactive classroom discussion (Clay-Warner & Marsh, 2000). Learners would be more willing to use mobile learning if they find that the technology can be easily used (Bao et al., 2013).

Contemporary classrooms in the Philippines may also embrace proliferation of digital games (Koh, Kin, Wadhwa & Lim, 2012) to encourage active participation of all learners. Integration of digital games in the classroom set up motivates learners to have fun while learning the concepts and principles of the subject. It makes learning more interesting while challenging their minds during the process. With students and teachers becoming more comfortable with them for recreation, it will be less of a challenge for teachers to use digital educational games (Koh et al., 2012). Moizer et al., (2009) stated that the significant linkages apparent between three broad barriers to teaching with simulations, games and roleplay: suitability, resource and risk. Further analysis of the interview transcripts facilitated the identification of a range of mechanisms which may be employed to overcome the aforementioned barriers: freeing up academics' time, providing training and development, enabling informal learning, providing resource support, facilitating access to networks and providing access to secondary information sources.

Majority of the countries from East Asia have a stand-alone, sector-wide ICT in education plan and this includes Malaysia and the Philippines while in Cambodia a stand-alone plan addressing only upper secondary education exists. Meanwhile for Indonesia, Myanmar, and Thailand, ICT is either mentioned in current education plans or education is mentioned in current national Master ICT Plans to cover several social spheres, including health, government and commerce, among others. Lao People's Democratic Republic has no plan on ICT in education (UNESCO Institute for Statistics database, 2011).

As the integration of ICT in education rises and evolves with evermore sophisticated tools, and participation and transition rates to higher levels of education increase, children and adults will increasingly need to develop digital literacy, not only for life skills but also to support their education throughout the secondary, post-secondary and tertiary levels. The early integration of ICT into primary and secondary curricula through formal recommendations is therefore vital and moreover acts as an important lever for ensuring the introduction and implementation of ICT into educational institutions and classrooms.

Indonesia, Malaysia and Thailand have started courses on basic computer skills at all levels. In countries that do not have objectives or courses on basic computer skills (or computing) at all levels, emphasis is placed on secondary education. For instance in Armenia, Bhutan, Lao People's Democratic Republic and the Philippines, basic computer skills and computing are emphasized beginning in lower secondary education, while in Cambodia and Myanmar, this occurs in upper secondary education (ADB, 2012).

The learner-to-computer ratio (LCR) refers to the mean number of learners sharing a single computer available for pedagogical use in national, aggregate education systems. At the primary level, data show that available computer resources are greatly overstretched in the Philippines (412:1) while very small ratio for Malaysia (17:1) and Thailand (15:1). Based on combined data for the primary and secondary levels, computer resources are also greatly overstretched in Indonesia with 136:1 (*UNESCO Institute for Statistics database*).

Table 10: Proportion of educational institutions with Internet, fixed broadband and Internet-assisted instruction by level of education

Country	Internet		Fixed Broadband		Internet Assisted Instruction	
	Primary	Secondary	Primary	Secondary	Primary	Secondary
Thailand	99	97	99	97	99	97
Singapore	100	100	100	100	100	100
Brunei	100	100	100	100	100	100
Malaysia	90	96	90	96	90	96
Indonesia	39	52	missing	missing	Missing	Missing
Philippines	7	40	3	17	4	28

UNESCO Institute for Statistics, 2012

In the Philippines where most schools have electricity (>80%), Internet and fixed broadband are only available in 7% and 3% of primary schools, respectively; however general Internet and fixed broadband connectivity rates do increase to 40% and 17% of secondary educational institutions. Similarly, Indonesia also prioritizes secondary schools for Internet connectivity. Whereas rates of available electricity are 80% for both primary and secondary levels in Indonesia, Internet is available in 39% of primary schools and 52% of secondary schools (Wallet, 2014).

In terms of proportion of combined primary- and secondary-level teachers teaching basic computer skills and subjects using ICT versus proportions trained, Philippines and Myanmar have only 2 percent of teachers trained to teach using ICT *(UNESCO Institute for Statistics, 2012)*.

In most countries, LCRs decrease from the primary to secondary level of education indicating greater levels of access. For instance, in the Philippines computer resources are greater in lower secondary education than in primary education where LCRs are 49:1 and 412:1, respectively.

Among the 55 nations included in the Information Society Index (ISI), the Philippines is ranked 48th in terms of preparedness and ability to absorb advances and growth in information and communication technologies (ICT). Recognizing the need for improvements in the use of ICT in education and training, the Philippines Government has enacted laws to foster the use of ICT for widening access to education, improving the quality of teaching and fostering the development of lifelong learning skills *(Rodriguez, 2008)*.

A survey commissioned in 2002 by the Philippine Senate Committee on Education, Arts and Culture to the South-East Asian Ministers of Education Organization Regional Centre for Educational Innovation and Technology (SEAMEO INNOTECH), examined the ICT infrastructure of elementary and secondary schools in the Philippines. Some of the survey findings are as follows: Two-thirds, or 66.07 percent, of the 36,368 schools surveyed have electricity. The regions with the highest electricity supply are the highly industrialized regions of Luzon namely: National Capital Region (NCR), Region I, Region III and Region IV; of the schools surveyed, 5,217 (14.28 percent) indicated they have computers. Only 726 (2 percent) have access to the Internet. There are 4,866 or 13.3 percent of the schools surveyed have access to landline telephones (Rodriguez, 2008).

Findings of the commissioned survey revealed that most common audio-visual and multimedia equipment in schools are traditional media equipment. Specifically, these are: radio-cassette players (42.22 percent of all schools); television (26.80 percent of all schools); and VHS players (17.19 percent of all schools). These electronic devices being used by school teachers in basic education are made useful in the delivery of instruction although considered old enough but some of these devices after a decade have changed to CD players and flat screen television.

Some schools have the necessary equipment to be used but the problem occurs among the teachers who do not want to move away from their comfort zones. Appropriate training has been already provided but the continuous application of teachers' learning through various teaching pedagogies where technology is suitable should be encouraged. Bay (2013) found out in his study of integrating technology in Photojournalism Course in one tertiary education in the Philippines that the technology-driven teaching strategies were often used; specifically, the PowerPoint presentation being the frequently used and video tutorial clips as the least used. PowerPoint presentations and digital cameras are highly effective in the delivery of instruction, along with Audio Video Presentation (AVP) and Video Tutorial Clips as effective strategies.

From the same survey, schools in the provinces in Mindanao (Regions IX, X, XI, XII, CARAGA and ARMM) have the lowest incidence of computers. Only one out of every seven schools has teachers who are computer literate. More schools have computer-literate teachers (6,632 or 18.24

percent) than have computers (5,217 or 14.28 percent). The percentage of trained teachers in ICT is still small to serve the needs and demands for learning using various technologies. In the survey of 27,042 school heads (74.36 percent) indicated they had received no training on any topic related to ICT in the past five years. The remaining 4,774 school heads (13.13 percent) indicated they had received some sort of ICT training. Support from various higher education institutions in a form of community extension service to public school teachers may provide great help to increase the number of teachers trained to use ICT in basic education. Knowledge and experience of facilitators in handling constructivist approach of learning process using modern technology in contemporary classroom is an essential factor in the sustainable integration of ICT. Training for teachers is an utmost requirement to effectively and efficiently maximize the full utilization of all the features of modern educational technology.

The Philippines received various support in ICT from different private national and international organizations. Some examples of projects include: the Department of Education "Modernization Programme" in 1996; "Adopt-a-School" programme, initiated in 1998; the Department of Transportation and Communication (DOTC), in partnership with the Science Education Institute (SEI) and Intel Philippines, provided Mobile Information Technology Classrooms (MITCs); Coca Cola Philippines' "Edventure"; and "e-Mage 2000" which means Math Games for excellence for secondary level (Rodriguez, 2007).

In June of 2011, Vibal distributed 1,000 tablets to public school students in Laguna that have built-in Rizaliana classics. Dubbed as "eRizal" tablets, they were distributed in commemoration of the 150th birth anniversary of the Philippine National Hero, Jose Rizal (Matikas, 2012). Text2teach is a pilot project being implemented in science classes in Grades 5 and 6 in elementary schools in the Philippines. It is the Philippines version of a global programme called BRIDGEit, an initiative that aims to improve the teaching of basic education in developing countries (Rodriguez, 2007).

Luistro said the DepEd has allocated P1.8 billion in 2012 to complete the Internet connectivity in the public schools. Speaking at the ceremony, Jaime Augusto Zobel de Ayala, Chairman and CEO of Ayala Corp. and co chairman of the Gilas project, said some 4.4 million students in 3,306 public high schools throughout the country now had access to cyberspace.

Barriers for Integration

The present condition of Philippine education has a great digital divide between private and public schools in terms of the integration of educational technology. With the high tuition fees in private schools where majority of the fees are being allocated to the development and improvement of instructional facilities and technological infrastructure, more students could be able to experience and utilize the benefits of modern equipment in teaching and learning processes compared to students from public schools where inadequate technological resources are at front as a huge challenge.

The Philippines is one of many developing nations that have turned to information and communication technology (ICT) as a tool to improve teaching and learning (Rodrigo, 2001). The author also identified major concerns in the integration of ICT in education: the absence of information on how ICT is actually used; a lack of coordination between public and private sector efforts; and insufficient teacher preparation.

Many aspects are being considered in making technology integration possible and measuring its impact could hardly get a few from the rest of the developing countries in ASEAN member states. It is always easier said than done those plans of integrating innovations in teaching and learning process. Some of the probable causes of educational technology integration in most developing countries are: inadequate financial support and infrastructure, human capital, management support, as well as behavioural and environmental aspects.

Economic strength or financial capability of developing countries in considered one of the major challenges in the integration and even the rest of the world. Lack of appropriation for ICT due to corruption and strong influence of politics might be some barriers to believe as reasons. Most organizations and industries from developed countries are giving out their support to alleviate the digital divide among nations. But only few stayed focus and committed from the beginning of the project until it has produced impact to the community and society at large. Huge amount of funds and human resources should be invested in such projects to become sustainable. Providing schools with the computer units without access to internet and other communication media could not serve its purpose into full extent.

Abcede mentioned some of the identified key problem areas for implementing ICT in the Philippine basic education: Teachers' fear of the technology; School principals' closed mindset to and non-appreciation of ICT in education; Constraints of the annual Education Budget; Maintenance of ICT resources and lack of technical staff; Sustainability; and Limited availability of education software and courseware.

Teacher preparation is insufficient (Rodrigo, 2001). The workforce must be well-equipped with the skills necessary to provide effective transfer of knowledge from the teachers and learners. Such technology is being used to support the delivery of instruction and to train students on how computer works and its fundamental operation as well as its applications in the development of an informed and educated community.

The infrastructure or facility where to place donated computers in an environment that can ensure temperature conducive to preserve the functionality of computer system is another story. The bill of the school will also increase and it will add up to their expenses. If the management will not adequate support in the utilization of computers in the delivery of instruction, conflicts will occur at times. Policies should also be clearly written and well-established for proper implementation and guidance of teachers and students.

The attitude and behaviour of teachers and school administrators regarding innovation in the constructivist (Shotsberger, 1996) point of view against the traditional approach to learning would also resist possible success in integration. Initiating paradigm shift is one way towards managing change in the school administration. Accepting new challenges must be well-communicated to all stakeholders so that everyone involved in the process could really adapt to the changing environment. The support of the management has primary importance in introducing such innovation replacing old techniques with new teaching approaches towards learning.

Rural youth for whom the Internet is more aspiration than avocation and whose schools may not even have electricity, let alone a computer, or for whom 'computer time' means the two hours a month spent in a crowded school computer lab learning how to use a word processing program while waiting, waiting, waiting for their desperately slow Internet connection to bring up a single web page: Such young people and circumstances represent the reality of current technology use in education across Asia as well (Trucano, 2014).

In order to gauge national capacity to support the integration of ICT in education, measuring the share of educational institutions with electricity and a telephone communication facility provides basic information for policymakers to assess current gaps in infrastructure, as well as help inform decisions about which ICT tools would be appropriate for short- and longer-term planning.

In Lao People's Democratic Republic, 19 percent of primary schools have electricity compared to 53 percent of secondary schools. Electricity is also rare in educational institutions in Cambodia, where 7 percent of all public schools are connected to a reliable power source to support the integration of ICT in the classroom.

Telephone communication facilities are more or less universal wherever electricity is widespread. However, in Malaysia, which has electricity in all schools, telephone communication facilities are just available in 88% of primary schools and 76 percent of secondary schools. In countries where electricity remains a challenge, telephone communication facilities are also typically less than universal. For example, telephone communication devices are present in 14 percent of primary-level and 38% of secondary-level schools in Lao People's Democratic Republic. Telecommunication devices are also uncommon in some schools with relatively high levels of electricity, for example in the Philippines. While privately-owned mobile telephones are excluded from the current definition, mobile units are increasingly used by teachers in developing countries for both pedagogical and administrative purposes (UNESCO Institute for Statistics database).

Naturally, in the best of all possible worlds, educational institutes could provide unlimited ICT support, but the reality is somewhat different as limited fiscal resources slow progress toward ICT implementation. Moreover, availability does not necessarily equate with usage (Elwood & MacLean, 2009).

Even though the Philippine government has initiated several programmes and projects for the use of ICT in education, real implementation in day-to-day learning is still limited. Teachers' fear of technology still hinders the optimal use of ICT-related skills in their teaching activities. Other constraints include the traditional mindset of the school principals, inadequacy of ICT facilities, the lack of adequate maintenance of the available/existing ICT resources, dependence for financial investment on the central government and dependence on ICT service providers for software/courseware (Andrada & Abcede, 2001). Despite various training programmes having been provided to teachers, there is still a need to embark on a comprehensive and sustained in-service training for teachers. Likewise, a systematic development programme for education managers needs also to be implemented to change the mindset of principals so they appreciate the value of ICT in education (Wallet, 2014). Considering the lack of technical staff for maintaining computers and computer networks, as well as providing user support for Internet-related activities, lease arrangements rather than procurement should be explored as an alternative. Another constraint that has had a significant impact on the use of ICT in classrooms is the availability of courseware.

Conclusion

Majority of the ASEAN member states belong to the classification of undeveloped to developing country only Brunei Darussalam and Singapore are considered graduating to developed economy and advanced/developed economy, respectively. Indonesia and Philippines have the highest total population while Singapore and Brunei have the least population but with the highest Gross National Income per Capita. In terms of literacy rating, Singapore, Thailand and Philippines obtained the highest percentage more than 96 percent while Laos and Cambodia obtained least with less than 80 percent. Singapore has the highest ICT Development index Value while Myanmar obtained the least.

Available computer resources are greatly overstretched in the Philippines (412:1) at the primary level while based on combined data for the primary and secondary levels, computer resources are also greatly overstretched in Indonesia (136:1). The use of technology is a burgeoning trend in all higher education (Karns & Pharr, 2001) but has limited use in basic education. Philippines has the least proportion of educational institutions with Internet, fixed broadband and Internet-assisted instruction by level of education while the.

Many secondary classroom teachers and academic administrators remain uncertain how to implement new technologies to replace outdated forms of classroom instruction. By relying on technology that is not completely understood, its potential benefits could be attenuated (Smith, 2012). Some of the probable causes of educational technology integration in most developing countries are: inadequate financial support and infrastructure, human capital, management support, as well as behavioural and environmental aspects. There is electricity divide (Trucano, 2014) between rural and urban areas in some parts of the country. Therefore, availability of electricity is also one of the problems facing by the school administration.

Gross National income is considered a factor that can directly or indirectly influence the Literacy rating and ICT Development Index value among the ASEAN Members states while the total population based on ranking of countries has nothing to do with the ranking of GNI, Literacy Rating and IDI value of each country.

Recommendations

Several multinational companies and industries have shared their financial and human resources in helping the developing countries to alleviate digital divide among primary or basic education from public and private schools located in rural and urban areas with or without supply of electricity. The issue of digital literacy among developing countries will continue to become subject of discussion until such time that the initiative of ICT integration in education will be coming from the school administration itself within the capacity of local community rather than from the national level. Positive views should be encouraged among the members of faculty and community to solicit support from the environment especially from the local government units and non-government organizations. The support of the government and private industries is well-rounded but the challenge of sustainability of ICT in education exists among the end-users on how they will improve the knowledge and skills acquired from the equipment and training provided to them is another part of the issue needed to address. The attitude of the people towards innovation has a great impact towards the achievement of the mission of having quality education through ICT integration.

Training of end–users like school teachers and maintenance technicians should also be given priority to fully utilize the functions of the computer. Various learning packages and educational software applications and courseware will also be needed to deliver interactive approach to instruction using the educational technology and media. There are many free downloadable educational tools and applications from the internet where teachers can use as supplementary materials to support the lessons. Various organizations made their resources available for all.

But there are times the overuse of educational technology on the same manner may result to "novelty effect," in which once a new technology becomes standard, students no longer find it exciting (Clay-Warner & Marsh, 2000). Various teaching pedagogy with appropriate creativity should also be developed in using educational technology in delivering instruction.

Questions on how to measure technology use is education are complicated in many countries by a lack of consensus on what can and/or should be measured, and how this measurement can and should take place. Lack of common sets of methodologies and indicators in this regard also hampers cross-national comparison of developments and the impact of related initiatives (Trucano, 2009b). Educational technology tools are increasingly common, although relatively little research has examined their impact and effectiveness (McAlister, 2001). While many school districts and academic policymakers are assessing online instruction as a replacement for current teaching practices, evidence supporting the effectiveness of the pedagogy is limited (Smith, 2012) therefore further studies may be conducted on this aspect.

If something has been already served and implemented, the next major concerns of the beneficiaries are the maintenance and sustainability of the projects where monitoring has an utmost importance. Learning how to protect the computer system and facilities from any kind of destruction would be helpful to reach the life span of the equipment or any electronic device.

Some of the developed countries are already talking about major breakthroughs in teaching science and technology but the undeveloped and developing countries are still trying to cope up with the challenge of having single computer unit in a classroom to make the instruction more interactive. Poverty still strikes among the third world countries in ASEAN member states that hold them back to provide adequate resources for its citizen especially the children from slums and rural areas.

Constant monitoring of implemented projects should be conducted to ensure the continuity and sustainability of the programs as well as its effectiveness and impact to the intended beneficiaries and to the society at large. How technology transformed the society and the Filipino culture in the context of how technology changed the way education should be delivered to the learners is the question still needs more exploration to understand the behaviour of young generation to get the picture of how the future of the Philippine education looks like in the coming years of more advanced information era.

References

Alper, M. (2013). Developmentally appropriate new media literacies: Supporting cultural competencies and social skills in early childhood education. *Journal of Early Childhood Literacy*, *13*(2), 175-196.

Andrada, L. M. & Abcede, V. (2001). "The Use of ICT in Basic Education in the Philippines and Efforts to Measure Its Impact", *http://gauge.u-gakugei.ac.jp/apeid/apeid02/papers/Philippin.htm*.

Arbaugh, J. B. (2000). How classroom environment and student engagement affect learning in Internet-based MBA courses. *Business Communication Quarterly*, *63*(4), 9-26.

Ball, S. B., & Eckel, C. C. (2004). Using technology to facilitate active learning in economics through experiments. *Social Science Computer Review*, *22*(4), 469-478.

Bao, Y., Xiong, T., Hu, Z., & Kibelloh, M. (2013). Exploring gender differences on general and specific computer self-efficacy in mobile learning adoption. *Journal of Educational Computing Research*, *49*(1), 111-132.

Bay Jr, B. E. (2013). Integration of Technology-Driven Teaching Strategies for Enhancing Photojournalism Course. *Educational Research International*, *2*(2), 155-164.

Belawati, T. (2003), Indonesia, Vietnam: ICT Use in Education, Metasurvey on the Use of Technologies in Education in Asia and the Pacific, UNESCO Bangkok.

Burke, L. A., Karl, K., Peluchette, J., & Evans, W. R. (2013). Student Incivility: A Domain Review. *Journal of Management Education*, 1052562913488112.

Cheung, A. (2013). Effects of educational technology applications on student achievement for disadvantaged students: What forty years of research tells us. *Cypriot Journal of Educational Sciences*, *8*(1), 19-33.

Chu, S. K., Lau, W. W., Chu, D. S., Lee, C. W., & Chan, L. L. (2014). Media awareness among Hong Kong primary students. *Journal of Librarianship and Information Science*, 0961000614551448.

Clay-Warner, J., & Marsh, K. (2000). Implementing computer mediated communication in the college classroom. *Journal of Educational Computing Research*, *23*(3), 257-274.

Dale, C., & Pymm, J. M. (2009). Pedagogy The iPod as a learning technology. *Active Learning in Higher Education*, *10*(1), 84-96.

Davis, K. (1944), Adolescence and the social structure, *The Annals of the American Academy of Political and Social Science*, 8-16.

Department of Education Five-Year Information and Communication Technology for Education Strategic Plan (DepED ICT4E Strategic Plan), url: http://planipolis.iiep.unesco.org/upload/Philippines/Philippines_ICT4E_Strategic_Plan_summary.pdf, date retrieved: March 20, 2016.

Di Blas, N., Fiore, A., Mainetti, L., Vergallo, R., & Paolini, P. (2014). A portal of educational resources: providing evidence for matching pedagogy with technology. *Research in Learning Technology*, *22*.

Elwood, J., & MacLean, G. (2009). ICT usage and student perceptions in Cambodia and Japan. *International Journal of Emerging Technologies and Society*, *7*(2), 65-82.

Foegen, A., Howe, K. B., Deno, S. L., & Robinson, S. L. (1998). Enhancing the potential of distance education: A case study involving groupware. *Teacher Education and Special Education: The Journal of the Teacher Education Division of the Council for Exceptional Children*, *21*(2), 132-149.

Gadanidis, G., Hughes, J., & Cordy, M. (2011). Mathematics for gifted students in an arts-and technology-rich setting. *Journal for the Education of the Gifted*, *34*(3), 397-433.

Geng, G. (2013). Investigating the use of text messages in mobile learning. *Active Learning in Higher Education*, *14*(1), 77-87.

Gross National Income per capita, World Bank national accounts data, and OECD National Accounts data files, date retrieved: March 25, 2016, url: http://data.worldbank.org/indicator/NY.GNP.PCAP.CD.

Gunter, G. A., & Kenny, R. F. (2012). UB the director: Utilizing digital book trailers to engage gifted and twice-exceptional students in reading. *Gifted Education International*, *28*(2), 146-160.

Guzman, A., & Nussbaum, M. (2009). Teaching competencies for technology integration in the classroom. *Journal of Computer Assisted Learning*, *25*(5), 453-469.

Hughes, C., Roche, A. M., Bywood, P., & Trifonoff, A. (2013). Audience-response devices ('clickers'): A discussion paper on their potential contribution to alcohol education in schools. *Health Education Journal*, *72*(1), 47-55.

Karns, G. L., and Stephen Pharr. 2001. Editor's corner. *Journal of Marketing Education* 23 (April): 3-4.

Koh, E., Kin, Y. G., Wadhwa, B., & Lim, J. (2012). Teacher perceptions of games in Singapore schools. *Simulation & Gaming, 43*(1), 51-66.

Latchem, C. (2013). Whatever Became of Educational Technology? The Implications for Teacher Education. *World Journal on Educational Technology, 5*(3), 371-388.

Lang, A. (2011). Exploring the potential of social network sites in relation to intercultural communication. *Arts and Humanities in Higher Education,* 1474022210394141.

Lemley, J. B., Schumacher, G., & Vesey, W. (2014). What Learning Environments Best Address 21st-Century Students' Perceived Needs at the Secondary Level of Instruction?. *NASSP Bulletin,* 0192636514528748.

Lin, G. (2009). Higher Education Research Methodology-Literature Method. *International Education Studies, 2*(4), p179.

Mahdzar, R. (2015). Using Technology to Improve Education for Cambodian Children, URL: http://geeksincambodia.com/using-technology-to-improve-education-for-cambodian-children/

Matikas, S. (2012). When digital classrooms become reality, url: http://technology.inquirer.net/9177/when-digital-classrooms-become-reality#ixzz42ltCoKLp.

McAlister, D. T. (2001). The editor's corner. *Journal of Marketing Education,* 167-68.

McCabe, D. B., & Meuter, M. L. (2011). A Student View of Technology in the Classroom Does It Enhance the Seven Principles of Good Practice in Undergraduate Education?. *Journal of Marketing Education, 33*(2), 149-159.

McCorkle, Denny E., Joe F. Alexander, and James Reardon. 2001. Integrating business technology and marketing education: Enhancing the diffusion process through technology champions. *Journal of Marketing Education* 23 (April): 16-24.

Miles, M., & Rainbird, S. (2014). Evaluating interdisciplinary collaborative learning and assessment in the creative arts and humanities. *Arts and Humanities in Higher Education,* 1474022214561759.

MoEYS (Ministry of Education, Youth and Sport, Cambodia) 2004, 'Policy and strategies on information and communication technology in education in Cambodia', http://www.moeys.gov.kh/Includes/Contents/Education/NationalPoliciesEducation/PolicyandStrategiesonICTinEducation.pdf.

Moizer, J., Lean, J., Towler, M., & Abbey, C. (2009). Simulations and Games overcoming the Barriers to their use in Higher Education. *Active Learning in Higher Education, 10*(3), 207-224.

More, C. M., & Travers, J. C. (2012). What's app with that? Selecting educational apps for young children with disabilities. *Young Exceptional Children,* 1096250612464763.

Murcia, K. (2014). Interactive and multimodal pedagogy: A case study of how teachers and students use interactive whiteboard technology in primary science. *Australian Journal of Education,* 0004944113517834.

Nichols, B. E., (2015), The Interactive Classroom: An Overview of SMART Notebook Software, General Music Today, Vol. 28(3) 28–32, DOI: 10.1177/1048371314568372

Peltier, J. W., Drago, W., & Schibrowsky, J. A. (2003). Virtual communities and the assessment of online marketing education. *Journal of Marketing Education, 25*(3), 260-276.

PREL, 2003, Laos, *Cambodia:* ICT Use in Education, Metasurvey on the Use of Technologies in Education in Asia and the Pacific, UNESCO Bangkok.

Rhodes, S. (2010, September). A Hand-held Data Tool Design for Teachers. In *Proceedings of the Human Factors and Ergonomics Society Annual Meeting* (Vol. 54, No. 7, pp. 626-630). SAGE Publications.

Richardson, J. W. (2011). Challenges of adopting the use of technology in less developed countries: The case of Cambodia. *Comparative Education Review, 55*(1), 008-029.

Ridener, L. R. (1999). The good, the bad, and the ugly in cyberspace: Ups and downs of the dead sociologists' society. *Social Science Computer Review, 17*, 445-450.

Rodrigo, M. M. T. (2001). Information and communication technology use in Philippine public and private schools. *Loyola Schools Review: School of Science and Engineering, 1*, 122-139.

Rodriguez, C. (2008). "Building teachers' capacity to make better use of ICT in Philippines schools", ICT in Teacher Education: Case Studies from the Asia-Pacif ic Region, United Nations Educational, Scientific and Cultural Organization (UNESCO), Thailand.

Shotsberger, P. G. (1996). Instructional uses of the Worldwide Web: Exemplars and precautions. *Educational Technology, 36*(2), 47-50.

Smith, J. G. (2012). *Screen-capture instructional technology: A cognitive tool for blended learning* (Doctoral dissertation, Saint Mary's College of California).

Sprague, E. W., & Dahl, D. W. (2009). Learning to click: An evaluation of the personal response system clicker technology in introductory marketing courses. *Journal of Marketing Education.*

Stecchini, L. (1964). Prospects in Retrospect: On Educational Technology. *Programs, teachers, and machines*, 25-33.

Teo, T., Ruangrit, N., Khlaisang, J., Thammetar, T., & Sunphakitjumnong, K. (2014). Exploring E-Learning Acceptance among University Students in Thailand: A National Survey. *Journal of Educational Computing Research,50*(4), 489-506.

Thurlow, M. L., & Kopriva, R. J. (2015). Advancing accessibility and accommodations in content assessments for students with disabilities and English learners. *Review of Research in Education, 39*(1), 331-369.

Trucano, M. (2009a). Comparing ICT use in education across countries, http://blogs.worldbank.org/edutech/UIS-indicators.

Trucano, M. (2009b). How to measure technology use in education, EduTech: A World Bank Blog on ICT Use in Education, url: http://blogs.worldbank.org/edutech/how-to-measure-technology-use-in-education.

Trucano, M (2014), Surveying ICT use in Education in Asia, EduTect, The World Bank, url: http://blogs.worldbank.org/edutech/surveying-ict-use-education-asia date retrieved: March 25, 2016.

Ueltschy, L. C. (2001). An exploratory study of integrating interactive technology into the marketing curriculum. *Journal of Marketing Education,23*(1), 63-72.

United Nations Population Division estimates. http://www.worldometers.info/world-population/ population-by-country/

UNESCO Institute for Statistics database; UNESCO Bangkok, 2011.

Viren, J., & Viren, C. (1999). Distance Learning Over ATM/Sonet: The Distance Learning Environment Demonstration. *Journal of Educational Technology Systems, 27,* 231-244.

Wallet, P. (2014). Information and Communication Technology (ICT) In Education In Asia A comparative analysis of ICT integration and e-readiness in schools across Asia, Information Paper No. 22, UNESCO Institute for Statistics, http://dx.doi.org/10.15220/978-92-9189-148-1-en

Waltz, S. B. (1998). Distance learning classrooms: a critique. *Bulletin of Science, Technology & Society, 18*(3), 204-212.

World Education, Inc.: Technical Brief, Using Computer Technologies to Improve Basic Education in Cambodia: Thin Client Labs, Boston, MA, URL: http://www.worlded.org/WEIInternet/inc/ common/_download_pub.cfm?id=13309&lid=3

Worley, K. (2011). Educating college students of the net generation. *Adult Learning, 22*(3), 31-39.

15

Achieving the Overall Philosophy of Nigeria: Can the Library Help?

Eme Ndeh *Ph.D CLN* & Mbuotidem Umoh *Esq.*

Abstract

This discourse focused on the concept of justice and equality as indicators of the overall philosophy of Nigeria. It further identified education library and law library in particular, as one of the machineries that would consolidate the change agenda of President Mohammadu Buhari in finding a long lasting solution of sustainable peace and harmony in Nigeria. The paper concluded that the only option for Nigerian leaders, politicians and policy makers is to advocate and institute laws that would mandatorily compel the building, equipping and use of functional law libraries.

Key Words: *Philosophy, Nigeria, Education, Library/Law Library*

Introduction

All over the world, there is widespread concern among people about education and the proper way to be educated. This is because; the rapid changes in contemporary life seem to impose fresh conditions with which the society must contend (Etuk, 2010). Etuk further explains that, that is why people, generally, do not fail to talk about values and education with which philosophy is chiefly concerned among other things. Etuk also argued that there is obviously, no society without a system, formal or informal, although there may be differences in practices and programmes. Such differences are in general reflections of diverse beliefs regarding values, knowledge, reality, human nature as well as the good society.

From the foregoing, it is very pertinent to affirm that for any society or nation to achieve great success in all facets of endeavour, there should be a well articulated and implemented, philosophy of such a nation. Idang (2008) asserted that philosophy helps people decide wisely and act consistently and to discover values and the meaning of things. Thomas (2014) is of the view that philosophy is a system of ideas about human nature and the nature of the reality we live in. It is a guide for living, because the issues it addresses are basic and pervasive, determining the course we take in life and how we treat other people. To this end, Snauwaert (2012) argued that philosophy constitutes a mode of inquiry and a discipline that enriches the capacity for reflection and rational deliberation and hence it is essential for both democracy and practice of education in a democratic society. The author concluded that philosophy makes this contribution by providing frameworks for understanding and generating ideas, methods of reflection and analysis and disciplines (exercises) for the cultivation of the capacity of reflection and rational deliberation. It is based on these that this paper examines the overall philosophy of Nigeria and how it has fared positively and negatively, what is to be done to improve the system and the explanation of the concept from home to national and to international levels. The paper also examines the impact of information and the overall need to establish and maintain digital law libraries in the country.

Nigeria's Overall Philosophy

Nigeria's overall philosophy as stipulated by the Federal Republic of Nigeria (2004) in its National Policy on Education, 4th edition in section I paragraph 2, which states as follows; that Nigeria will:

- Live in unity and harmony as one indivisible, indissoluble, democratic and sovereign nation founded on the principles of freedom, equality and justices.
- Promote inter-African solidarity and world peace through understanding.

The next section of this paper, therefore examines the issues of justice and equality in the Nigerian society.

The Concept of Justice and Equality in Nigeria

The development of any nation depends on how she manages, handles, coordinates and regulates the tripod concepts of justice, equality and freedom. The three concepts work in tandem. The principle of justice simply explained, is to give each person or group of persons whether weak or strong what is his/her due and do demand the contribution of each on the basis of equal contribution. Aquinas (1969) views justice as the constant and perpetual will to render to everyone what is due to him; however, what is due is often expressed in a right, which is determined by national and conventional laws. If a person has a right, to have or do something, others have the duty to respect that claim on the balance of equal protection and reciprocity. He further stated that justice is a moral virtue which inclines the will constantly and perpetually to render to others their due in time and place and in a given set of circumstance. In affirmation, Ayeni (2013) stated that justice is the quality of being just, impartial, rightness, legitimacy, equity and fairness in awarding of what is due. Furthermore, the concept of justice cannot be properly understood within the context of this paper without due attention to the three major classical schools of thoughts of Justice. Hence;

- The Social Contract concept
- The Utilitarian concept
- The Respect concept

According to Ayeni (2013), the social contract concept of justice believes that a society such as Nigeria, is just, if its members mutually and freely consent to the rules or codes of the society, which in the short-run or in the long-run is advantageous to all, or for mutual self interest. One of the basic premises of this is that, societies are built around a set of norms, rules or do's or don'ts which are backed by sanctions to the content that conformists are rewarded while the deviants are penalised.

Positively, justice has prevailed in Nigeria as seen in the probing into the financial records of some citizens irrespective of their status in the society, who deviated from the ethics of their professions. Example of such included the likes of former speaker of the House of Representatives, Hon. Dimeji Bankole; former Central Bank of Nigeria Governor, Alhaji Sanusi Lamido Sanusi and former Governor of Bayelsa State, Mr. Depriye Alamieyeseigha among others.

However, from the negative point of view, justice has failed to prevail politically, educationally and financially among others. In the political scene, justice has failed in several instances such as the case of Late MKO Abiola who won the June 12, 1993 presidential elections but was denied, imprisoned and killed. The prevailing issue of "godfatherism" in the polity, where political positions are attained through selection "man-know-man" and not elections. Educationally, justice has failed in that teachers at all levels of education are victimised underpaid and treated without respect. This treatment has so negatively influenced children who opt for other professions because they wish to receive the reward for their labours here on earth even as they popularly chant that "a teacher's reward is in heaven".

The case also abounds of injustice meted out to the University of Uyo, over the government's refusal to pay its take off grant since its inception in 1991. From the financial aspect, injustices have been meted out to local governments and states where revenues are allocated not according to the derivation formula; not to mention the case where local governments' allocations are hijacked by the state governors who utilise it for their personal aggrandisement while the local governments are left struggling to meet its wage bill. All these have threatened the existence of Nigeria as one indivisible and indissoluble entity.

The utilitarian concept of justice maintains that a society is just if it guarantees the greatest happiness to the greatest number. This is evident in the Nigerian society where the government has also tried to satisfy the majority tribes of Hausa, Igbo and Yoruba to the neglect of minority groups. This has not fostered unity and harmony in Nigeria. The respect concept of justice maintains that the just society is that which people are treated as ends in themselves and never merely as means to an end. It also stated that, in a just society under this, people are respected because they are human beings not as a result of their social graces or bourgeoisie trappings.

This is however not applicable in the Nigerian society, in that, only the very rich, mighty, influential and political office holders are respected and treated as ends in themselves. The poor, down trodden and the no bodies are usually treated as just means to an end whose deaths, situations, rights and dues are nothing to take into consideration. This to a very large extent has threatened negatively the unity and harmony of the country.

The Concept of Equality in Nigeria

This is a very complex, but highly related and strongly attached concept to justice. Equality as a concept has the notion that each person is to have an equal right to the most extensive system of basic liberties, compatible with similar system of liberty for all and secondly, social and economic in equalities are to be arranged so that they are attached to positions open to all, under conditions of equality of opportunity and are to the greatest benefit of the least privileged. Negatively, Ayeni (2013) argues that when the principle of equal opportunity is not observed; then there is a discrimination between classes and groups with little or no social mobility, where the natural resources which nature provides for the benefit of all is placed in the hands of a few who exploit the labour of the rest or where a great majority of the population live on the level of abject poverty or near poverty becomes the order of the day.

This situation is found in Nigeria where the monies derived from one part of the country (South-South, South- East and some part of South-West) are used to develop the other parts of the country such as the Federal Capital Territory, Abuja, furthermore, the Nigerian entity has six geopolitical zones with six states each, except for the south East with five states. It is a recognised fact that all these in equalities have directly or indirectly led to several protests, kidnappings, killings, youth restiveness and more recently political and social insurgencies such as the Boko Haram in the North, the Niger Delta Avengers in the South and MASSOB in the East among others. This in turn, affects the unity and harmony of Nigeria as one indivisible and indissoluble entity.

Steps towards the Improvement of the Unity and Harmony of Nigeria

Nigeria is blessed in every way; but the interplay of social forces, the struggle for power and primitive accumulation, mediocre leadership and the weak structures of the state have continued to complicate life for the ordinary citizen. It is as if ordinary Nigerians are being punished for being citizens of this country (Ihonvbere, 2014). The author further stated that to ensure a steady and qualitative improvement in the lives of the people, in their socio-economic, political, cultural and spiritual development, the protection of their environment, the decolonization of their minds and putting in the middle of holistic and sustainable growth and development, 5 basic steps must be put in place. These are to:

- Strengthen the Nigerian state
- Redefine and strengthen leadership at all levels
- Generate positive political will for positive action
- Review the constitution: Build it on the people
- Reform political parties for democracy

Generating Positive Political Will for Positive Action

It is obvious that one of the major problems of Nigeria is that people often tend to think small. There is the lack of capacity for vision. To this end, Ihonvbere (2014) opined that until the Nigerian polity generates the political power to address issues that are critical to our development especially food production, industrialisation, infrastructural development, power, housing, education and tourism the Nigerian society would not live in unity and harmony. The author also stated that it should be indisputable that the will to terminate poverty, pursue justice, and respect, the rule of law must guide individual and collective determination to move Nigeria forward and improve the unity and harmony of the country.

Reforming Political Parties for Democracy

In Nigeria, politics is war. Former President Olusegun Aremu Obasanjo was credited with saying that election is a 'do or die' affair thus candidates are sponsored for political positions not necessarily based on competence but on their predisposition to being manipulated and ability to pursue narrow interests. To solve this problem, modern democracies should be built on political parties with well and people oriented manifestoes, periodic competitive elections, public policy and programmes, by this achievement, the country will be united and live in harmony.

Reviewing the Constitution: Building it on the People

Constitution making process, properly anchored on the people, their communities and constituencies is often an opportunity to popularise the constitution, mobilise the people, increase political awareness and education, strengthen people discourses on contemporary issues and build new platforms of unity and harmony. For Nigerians such a process would provide an opportunity to deal with issues of re-federalisation, fiscal federalism, local governance, structures of governance, socio-economic and human rights and other issues that have been raised in related debates; by so doing, the Nigerian government would have produced a document that would engender peace, stability, dialogue, tolerance, diversity, democracy and most importantly, unity and harmony in Nigeria.

At this point, it should be noted that the Nigerian government should evince the political will to be guided by the provisions contained in such document as such documents are generally regarded as the grundnorm in foreign climes.

Unity and Harmony from Home to National and International

It is vital to maintain unity and harmony in the multi-ethnic and multi-religious country of Nigeria with more than 250 ethnic groups and various religious beliefs divided across geo-political lines of Muslim North and Christian South, with the nation's unity and harmonious existence being woefully threatened by non compliance in totality with the principles of freedom, equity and justice. To this and, the concept of home becomes important not only in maintaining unity in Nigeria, but in upholding peace and tranquility among Nigerians.

Accepting this stance, Suhails (2012) posited that Nigerians should regard all and sundry as one and that parents at home and teachers in schools should orient the children about the importance of equality.

Nationally, the Nigerian entity was built on the foundations of tolerance and solidarity. As Nigerians, we should uphold the Nigerian dream of unity in diversity and stay strong, peaceful, and united despite the bitter economic challenges that are facing us today. The Federal Government must step in to enlighten the general public, especially the ignorant and illiterate population about unity and harmonious co-existence among the citizenry with the central theme of equality, freedom and justice. This can be achieved by the encouragement and revitalisation of activities that bring the country together such as the National Youth Service Corps (NYSC), sports festivals, cultural festivals, federal and unity schools among others.

The Library as a Mechanism of Justice and Equality for Sustainable Unity and Harmony in Nigeria

Education is an instrument par excellence for the development of any nation that is serious and focused on its destination; this is because it involves the wholesome development of the individual in every facet of his life whether intellectually, psychologically, socially, vocationally, religiously or morally. Okiy (n.d) affirms that education is a process through which people are formally and informally trained to acquire knowledge and skills. The formal training comes from established schools from the basic level to the tertiary level while the non-formal education is got where people are tutored in various skills set/knowledge in non-formal surroundings; through the process of formal education however, people are expected to obtain knowledge and relevant skills and hence specialise in specific fields of study.

It is pertinent at this point to emphasize that it is only through this process of acquiring relevant skills-set and knowledge that people will be empowered intellectually to arise and participate in national discourse thereby holding political office holders accountable to fulfill their electoral promises which will directly contribute to national development as well as sustain unity and harmony in the polity.

Okiy (n.d.) citing Aboyade, 1984; Brooks, 1990; Mohammed; (1996) explained that National Development involves economic growth modernisation, equitable distribution of income and national resources and socio-economic transformation for improved living standards of people through the use of a country's human, natural and institutional resources. She goes further to argue that it is the level and quality of occupational participation and productivity of a populace that are important contributory factors to the level of economic and overall development of any nation.

The library is focal to the provision of the right type of information resources in the suitable format that empowers the educational institutions to produce extremely ingenuous people who will in turn be interested enough to exert a positive influence on the development of any nation such as Nigeria.

It is no longer news that in this 21st century, information and communication technology (ICT) has come to stay; it has permeated every aspect of the nation, no profession is immune from it; even the conservative legal profession has had no choice but to embrace and accept it, vocations such as welding, car repairs (mechanics) have all gone digital as some of the educated mechanics conduct online searches to diagnose correctly the faults in the vehicles brought to them for repairs.

Most libraries have gone digital while some simply have digitised collections in a traditional setting; be that as it may; law libraries are not being left out in this move to transform resources and services to serve clients better in this technological era. In all this however, it is only the nation that is conscious of the relevance of information and libraries in the drive towards the quickened development of a nation that can survive and flourish in the comity of nations in this information age.

In tracing the evolution of education with libraries, Information Science Today.org (2009) narrates that educational materials and Buddhist scriptures, were stored in "pitakataik" a library that was founded by King Mindon Min during the pre-colonial era and this further reinforced the destinies of libraries with education. Libraries and education thus became symbiotically and inexorable dependent on each other. Over the years, we have learned that the library, education, literacy and national development always went hand in hand and have influenced everyone from the primary school students to those at the highest levels of education. The foregoing goes to show that education and libraries are dependent on each other; where one survives: the other thrives and where one is non-existent, the other ceases to exist. This goes to show that both work hand-in-hand to produce the intellectuals, philosophers, heroes and leaders who arise in the society and chart the course for the future.

Onoyeyan and Adesina (2014) citing Forsyth (2005) claim that libraries are integral to community development as they provide access to information and works of imagination in a variety of formats. Onoyeyan and Adesina (2014) citing Makotzi (2004) stress that libraries go beyond formal education; they encourage and sustain literacy and support development. The authors further espoused that the role of libraries in the provision of information for development is trite. They further stated that no nation can be developed without relevant information to drive its developmental sustainability.

The business of libraries is the acquisition, organisation; dissemination and preservation of information for development. Law libraries are a type of libraries which are often described as special.

They are distinct from other types of libraries because they stock different type of information resources such as legal textbooks, legal journals, law reports, law digests, official gazettes, statute books etc.

Law libraries also service a specific kind of clients. They are established primarily to meet the information needs of the law makers, judges, lawyers, barristers, solicitors, law teachers, law students, people interested in legal research etc.

The afore mentioned groups of people have a fundamental role to play in the development of a nation as they determine the state of the nation in terms of long-lasting peace, tolerance, regional acceptance among others, thus, there is need for an effective and speedy information dissemination to this group as well as other policy formulators and implementators.

The Way Forward

The sole agenda of the present administration includes: good governance, tracing and recovery of stolen government loot by political office holders and ridding all tiers of the Nigerian society of corruption. In other words, this present administration led by President Mohammed Buhari is on a quest to ensure a corruption free society as well as to ensure the recovery of Nigerian money from foreign nations. However; this feat can only be achieved through adequate organisation and dissemination of all forms of information for future reference; such information must be kept in an organised manner for easy accessibility and retrieval by qualified citizens with the requisite platform to articulate and agitate for positive changes in government policies etc. This can only be possible when the information has the law implications, which can only be made available by the law library.

The change agenda as vigorously pursued by this government can speedily become a reality through development of standard digitalised law libraries which would serve as the information bank of the nation. In other words, this nation cannot achieve good governance, strengthening of the Nigerian currency (Naira), recovery of the nation's resources and a corrupt free society through defeating corruption without first putting in place well developed digitalised law libraries in all universities.

Since the law library can be described as a place where legal books and non-book materials are kept in an organised manner for easy identification and retrieval, the change agenda of the present administration can be attained and sustained through development of legal institutions with standard digitised law libraries that could collect, organise, preserve, retrieve and adequately disseminate legal information to her patrons who comprise mainly of lawyers, barristers, solicitors, judges, law makers, law teachers etc. It is this group of people, who armed with a firm grasp of the law, can articulate people-friendly policies, sponsor bills which are hinged on justice, equity and fair play, lead local, national and international advocacy on addressing the many injustices that abound in the Nigerian state.

It is this same group of enlightened individuals who by their training are well suited to draw the attention of international bodies to the apparent and perceived irregularities in the country, unfavourable government policies, suppression of the public will, favouritism, unequal development of the different regions in the country etc. This group of people who after conducting well-balanced research in the law libraries will be well equipped to promote justice, equity and advocate for a truly egalitarian Nigerian nation where all men will be treated as equals regardless of race, tribe and religious affiliation. It is only and when this is done, that the philosophy of Nigeria can be attained and further sustained for National Development.

Conclusion

The problems, challenges and contradictions of the Nigerian society is not created by any supernatural being. They were created by Nigerians, most of whom are well known, and therefore the problems must be solved by same people. Nigerian leaders must promote justice, equity and freedom towards the realisation of the philosophy of the nation which is built on unity and harmony as one indivisible, indissoluble, democratic and sovereign nation.

The paper concludes that the options before the Nigerian leaders, politicians, policy makers, government and indeed all, are to build a well equipped and digitalized law library with state of the art facilities in Information and Communication Technology; recreate a mindset that is free from tribalism and selfish thoughts. They have to also take themselves and the people seriously by making tangible efforts to fulfill their electoral promises to the electorate, improve on their environment and living conditions of the people or be ready to face the revolutionary pressures and militant actions springing up from all facets of the Nigerian society.

References

Aquinas, T. (1969). *St Summer Theological*. New York: Image Books.

Ayeni, M. A. (2013). Justice, Equality and Peace: The Necessary Tripod for National Development. *Greener Journal of Social Sciences*. 3(1) 033-038.

Etuk, U. A. (2010). Philosophy and Logic in Education. In F. E. Etim (ed.) *Beyond Academic Process: A Festschrift in Honour of Chief Ernest Elijah James Etim*. Uyo: Abaam Publisher Co.

Federal Republic of Nigeria (2004). National Policy on Education NERDC: Lagos.

Ihonvbere, J. (2014). Nigeria: How far have we gone as a Nation and People? The *Nigerian Observer*. Monday 18 August, 2014

Information Science Today, (2009). The Role of Libraries in Education. Retrieved from www.google.com on 10/5/2016.

Okiy, R. (n.d). Using Libraries in Nigeria as Tools for Education and National Development in the 21st Century. Retrieved from www.google.com on 7/5/2016.

Online Philosophy Club (2010). What freedom means to Me. www.//onlinephilosophyclub.com.

Onoyeyan, G. and Adesina, O. (2014). A Literature Review of the Role of Libraries in the Provision of Information towards the Attainment of the United Nations Millennium Development Goals (MDGS) in Nigeria. *Library Philosophy and Practice*. Retrieved from www.dogpile.com on 2/4/2016.

Snauwaert, D. T. (2014). The Importance of Philosophy for Education in a Democratic Society. *In Factis Pax* 6 (2) 73-84.

Thomas, R. (2014). What is Philosophy www.atlassociety.org. Retrieved on July 20, 2014.

16

Institutional Repository: Expectations of Academic Librarians in the Information Technology (IT) Age

Mercy Ebong *Ph.D*, Etido E. Nelson & Godwin B. Afebende

Abstract

*T*his paper focuses on the actualization of institutional repository (IR) and the expectations of academic librarians in the information technology age. A brief history of IR, its benefits and steps on how to build an effective IR are highlighted; and the need for institutions to collect and organize their intellectual output for effective global access through an IR are also elucidated. The paper recommends that all academic and research institutions should establish and maintain an institutional repository (IR) for effective information service delivery.

Key Words: *Institutional Repository, Academic Librarians, Information Technology*

Introduction

One aspect of development which information technology has brought for institutions of higher learning is the improvement and chances of access to global knowledge through institutional repositories. Some institutions especially in developing countries, are still dabbling with the evolving new culture of technology. Utulu and Akadiri (2010), noted that, such institutions of higher learning are still at the base of knowledge creation. In this electronic or digital age of intellectual and scholarly research, academic institutions in Nigeria are not exempted from this evolving technology, and as such, they are expected to create, disseminate as well as preserve knowledge for accessibility and utilization. Librarians have equally recognized the importance of an institutional repository (IR) as an essential infrastructure for scholarly dissemination.

For centuries, libraries and scholarly publishing have been the conventional models adopted in preserving and disseminating knowledge from academic institutions. Whereas institutional libraries housed research outputs in the form of grey literature, thus playing the role of preservation than dissemination. Scholarly publishing played a much greater role in terms of dissemination through scholarly journals. Over the past decades, however, the economics, marketing and technological foundations that sustained this symbiotic publisher –library market relationship had begun to shift. This shift according to Benkler (2006) is called "networked information" which is gradually displacing the "industrial information economy" that typified information production from about the second half of the nineteenth century and throughout the twentieth century. This shift perhaps is also made possible with the emergence of information technology (IT).

Information technology (IT) continues to transform the scholarly environment and management of higher education institutions especially in digital publishing thereby making scholarly researches visible and accessible to users at any point in the world, thus, making the world a "global information village". As librarians harness the power of technology and the expertise of the computer professionals to handle the technology aspect of operations, it is recognized that greater proportion of institutional intellectual output which are valuable literature to users in this digital age have been lying waste; while some are being hoarded by their respective authors and publishers waiting to be bought by people;as such, many people who could have utilized these resources are unable to due to lack of visibility and access. Such output include: journal articles, conference papers, reports, theses and dissertation, teaching materials, artworks, research notes, and research data. Librarians in recognition of this challenge, have been grappling with how to collate, organize and disseminate these intellectual output produced by researchers in their institutions. It is against this background that this study is conducted to examine how to set up, manage and disseminate these vital research outputs.

Concept of Institutional Repository (IR)

According to Jain, Bentley and Oladiran (2008), an Institutional Repository (IR) is a digital research archive consisting of accessible collections of scholarly work that represent the intellectual capital of an institution. It is a means by which institutions create and manage the digital scholarship produced by their community members, and maximize access to research outputs before and after publication, and increase the visibility and academic prestige of the institutions and authors.

The development of open access movement in the academic world brought the institutional repositories. Institutions started collecting the intellectual output of their organization's faculty, researchers, and often students. These records that make up these repositories range from journal publications and articles, research projects, and even materials used to facilitate classroom learning. In many situations, the number and time of staff available to facilitate the process of submitting something to the repository limited. As a result, many institutions have self-submission or self-archiving policies in place. These policies put the responsibility on an outside individual, often the document's creator or a departmental liaison, to submit the document and create associated metadata. Repositories manage ingest, storage, and retrieval of items deposited in them; those that are affiliated with a specific institution are known as institutional repositories. Raym Crow (2002) defines institutional repositories as "digital collections capturing and preserving the intellectual output of a single or multi-university community" (p. 4). Paul Genoni (2004) describes them as a means by which libraries can support the communication of the research output of universities and other research organizations.

Mellon (2006) stated that Institutional Repository is a net-worked system that provides services pertaining to the collection of digital objects. Akpokodje and Akpokodje (2015) on their part averred that IR has been used unduly by many academic institutions to communicate and preserve knowledge. To this end, Wikipedia, the Free Encyclopedia (2012) sees it as an online locus for collection, preserving and disseminating – in digital form, the intellectual output of an institution, particularly a research institution. According to the Scholarly Publishing and Academic Resources Council, "a digital institutional repository can be any collection of digital material hosted, owned or controlled, or disseminated by a college or university, irrespective of purpose or provenance" (Johnson, 2002). Other scholars explain that an institutional repository "is an information system, specifically a web-based database or repository of scholarly material which is institutionally defined, and which makes that scholarly material widely accessible to the community using open access technologies and protocols" (Kennan & Wilson, 2006).

The growth of institutional repositories has been remarkable in developed countries as well as some developing countries like Brazil, India and South Africa. The concept of the IR is relatively new in Nigeria as some research institutions in Nigeria are yet to develop their IRs (Christian, 2008). An 'Institutional Repository' is a digital archive of the intellectual product created by the faculty, researchers, staff, and students of an institution and accessible to end users both within and outside of the institution (Crow, 2002). To buttress this, Lynch (2003) sees an IR as a set of services that a university offers to the members of its community for the management and dissemination of digital materials created by the institution and its community members. An increasing amount of research and scholarship exists in digital form, thus, collecting and preserving these materials serve multiples purposes. When an IR is established, it will allow authors to disseminate their research articles for free over the internet and it helps to ensure the preservation of these articles in a rapidly evolving electronic environment. This means that research outputs in academic institutions will be made visible and accessible. Lynch (2003) succinctly states that "a university-based institutional repository is a set of services that a university offers to the members of its community for the management and dissemination of digital materials created by the institution and its community members. It is most essentially an organizational commitment to the stewardship of these digital materials, including long-term preservation where appropriate, as well as organization and access or distribution.

No wonder Wikipedia (2007) defines an institutional repository as:

> "an online locus for collecting, preserving and disseminating – in digital form – the intellectual output of an institution particularly a research institution. For a university, this would include materials such as research journals articles, before (preprints) and after (post prints) undergoing peer – review, and digital assets generated by normal academic life, such as administrative documents, course notes or learning objects".

The above definition goes beyond digital publishing of research and into the visibility of the parent institution. The expression of "institutional repositories" goes along with the idea of creating a digital library. Jones *et al* (2006)regard repositories in this way as constituent elements of digital libraries, providing them with the selections of collections they present as libraries, whether institutional or disciplinary. The distinction between institutional or disciplinary is due to the scope of a repository or a digital library whether it serves a single institution or collects materials belonging to a specific discipline.

Brief History of Institutional Repository

Institutional repository began at the same time as the World Wide Web (www) itself. The first online repository centered on theoretical physics was established in 1999 by physicist Paul Ginsparg at the Los Alamos National Laboratory in New Mexico and it was known as "arxiv" (pronounced "archive"). Currently, it is housed in Cornell University in New York.

Since the establishment of arxiv, it has expanded to include most other areas of physics as well as mathematics and computer science. Its success led to the establishment of other institutional repositories such as Repec (Research Papers in Economics), Cogprints and Education Line respectively in 1997. They eventually led to the Open Archives Initiative (OAI) in 1999 which enables institutional repositories to operate together, a phenomenon known as "interoperability".

In 2001, the software known as e-prints was conceived for IRs. Since then, other types of software for use by digital repositories have emerged such as Dspace launched by the Massachusetts Institute of Technology (MIT) in 2002 "to build a stable and sustainable long term digital storage repository that provides an opportunity to explore issues surrounding access control, rights management, versioning, retrieval, community feedback, and flexible publishing capabilities" (Dspace Project, 2000).

The emergence of the above technology has resolved the issue of grappling with how to manage the digital intellectual output of academic and other research institutions. This has made possible instantaneous access. All too often many information materials are not usually made accessible to many users and these materials remain marooned in the author's computers. About 80-85% of digital intellectual output of universities was never made accessible to the public (The Open Citation Project, 2004). Besides, the escalating cost of online journals prohibits subscription and it is becoming more unrealistic and challenging for libraries to subscribe to all, or even most of the online academic journals (Warren, 2003). However, Dpsace which is institutional in scope is responding to the above conditions by creating IRs.

Steps to follow in setting up an Institutional Repository in Academic Institutions

The rapid publications of journal articles, research papers, theses and dissertations, book chapters, conference papers and the production of teaching materials, works of arts, photographs and video recording have made it imperative for academic institutions to have institutional repositories in order to create access for public consumption of their intellectual output to aid research activities. In setting up an IR, the following steps are to be followed;

a. Planning
b. Choice of software platform

Planning: In planning, the question of what does the institutional repository mean to the academic librarian should be clearly answered. That is the librarian should have an outline to state the purpose and drivers of IR establishment in the institution.

- Define vision and initial goals clearly.
- Plan how to position the IR within wider information environment.
- Define target content of the repository e.g. research papers and data, electronic theses, teaching and learning resources etc
- Do a holistic stakeholder analysis to include them in planning and implementation processes.
- Stakeholders are senior institutional managers, departmental leaders, and those who are expected to contribute content.
- Have an institution wide Intellectual Property Right (IPR) policy working group.

- Put in place financial arrangements to support institutional repository work in the short/medium/long term.
- Have a name for the repository; it should be easy to remember, easy to type etc.
- Have persistent URL for repository with no redirect, for example *http://www.abcuniversity.edu.ng/repository*.

Choice of Institutional Repository Software Platform

Having done with the setting up of plans, the next step is to have a choice of software platform to suit the need of the type of IR. Academic librarians need to balance the need to innovate in managing digital archives with available resources and budget constraints. Each IR platform has unique strengths and some of the software providers are DSpace, Archimedes, E-prints, CDSware, Bepress, Greenstone, open repository etc. The cost and user-friendliness of the software should be considered as workability of the IR depends on the choice of software.

Components of an Institutional Repository System

The essential components of an IR according to Barton and Waters (2005) are;

- Interface for adding content to the system.
- Interface for searching/browsing/retrieving content
- Content database for storing content.
- Administrative interface to support collection management and preservation activities.

One of the primary concerns of IRs deployment is document dissemination and accessibility. Ways to create the academic contents of IRs are as follows:

- Awareness creation among the academics: awareness can be created through the issue of notices to faculties and all members of staff of development and importance of IR to academic community
- Making requests for individual research output be submitted to IR unit. This will result from the awareness level among academic staff and the entire university community of the importance of IR.
- Develop strategies that will speed up the rate document are provided for publication in the IR.
- Develop policy to handle the problems of copyright issues

Hardware and software concerns could be problematic when establishing an IR. The fact that most institutions are adopting IRs and they have gotten previous experiences in the use of the internet, websites and specialized applications software and hardware requirement, one may have to consult in case of such problems. Another challenge may come from copyright issues. Utulu and Adebayo (2010) say that such issues should have been answered to provide a level ground for implementation of IR: who owns the deposited works and which kind of already published work should be accepted for IR publication. It is advisable for institutions to develop a working policy to avoid the occurrence of court litigation in case of copyright violations and other forms of litigations.

Benefits of Institutional Repository (IR)

Researchers and institutions benefit from institutional repositories in the same way. The most prominent benefit is the increase in visibility and impact of research output. Building up and maintaining reputation in the scientific community is essential for academics and institutions. To Pickton and Barwick (2006) the benefits of institutional repositories can be grouped into the following categories;

To the Institution, an IR offers:

- Increasing visibility and prestige. A high profile IR may be used to support marketing activities to attract high quality staff, students and funding.
- Centralization and storage of all types of institutional output, including unpublished literature.
- Support for learning and teaching. Links may be made with the virtual teaching environment and library catalogue.
- Ability to keep track of and analyze research performance.
- Breaking down of publishers' costs and permissions barriers.

To Authors, an IR enhances

- Dissemination and impact of scholarship, for example, some studies have estimated that open access articles are cited 50% to 250% more than non open access articles. In some disciplines, online files receive an average of 300% more citations than materials available in paper format (The open citation project, 2004). Google Scholar gives preferential treatment to materials in IRs; a paper picked up from an IR would appear higher up on the Google results list (Ashwork, 2006).
- Feed back and commentary from users: Authors are able to receive and respond to commentary on pre-prints.
- Added value service; such as hit counts on papers, personalized publication lists and citation analyses (bibliometrics).
- a central archive of a researcher's work.
- benefits to researchers and their institutions in terms of prestige, prizes and grant revenue.

To summarize, the potential uses of an IR are: disseminating scholarly communication, managing and storing of learning materials, developing electronic publications and research collections; preserving of digital research work, building university profile by showcasing academic research work; providing an institutional leadership role for the library; providing avenue for research assessment, encouraging open access and housing of digitized collections.

Creation and Management of Institutional Repository

Providing guidelines in terms of appropriate content, acceptable formats, and creating metadata is critical to the creation and management of an effective and successful repository. Kurtz (2010) describes metadata as "an attempt to capture the contextual information surrounding a datum"

Metadata accompanies material that is submitted to repositories and serves a bibliographic function, making its associated material identifiable and searchable. Park and Tosaka (2010)equally state that "the core functions of bibliographic control in facilitating the discovery, identification, selection, and use of digital resources need by end users, not to mention the newer functions of administration, provenance, rights management, and preservation, depend on metadata. Metadata plays a crucial role in the functioning of individual repositories, and also networks of open access repositories. Consistent and complete use of metadata in a repository helps ensure its interoperability with other repositories, as well as its usefulness outside a local context. Yeates (2003) explains that interoperability strengthens "the long-term security of repositories generally, beyond any federation using a single technical platform while allowing "dynamic cross-boundary communications services that, nevertheless ever more tightly engage scholars in dissemination and exploitation of their work

Because of the crucial role that metadata plays in making the content of repositories discoverable and searchable not only within an individual repository, but also within a network of them, its creation is an extremely important step of the submission process. Guidelines for creating metadata in self-submission systems are fundamental in ensuring that at least a minimum level of consistency is maintained within a single repository's collection and across a network of repositories. Some institutions include extensive metadata creation guidelines to guide users as they submit documents. Even though it takes considerable, and therefore results in greater costs, other institutional repositories have actually committed to creating metadata for submissions (Howard, 2010). Despite the challenges of time and funding, it is suggested that there are benefits to staff members creating metadata for submitted materials. A study by Kurtz (2010) investigated three university repositories, one of which used librarians to archive metadata for contributed work, while the other two used other methods. All three universities used the same repository system, DSpace, but the one that used librarians to oversee the metadata process had the greatest accuracy and most complete records. Consistently, and not surprisingly, those contributor-generated metadata fields had the inconsistencies and lower quality metadata.

In terms of the metadata standards used by institutional repositories, a 2010 study by Park and Tosaka found that Dublin Core was the most frequently used non-MARC metadata scheme in the digital repositories that they profiled. Many repository systems, such as DSpace, base their metadata creation systems on Dublin Core, but may use more recognizable and understandable terms for contributors who are creating their own metadata. Other repositories have created their own metadata tags to be populated upon submission. No matter what approach is used, it is important that the procedure be carefully regulated and there be established policies decidedly in place.

Lastly, metadata creation is an important factor to be considered in the preservation of material within a repository. Hockx-Yu (2006) emphasizes that "much could be done to consider digital preservation from the outset, to involve the authors in contributing preservation metadata during the creation and ingest process and to embed digital preservation into the repositories work flow, which will ease the later preservation tasks.

Institutional repositories typically store the academic output of the institution, their content ranging from scholarly publications and learning tools, to course syllabi and student work.

Considering the academic nature of the e-Portfolio items, creating metadata for them would provide an experience somewhat comparable to that of individual self-archiving academic documents in an institutional repository. As Park and Tosaka (2010) stress, institutional repositories should consider a number of issues when selecting which metadata system to use. When surveying institutional repositories about their metadata selections, the most common considerations were the types of resources needing metadata, the target users and audience of the resources, as well as the subject matter of the resources. Institutional repositories should also consider how metadata structures will affect their interoperability among other repositories. Dunsire states that "community agreement on a single metadata structure richer than unqualified DC is likely to be hampered because there is wide variation in the scope of resources to be described within a local repository, leading to divergent functional requirements between the institution and the community" (2008). Consistency in metadata systems is an issue that must be addressed by institutional repositories as they make policies and decisions that will have an effect on not only their own collections, but those of other institutions they may be linked to. Regardless of an institutional repository's choice of metadata system, it is essential to provide guidance to users during the self-archiving process (McCallum, 2004). These "guidelines seem to be fundamental in ensuring a minimum level of consistency in resource description within a collection and across distributed digital repositories" (Park and Tosaka, 2010). The Metadata Object Description Schema (MODS) Guidelines from the Library of Congress made the task of creating MODS records less complicated, because detailed descriptions of each element, sub-element, and attribute were listed alongside examples of accurate MODS records. While not offering quite as many examples as the MODS user guide, the Dublin Core user guide also offered examples of appropriate ways to describe elements. Having a number of examples to reference when creating records, make the process easier and increases the accuracy and completeness of the record.

Expectations of Academic Librarians on Institutional Repository in the Information Technology (IT) Age

There is no gain saying that this present age is referred to as the information technology era where information can be created, stored and disseminated to billions of people across the globe in whatever form to enhance teaching, learning and research at any point. And in building a research reservoir such as an IR, academic librarians according to Nixon (2002), should act as the "library's eyes and ears" so as to collect organize and disseminate relevant information to the users who are always eager to read and research. They understand users' needs and perceptions and therefore act as subject selectors. Academic librarians are expected to be involved in the planning, implementation and operation of IR. The expectation of academic librarians in building an IR is summed up in the following ways:

- **Advocacy:** Librarians, especially academic librarians, need to know all about IR, its principles, benefits and operational processes in order to promote it and act as IR evangelists. They will need to develop advocacy programmes, publicize the IR through institutional news media and respond to questions by the stakeholders.
- **Building Content:** Academic librarians can employ advocacy and marketing strategies to promote engagement with faculty members and help to generate content. They can also assist by proactively searching for content independently.
- **Collection Administrators and Metadata Specialists:** Librarians have potential roles as collection administrators and metadata specialists. For effective implementation of IR, libraries will need to recruit or train librarians for digital collection management.
- **Training:** Academic librarians should be able to train staff and students through user education to use the IR and help them prepare their digital products.

Challenges of an Institutional Repository

Despite the above benefits of an IR, it is not without challenges which may hinder its success. These challenges are summarized thus:

- Cost: The initial cost for an open source software adopted by most institutions for creating IRs is not high but the recurrent costs, especially staff costs (e.g., time spent drafting policies, developing guidelines, publishing, training, supporting users and creating metadata, specialist IT consultancy) is insignificant.
- Difficulties in Generating Content: A successful IR depends on the willingness of authors and other researchers especially lectures and students to deposit their work voluntarily. There may also be local barriers and hindrances to be overcome.
- Rights Management Issues: Sometimes researchers are apprehensive about infringing publishers' copyright and lack adequate awareness about their own intellectual property rights. They may be uncertain about making their work available online before it is published by traditional publishers.
- Lack of Incentive: In the absence of any incentive, academics may feel reluctant to provide even bibliographic details of their scholarly output especially when they know that incentives are available in other institutions.
- Time Factor: Contributing content to user generated or 'self-service" sites is time consuming; and time is something which academics often lack. They may be willing to contribute content but reluctant to do it themselves. This calls for mediated deposits service for them.

Conclusion

From the above, it is pertinent to conclude that institutional repository is sine qua non to academic and other research institutions if their researches are to be seen, accessed, retrieved and utilized for development of mankind. Institutional repository in no small measure collects and organizes researches produced in an institution, and when properly managed, it gives prestige to both the author and the institution in the global arena. There is therefore the need for academic institutions to critically study the concept of institutional repository along with its benefits and provide one for their researches with the help of librarians who are specialized information custodians.

Recommendations/Suggestions

- In order to secure full institutional accreditation, National Universities Commission (NUC) should, as a matter of necessity, make institutional repository a major requirement.
- In order to secure IR content, heads of departments in academic and other research institutions should ensure submission of any research output of their institutions to their libraries for creation of IRs.
- Librarians should be trained about all aspects of institutional repositories and act as advocates of IR, considering its vital role in provision of research information.
- An institution willing to establish an IR should, as a matter of fact, study this paper.

References

Akpokodje, V. N. And Akpokodje, E. T. (2015). Availability and utilisation of institutional repository as indicators to institutional WEB BANKING. *European Journal of Computer Science and Information Technology, 13(2), 29-40.*

Ashworth, S. (2006).Role of librarians in the development of institutional repositories. Retrieved on April 8, 2013 from *http://pfsl.poznam.pl/oa/2.ppt*

Benkler, Y. (2006). The wealth of networks: how social production transforms markets and freedom. Yale: Yale University Press.

Christian, G. E. (2008). Issues and challenges to the development of open access institutional repositories in academic and research institutions in Nigeria. A research paper prepared for the Internal Development Research Centre (IDRC) Ottawa, Canada.

Crow, R. (2002). *The case for institutional repositories: a SPARC position paper.* The Scholarly Publishing & Academic Resources Coalition, retrieved from http://www.arl.org/sparc/bm~doc/ ir_final_release_102.pdf

Digital Case (2009). *Retrieved February 28, 2011 from http://library.case.edu/digitalcase/index.aspx*

Dspace Project (2000). *MIT Faculty Newsletter,* xii (4) Retrieved on April 8, 2003 from *http://www. dspace.org//news/articles/dspace-project-html.*

DRUM (n.d.). *Retrieved March 1, 2011 from http://drum.lib.umd.edu/*

DSpace@MIT (n.d.). *Retrieved February 28, 2011 from http://dspace.mit.edu/*

Genoni, P. (2004). Content in institutional repositories: A collection management issue. *Library Management, 25(6-7), 300-306.*

Howard, J. (2010). Digital repositories foment a quiet revolution in scholarship. *Chronicle of Higher Education, 56(38), A12-A11.*

Jain, P. Bentley, G. &Oladiran M. T. (2008).The role of institutional repository in digital scholarship communications. Gaborone: University press.

Johnson, R. (2002). Institutional repositories: Partnering with faculty to enhance scholarly communication. *D-Lib Magazine, 8(11),* retrieved March 3, 2011 from http://www.dlib.org/ dlib/november02/johnson/11johnson.html

Kennan, M., & Wilson, C. (2006). Institutional repositories: review and an information systems perspective. *Library Management, 27(4/5), 236-248.*

Kurtz, M. (2010). Dublin Core, DSpace, and a brief analysis of three university repositories. *Information Technology and Libraries, 29(1), 40-46.*

McCallum, S. (2004). An introduction to the Metadata Object Description Schema (MODS). *Library Hi Tech, 22(1).*

Park, J., & Tosaka, Y. (2010). Metadata quality control in digital repositories and collections: criteria, semantics, and mechanisms. *Cataloging & Classification Quarterly, 48, 696-715.*

PREMIS (2011). *Retrieved March 5, 2011 from http://www.loc.gov/standards/premis/*

Lynch, C. A. (2003). Institutional repositories: Essential infrastructure for scholarship in the digital age *ARL*. 226 p.1-7.

Mellon, A. W. (2006). "Augmenting interoperability across scholarly repositories. http://msc.mellon.org/meeting/interiop. Retrieved on June 18, 2016.

Pickton, M. & Barwick, J. (2006). *Librarian's guide to institutional repositories.* Loughborough: Loughborough University press.

The Open Citation Project (2004). The effect of open access and downloads on citation impact: a bibliography of studies. Retrieved April 8, 2013 from *http://opcit.eprints.org/oacitation-biblio.html*

Warren, B. (2003). Current challenges and choices in scientific publication. *Baylor University Medical Centre Proceedings* 16(4). Retrieved April on 8, 2013 from *http://www.baylorhealth.edu/proceedings/16/warren.pdf*.

Wikipedia, the Free Encyclopaedia (2012). Institutional repository. http://en.wikipedia.org/wiki/institutional_repository. Retrieved on June 20, 2016.

Yeates, R. (2003). Over the horizon: Institutional repositories. *VINE: The Journal of Information and Knowledge Management Systems, 33(2), 96-100.*

SPECIAL EDUCATION ISSUES

17

Creating a Differentiated Learning Environment for Holistic Learning in Nigeria Schools

Stella N. Nwosu *Ph.D* & Gibson Okworo *Ph.D*

Abstract

*T*he chapter advocates for provision of holistic learning experiences in schools through differentiated learning environments to engender high- quality educational attainment among Nigerian youths. This implies catering for every aspect of the learners needs during schooling; physical, cognitive, and psychological. It describes the learning environment and the features of a 21ˢᵗ century learning environment and compares this with the existing learning environment in Nigeria. The term differentiation, it's meaning and theoretical basis is highlighted. The use of differentiation in the context of the learning environment is explained. And the attributes of a differentiated learning environment; the physical facilities; instructional strategies and psychological are discussed. It concludes that differentiating the school environment is essential for creating complete learners, individuals who are relevant academically and socially in the society. The role of the teacher, school administration and government in providing a differentiated learning environment is recommended.

Key Words: *Learning Environment, Differentiation, holistic learning, Nigeria Schools*

Introduction

To facilitate optimal learning is the ultimate goal of all educational endeavors. And to make this possible, care must be taken to provide the enabling environment for it to take place. Learning cannot occur in isolation of the conditions under which it is expected to take place, there should be a conducive atmosphere that satisfies most of a learner needs. We can then ask, "what should be the best environment for effective learning"?

By definition, 'Learning environment' refers to the diverse physical locations, contexts, and cultures in which students learn. Since students may learn in a wide variety of settings, such as outside-of-school locations and outdoor environments. Alibi, Oduwaiye and Fasai (2012) describe learning environment as the totality of internal and external influence surrounding a school. The term is often used as a more accurate or preferred alternative to classroom, which has more limited and traditional connotations—a room with rows of desks and a chalkboard, for example. The term also encompasses the culture of a school or class—its presiding ethos and characteristics, including how individuals interact with and treat one another—as well as the ways in which teachers may organize an educational setting to facilitate learning..." (Bates, 2015). This definition indicates that learning environment is not just the physical environment (such as class rooms, lecture theatres, laboratories and delivery technologies) which readily comes into mind but includes also the conceptual, socio-cultural and psychological environment. This definition implies that students learn in many different ways in very different contexts. Since learners are in school to learn, then the system should create a learning environment that optimizes the ability of students to learn. Learning environments must be adapted to meet every aspect of students' needs. Globalization and social changes have transformed the world and societies, thus placing new demands on the educational system, and this must be reflected in our school system. There is really not any specific ideal learning environment but rather an infinite number of possible learning environments. Therefore, developing an appropriate learning environment for students in a particular course, program or school setting, requires creativity from teachers and responsibility on the part of the school administration and government. However, what should be the components of an appropriate learning environment for the 21st century learner.

According to Osborne (2013), a modern learning environment not only supports traditional pedagogy such as direct instruction but should offer more facilities, such as: flexibility to combine classrooms and split them with small groups; Openness: fewer walls, learning hub or central teaching and learning spaces that can be shared by several classes. There should also be access to resources including technology. Such learning environments should support a range of pedagogies including, applying, creating, communicating and decision-making. Osborne (2013) proposed that quality learning should be a combination of:

- *Personalized learning: Learning in our own unique way.*
- *Socially constructed learning: The collaboration, peer tutoring and reciprocal teaching that takes place when students work together, results in deeper understanding.*
- *Differentiated learning: The getting to learn at one's own pace, content and context*
- *Learning initiated by students themselves*
- *Learning that is connected to the physical world and authentic contexts, through interaction with others and the physical world and not from textbooks.(p12)*

Similarly, the Partnership for the 21st century skills (2016), describes the 21st century learning as the support systems that organize the condition in which humans learn best – systems that accommodate the unique learning needs of every learner and support the positive human relationship needed for effective learning. Thus, to educate the whole child, schools must devote themselves to more than the mind-body connections. They must attend to the emotional and social learning needs of children, as well as the traditional objectives of academic achievement and physical education. This is far from being the case in the Nigeria schools.

State of Nigeria Learning Environments

The Nigeria Federal and State governments have over the years initiated diverse educational policies aimed at improving the standard of education and create a more literate society. These includes: the free Universal Primary Education(UPE) of 1976; the 6-3-3-4 system,(that is 6 years primary, three year junior secondary, 3 year senior secondary and 4 year university education) of 1980; the Universal Basic Education (UBE) programme of 1988 (Igwe, 1988). In similar developments, the new National Policy on Education, highlights the need for citizen self learning. To this end, educational resource centres are to be established in the federal, states and local governments (FGN, 2004). Some of these policies have had positive impacts on educational attainment of the citizenry. However, the crux of our concerns here is the kind of education the children are getting. While governments and the school administrators are striving to improve literacy levels, they should also take a closer look at the nature of learning experiences Nigerian children encounter while in school.

Nigeria's schools have essentially not been able to provide the required environment for effective learning. The Nigeria learning environment was far from conducive: most schools had dilapidated buildings and lack necessary infrastructure. This has generated a negative attitude of students towards schooling and poor performance (Ohakamike-obeka, 2016). Many schools in Nigeria are not learner friendly nor do they have infrastructural facilities such as chairs, desks, toilets, facilities for the disabled children (Oluremi, 2016). According to Alibi, Oduwaiye and Fasai a positive learning environment is where the physical, emotional, social and academic development of a child is adequately taken care of. The challenges facing Nigeria learning environment is the inadequacies of qualitative human and material resources as well as inappropriate facilities. These conditions are not uniform in all schools while evaluation criteria is the same in all schools. They recommend the arrangement of the classroom that would engender learner centered approach to teaching and improved provision of school plant facilities. Ajaji, Ekundayo and Osalusi (2010) in a study conducted in western Nigeria found a conducive secondary school learning environment that is effective in the affective and psychomotor domains of learning but not that effective in the cognitive domain.

What is Differentiation?

The term "differentiation" is concerned with pedagogy. Differentiation is concerned with providing instruction that accommodates individual differences in learning and tries to develop learning potentials of every learner. It accommodates individual learning style and develops learning skills. Several authors (Kolb, 1984:: Keefe, 1988: McCarthy, 1989: Tomlinson, 2003) are strong advocates of differentiated instructional approach and have developed models and strategies for implementing it in the classroom. According to Carol Ann Tomlinson, professor of educational leadership, foundations and policy at the University of Virginia, a leader in the area of differentiated learning (Tomlinson, 1999), differentiated instruction is factoring students' individual learning styles and levels of readiness first before designing a lesson plan. Differentiation in the context of learning environment implies the learning environment that provides for the physical, conceptual, socio-cultural and psychological needs of the leaner.

Nwosu, Etiubon and Udofia (2014) showed that the concept of differentiation can be applied in other situations other than pedagogy. As it was adopted in the mentoring of school girls in order to provide a more holistic mentoring approach that meets the girls mentoring needs. Differentiating the learning environment implies providing a learning environment in the school that will meet all aspects of the learners needs in the school/classroom, so that they can achieve optimal learning. These include cognitive needs:-effective teaching strategies, books. Psychological needs:-counselling, creating good interpersonal relationship among students, between teachers-student and the school administration etc. Physical needs: - well equipped classroom, library, and infrastructure.

Theoretical Bases of Differentiation

Differentiation stems from the constructivist theories of education. It has been defined as an approach to teaching in which teachers proactively modify curricula, teaching methods, resources, learning activities and student products to address the diverse needs of individual students and small groups of students to maximize learning opportunity for each student in a classroom (Bearne, 1990; Tomlinson, 1999). The constructivist learning theory lends its self to the concept of differentiated instruction. According to the constructivism, we construct new knowledge rather than simply acquire it via memorization or through transmission from those who know to those who do not know. The constructivist view is that meaning and understanding is achieved by assimilating information, relating it to our existing knowledge and cognitively processing it (that is, constructing it based on our unique previous knowledge and experiences) an active not passive process. The theory of knowledge being crated originated from the cognitive learning theorists Jerome Bruner (19066) and David Ausubel (1968). Experience plays an important role in the learning in the learning process. This perspective of learning is tied to the theories of Dewy (1938) and Piaget (1952). These theories are the foundation of what is known as the "Experiential Learning" Kolb (1984) through the experiential learning theory developed a holistic integrative model of learning that combines experience, perception, cognition and behaviors. This model forms a perspective for differentiating instruction. A major outcome of the constructivist theory is that each individual is unique, because the interaction of their different experiences and their search for personal meaning results in each person being different from anyone else. The idea of differentiation is to create learning experiences that conform to individual learner needs creating a meaningful experience that is aligned with their schema. The cognitive theory takes a stand that learners tend to recall things that are meaningful to them, constructivism, works with prior knowledge, here prior knowledge is referred to as "Schema" or internal knowledge structure (Mergel, 1998).

If academically responsive or differentiated teaching is to take place in schools, effective support must be given to change systemic factors that impede attention to differences in learning such as getting to be familiar with wide range instructional approaches, effective classroom management on the part of the teacher and provision of both psychologically and physically friendly atmosphere by the school administration and government. However, engendering a differentiated learning environment does not only call for teacher transformation in thinking and practice but a common orientation among teachers, administrators, government, parents, students and community to develop schools that understand, respect and respond to individual differences. It requires a permanent and sustained commitment and action among stake holders in the Nigeria Education System to generate knowledge, understanding and skills that largely do not exist in our schools.

In Support of Differentiation

Studies have shown (Bearne, 1990; Tomlinson, 1999; Nwosu, Etiubon and Udofia, 2014) that differentiation is not only effective in engendering better learning and learners; it also creates holistic learning experiences. Tomlinson, Brimijoin and Narvaez (2008) found in a longitudinal study of elementary and high schools a positive and sustained achievement gains for students in all segments of the achievement spectrum and in a range of subject areas as a result of differentiated instruction. Tieso (2002) also reported achievement gains across economic and achievement levels through pre/post-test results of students in effectively differentiated classroom. Similarly, summary of research by

Strong (2002) reveals that effective teachers in contemporary classrooms develop classroom routines that attend to rather than ignore learner variance. Rasmussen (2006) showed that students in a Chicago high school receiving more instruction from a differentiated instructional methodology out performed students receiving less instruction from a differential methodology on American College Testing (ACT) English, Mathematics, Reading and composite.

When student's basic psychological needs (safety, belonging, autonomy and competence) are satisfied, they are likely to become engaged in school (school bonding). They act in accord with school goals and values, develop social skills and understanding, contribute to the school and the community. When students need for belonging, competence, autonomy, are not satisfied students are more likely to become: less motivated, more alienated and exhibit poor academic performance (Schneider, 2003).

Nwosu (2009) provided a practical guide to differentiating instructions and stressed that the approach provide each learner with an opportunity to become more proficient learner, enhance learning skills and thus, achieving balance learning experience. Differentiation maximizes learning for all student regardless their skill level or background. Nigerian schools can improve the quality of education the children receive through differentiation that is providing a more holistic learning environment and experiences.

Differentiating the Learning Environment

How can we ensure the learning environment is differentiated? According to Tomlinson and Allan (2003) the learning environment not only includes;" the operation and tone of the classroom-class rules, furniture arrangement, lighting, procedures and processes", (p3). It also involves:

- Considering the look and feel of the classroom
- Providing a safe and positive environment for learning
- Allowing for individual work preferences
- Managing the learning space". (p 4)

Thus, in providing a differentiated learning environment all aspects of the learning environment should meet the leaner's needs and expectations, starting with the physical learning environment.

Physical Learning Environment

The physical learning environment should be appealing to the learner. The physical elements such as lighting, air, noise, the colour of the walls, the arrangement of the seats should be to create better learning environment. There is strong consistent evidence that these physical variables affect learning. Maxwell (2000) found that children considered that colour was important to them and needed less uninviting and boring classroom wall colours. In the case of Noise (Schneider, 2000): found that good acoustics are fundamental to good academic performance. Similarly, some physical elements in the classroom such as chairs, classroom arrangement can improve comfort, wellbeing, and thus improve achievement (Hannah, 2013). Physical elements in the school environment have shown to have measurable positive effects on both the learning and attitudes towards schooling. A classroom with fresh air can create an atmosphere conducive to learning. Noise sound can play a very important role in the attention and success of a student, simple noise such as noisy hallways, slamming doors, taping pen on disks can greatly distract students thus hampering learning. (Hannah, 2013)

The seating arrangement also affects student's productivity. A differentiated classroom seating arrangement should be one in which there are no "back benchers". And no student is ignored, the troublesome ones are made to lead in group work or conservations so that they get the attention they desire A teacher should be mindful of not only where in a room a student is seated, but also by whom they are seated (Grabugh & Houston,1990) A teacher can organize the students according to behaviours, interests, cognitive abilities, or randomly, each arrangement has its purpose and strengths and weaknesses. A differentiated classroom arrangement is one that will enable each student to participate in class activities and get attention. This can generally be done physically through different patterns of disk arrangement, prop-control of classroom interactions, grouping the students according to various tenants and rotating leaders according to talents.

Class Room

In most Nigerian classrooms today, teachers are keenly aware of their students' learning differences but the question is whether they can figure out how to address those differences in ways that benefit both the individual learners and the class as a whole. One of the best teaching practices employed with widely reported favourable academic outcomes is the differentiated approach. Differentiated instructional approach is a way of thinking about the classroom that involves attending to individual and small group needs while moving the whole class ahead in knowledge, understanding, and skill. Differentiation therefore means tailoring instruction to meet individual and group needs. Teachers achieve this in four broad ways, namely, differentiating content, process, product or learning environment. This section would expatiate on these differentiating component possibilities in the Nigerian school setting.

Research on the effectiveness of differentiation shows this method benefits a wide range of students, from those with learning disabilities to those who are considered high ability. Differentiating instruction may mean teaching the same material to all students using a variety of instructional strategies, or it may require the teacher to deliver lessons at varying levels of difficulty, based on the ability of each student. Formative assessment is an essential ingredient of this method. Tomlinson & Allan (2000) in their book "Leadership for differentiating schools and classrooms" expounded the four different ways teachers can differentiate instructions to include:

1. Differentiating Content: This refers to what the student needs to learn or how the student will get access to the information. The teacher should observe, evaluate and determine students' capabilities and:

- use 'hands on' activities for some learners to help them understand a new idea
- use texts or novels at more than one reading level
- present information through both whole-to-part and part-to-whole
- use a variety of reading-buddy arrangements to support and challenge students when working with different texts
- re-teach students who need further demonstration or exempt students who already demonstrate mastery from reading a chapter or sitting through a re-teaching lesson
- use texts, computer programs, tape recordings and videos as a way of conveying key concepts to varied learners

- use Bloom's Taxonomy (a classification of levels of intellectual behavior going from lower-order thinking skills to higher-order thinking skills) to encourage thinking about content at several levels. The six levels coverable are: remembering, understanding, applying, analyzing, evaluating and creating.

2. Differentiating Process: This refers to activities in which the student engages in order to make sense of or master the content which includes:.

- use tiered activities through which all learners work on building the same important understandings and skills but proceed with different levels of support, challenge or complexity
- provide interest centers that encourage students to explore subsets of class topics that are of particular interest to them
- develop personal agendas (task lists written by the teacher and containing both 'common' work for the whole class and work that addresses the individual needs of learners) to be completed either during specified 'agenda time' or if students complete core work ahead of time
- offer 'hands-on' supports for students who need them
- vary the length of time a student may take to complete a task in order to provide additional support for a struggling learner or to encourage an advanced learner to pursue a topic in greater depth
- provide access to a variety of materials that target different learning preferences and readiness
- develop activities that target auditory, visual and kinesthetic learners
- establish areas/stations for inquiry-based, independent activities
- use flexible grouping to group and regroup students, for example according to content, ability, interests.

3. Differentiating product: This refers to culminating projects that ask the student to rehearse, apply, and extend what he or she has learned in a unit which may include:

- allow students to help design products around learning intentions/goals
- encourage students to express what they have learned in varied ways
- allow for varied working arrangements – alone, with a group
- provide or encourage the use of varied types of resources in preparing products
- provide product assignments at varying degrees of difficulty to match student readiness
- use a wide variety of assessments
- work with students to develop rubrics that match and extend students' varied skill levels
- use a continuum -
    - simple to complex
    - less independent to more independent
    - clearly defined to 'fuzzy' problems.

4. Differentiating the learning environment: This refers to the physical, conceptual, socio-cultural, and psychological environment

- make sure there are places in the room to work quietly and without distraction as well as places that invite student collaboration
- provide materials that reflect a variety of cultures and home settings
- set out clear guidelines for independent work that matches individual needs
- develop routines that allow students to get help when teachers are busy with other students and cannot help them immediately
- help students understand that some learners need to move around to learn while others do better sitting quietly
- vary the places where learning occurs – for example the lab or outside.
- use alternative seating
- identify classroom management procedures that would make the learning environment safe or more supportive.

Tomlinson (2003) suggest the following strategies to be used frequently or occasionally in differentiated classroom:

Complex Instruction
Students work in small instructional groups that

- draw upon individual's intellectual strengths
- allow for a variety of solutions and solution routes
- interest students
- use real world connection
- integrate reading and writing
- use multi-media
- require different talents to complete whole task

Orbital Studies
Students select a topic from a larger theme in the curriculum and

- investigate independently
- have guidance and coaching from the teacher
- develop more expertise on topic
- learn how to become an independent investigator

Stations
Students go to different spots in the classroom to work on various tasks simultaneously. This strategy

- allows students to work on different task simultaneously
- invites flexible grouping and timing
- includes a variety of assignments, materials, and product options based on rotation
- allows choice of station as a result of teacher, student, or shared decision

- may include the following examples: Teaching Station, Practice Station, Project Place, Thinking Place, Proof Place (peer conferencing, peer editing, etc).

Centers

Students go to different areas that contain collections of materials or activities designed to teach, reinforce, or extend a skill or concept. Teachers

- use materials and activities addressing a wide range of reading levels, learning profiles, and interest
- plan activities that vary from simple to complex, abstract to concrete, structured to open-ended include instruction about what a student should do if help is needed or the assignment is complete
- use a record keeping system to monitor quality and completion level
- include a plan for ongoing assessment to allow for adjustment in center tasks
- focus on mastery or extension of specific skills

Agendas

Students complete a personalized list of tasks in a specified time. The teacher

- creates the agenda that will last the student two to three weeks
- includes special instructions for each task
- allows the student to determine the order of the tasks
- sets aside a particular time (daily, weekly, etc) to work on agenda activities
- moves to individual students to monitor progress and to coach
- may instruct small group of students having difficulty with like tasks or skill

Entry Points

Teacher uses students' learner profiles (Multiple Intelligences) to plan instruction. Teacher presents topic or concept. Student is given the choice of avenues to begin studying the topic or concept, either individually or in small groups

- (Narrational Entry Point)- presents a story or narrative
- (Logical-Quantitative Entry Point)- uses numbers or deductive scientific approach
- (Foundational Entry Point)- examines the philosophy and vocabulary of the topic
- (Aesthetic Entry Point)- focuses on the sensory features
- (Experimental Entry Point)- uses a hand-on approach

Tiered Activities

Teacher plans tiered activities that focus on different levels of complexity, abstractness, and open-endedness. The teacher;

- selects the concept or skill to be learned
- assesses the students' readiness level

- creates an activity that is interesting, high level, and develops or teaches the skill
- charts the complexity of the activity (high complexity to low complexity)
- clones the activity to ensure success and assess in terms of materials (basic to advanced), form of expression (familiar to unfamiliar), and experience (from personal to removed from personal)

Learning Contracts

Teacher negotiates a contract with student to give freedom, decide what is to be learned, working conditions, and how information will be applied or expressed. The contract

- specifies working conditions which may include behavior, time constraints, homework, class work involvement
- sets positive and negative consequences
- establishes criteria for successful completion of work
- includes signatures of agreement by both teacher and student.

Other Strategies

There are many more strategies a teacher can employ in the classroom to create differentiated learning, where every student gets a chance to be at his best. These include:

Compacting

Teacher pre-assesses what the students know or do not know about the topic or skill. Teacher provides a meaningful and challenging use of time for the students who have already mastered the topic or skill this gives them confidence.

Problem-Based Learning

Teacher presents the students with a complex, unclear problem. Students then seek additional information. Define the problem, locate and use valid resources, make decisions about solutions, pose a solution, communicate that solution to others, and assess the solution's effectiveness. This enables critical thinking and "Analytic Learners" (McCarthy, 1989) will excel in it.

Group Investigation

Teacher guides students through the investigation of a topic related to something else being studied in the class. Groups are divided by learner interest. Teacher assists in planning and carrying out the investigation, presenting the findings, and evaluating outcomes.

Independent Study

Teacher guides students in pursuing topics that interest them, identifying intriguing questions, setting goals and criteria for work, and assessing progress according to those goals.

Choice Boards

Students choose assignments from Choice Board with pockets containing varied tasks and instructions based on the core concept being taught. Students choose from a row and topic suited to their multiple intelligences or learning styles and readiness level.

4MAT

Teachers plan instruction based on the four preferences (mastery, understanding, personal involvement, and synthesis) during the course of several days on a given topic, organizing students, and the classroom structures to enhance learning; he not only has to provide the best instruction that will meet the learning needs at the diverse personalities in his class(McCarthy, 1989). He will not be teaching cognate alone but social skills. He is must mentor to his student in a way that promotes positive interactions (Lindbald, 1994).

In a differentiated classroom environment, each student is allowed to utilize his/her potentials, they have opportunities to use their unique skills and abilities to benefit the class as a whole hoping that the students can realize they have talents that others can benefit from, and that they will use those skills selflessly to benefit society (Hannah 2013), thus, creating potentially beneficial and productive members of society. In a differentiated classroom, the teacher should make students feel that everyone of them is important and has the potential to learn, thus a teacher becomes a psychologist using the right words and attitude to make his students feel important and relaxed in his class.

On the whole, the classroom environment plays a crucial role in keeping students engaged and enabling them to be successful learners. This can be achieved by the teacher through not only cognitive strategies as enumerated above but also through maintaining good psychological atmosphere and conducive physical environment, but the major forces should be to create an environment in which every student is given an opportunity to realize his potentials and talents.

Conclusion

This chapter has highlighted the facets of differentiation of the learning environment. Stating the possible outcomes of a differentiated learning environment to include; creating complete learners that they enjoy schooling and are able to realize their potentials and are confident to pursue them. It is advocated here that differentiation should not be limited to just instruction but extended to all aspects of the learning environment including physical and psychological needs of the students. In this way the school provides optimal, meaningful and relevant learning experiences for Nigeria students to create complete learners. The school can become a place where they not only acquire cognitive/intellectual knowledge, but also develop good self concepts and other social skills. These traits work together to make the students intellectually and socially connected members of the society.

Recommendations

- **The Role of the Teacher**

Most of the time a student spends in school is spent sitting in the classroom; this is where more of the learning takes place. It is an important aspect of the school. It is the major learning environment. Thus everything about the classroom should be set as a with the objective of enhancing students learning, it should be a place where students can thrive Hannah (2013) This puts a lot of pressure on the teacher and to some extent the school administration. For the teacher he must exhibit several traits to create a conclusive classroom for learning.

- **The Role of Administrative Stake Holders**

Are they forced to share desks, chairs, sit in hot poorly ventilated classrooms with poor understanding of what is being taught,afraid of the teacher and the school authority, with little or no direction or what he is good at or what he can do.

While educating the mind let the good characters be built, let talents be harnessed, let potentials be developed and the thought of schooling be pleasant ones. Thus, governments and the school administrators need to consolidate the existing educational structures provide more learner friendly physical structures to take care of the learners physical needs. Support more teacher continuing professional development in acquisition of differentiated instructional skills,interpersonal skills that would cater for the learners cognitive needs; provision of a stable counseling services in schools for both the teachers and students to handle affective (psychological) hindrances' to learning and character building.

References

Ajayi, I. A., Ekundayo, H. T. & Osalusi, F. M. (2010). Learning environment and secondary school effectiveness in Nigeria. *Kamla—Raj* 4(3), 137-142.

Bates, A. W. (2015). Teaching in a digital age, guidelines for designing and teaching, Available at: http://opentextbc.teachingatadigital age/

Diget,.J. (1952). *The origins of intelligence in children*. New York: International University Press.

Deweg, J. (1938). *Experience and education*. New York: McMillan

Federal Republic of Nigeria (2004). *National Policy on Education.* Lagos: NERDC Press.

Grabugh & Houston (1990). Establishing a classroom Environment that promotes interaction and improved student Behavior. *The Clearing House* 63(8) ps75-379.

Hannah, R. (2013). The effect of classroom Environment on student learning "An honors thesis Lee Honors College, Western Michigan University.

Igwe S. O. (1988). The concept of the 6-3-3-4 system of the education and its implications for Nigeria. In G. O. Akpa and S. U. Udoh (eds). *Towards Implementing the 6-3-3-4 System of Information in Nigeria.* Jos: *Top Educational Series.* Pp 73-79.

Keefe J. W. (1988). (Ed). *Profiling and utilizing learning style.* Boston VA: National Association of Secondary School Principals.

Kolb (1984). *Experiential learning and Development* Englewood Cliffs: Prentice Hill.

Lindbald, A. H. (1994). You can avoid the traps of cooperative learning. *The Clearing House,* 67(5), 291-293.

Maxwell, L. E. E. and Evans G. W. (2000). The effects of Noise in pre-school children's pre-reading skills. *Journal of Environmental Psychology* 29, 91-97.

McCarthy, B. (1989). *The 4mat system. Teaching to learning style and right left mode technique4s.* Barrington: Excel. Inc.

Nwosu, S. N. (2009). Differentiating instruction: A strategy for the attainment of educational goals. *Journal of Educational Teaching and Instruction* (1):41-46.

Nwosu, S. N., Etiubon, R. U. & Udofia, T. M. (2014). Tackling inhibitions to careers in science and technology through differentiated mentoring approach. *International Education Studie*s 7(8) p 124-130.

Ohakamike– Obeka (2016). The school learning environment and students' language. *Research on Humanities and Social Science* 16(2) 31-33.

Ofsted, Annual Report 1999/2000. Available at: http://www.archive.official – documents. co. Uk/ document/opsted/hc 102/102/htm

Olurenmi O F. Creating a Friendly school learning environment for Nigeria children. *European Scientific Journal* 8 (8) p10

Osborne, M. (2013) Modern learning environment CORE Education New Zealand. Available at http//; open text bc. ca /teachinginadiquatal age I:15-2 what islearningenvironment.

Partnership for the 21st century skills (2016) 21st century learning environments available at hppt/;www. p21.ori/storage/document/te white papr ipdf.

Rasmussen, (2006). Differentiated instruction as a means for improving achievement as measured by the American college Testing (ACT). A dissertation submitted to the Loyola University of Chicago School of Education.

Schneider, M. (2003). Linking school facilities conditions to teacher satisfaction and success Available at: http// www edfacilities.org/pubs/teacher survey.pdf.

Stronge, J. (2002). *Qualities of effective teachers.* Alexandria, V. A; Association for supervision and curriculum Development.

Tieso, C. (2002).*The effect of groping and curricular practices on intermediate students' math achievement.* Hardford, CT: National Research center on the Gifted and Talented University of Connecticut.

Tomlinson, C.A & Callahan C. (1997). Challenging expectation: casa students of high-potential culturally diverse young children. *Gifted Quarterly* 14(2), 5-17.

Tomlinson, C. (1999). *The differentiated classroom: responding to the needs of all learners.* Alexandria, VA: Association for supervision and curriculum development.

Tomlinson, C. (2003). *Fulfilling the promise of the differentiated classroom: strategies and tools for responsive teaching.* Alexandria, VA: Association for supervision and curriculum Development.

Vygotsky, L. (1978) mind in society. Cambridge, MH. Harvard University Press.

18

Effects of Domestic/Family Violence on the Educational Development of Children in Nigeria

A. D. Oghiagbephan *MISPON, MCASSON, MNISEP, MASSE*

Abstract

*D*omestic/Family violence is a daily reality for millions of families around the world including Nigeria, affecting Nigerian children of all ages, all social contexts and in every part of their lives – their homes and families, schools, institutions, and communities. Domestic/family violence is a health, legal, economic, educational, developmental, and above all, a human rights issue. The paper, therefore, focuses on family violence as one of the most prevalent yet relatively hidden and ignored forms of violence globally. The paper highlights the concepts of violence, domestic/family violence, theories of violence, violence in the home, what constitutes domestic/family violence in the home, domestic/family violence and its effects on the Education of the Nigeria child and strategies for preventing domestic/family violence. The paper also recommends the need for coordinated and integrated efforts among counsellors, psychologists, educationists, scholars and significant others in educating Nigerians on the deadly effect of family violence on educational development of children in Nigeria.

Key Words: *Domestic, Family Violence, Children, Victims, Physical and Emotional*

Introduction

One negative aspect of family's life is the effect of family violence on children, either as witnesses to, or victims of the conflict. Children could be severely traumatized by witnessing family violence, otherwise known as domestic violence or themselves being victims of this violence (Imhonde, Aluede and Oboite, 2009). Children are in great danger in the place where they should be safest: within their families. For many, 'home' is where they face a regime of terror and violence at the hands of somebody close to them – somebody they should be able to trust. Those victimized suffer physically and psychologically. They are unable to make their own decisions, voice their own opinions or protect themselves for fear of further repercussions. Their human rights have been denied and their lives are stolen from them by the ever-present threat of violence.

Violence in society is rooted in the family as a basic unit of society. It is now a conclusive fact that the family plays the most crucial role in child and family violence in Nigeria (Egwu, 2004). It is within the family circle that individual child learns first before moving to the formal education to acquire more knowledge. Life at the human level starts within the family. Family violence is one of the tools of developmental setbacks to education of Nigerian children and women and children have been the worst hit. Every Nigerian child is born into a family where such a child is supposed to be cared for, nourished, stimulated, socialized and sent to school in preparation for meaningful living in the society. However, due to the family violence, the quality care, good nutrition and stimulation needed for the child's healthy growth and educational development, most especially at the childhood stage cannot be readily achieved (Ezurike, 2004). The outlook described above, is worrisome and the future of the Nigerian child glooms because a family full of violence will never provide conducive environment which can promote early stimulation to learning in the Nigerian child. It is in the light of the above that this paper sets out to examine the impacts of family violence on the educational development of the Nigerian child.

Definition of Violence

Violence could be defined as a situation of unequal relation between members of a family particularly between the husband and wife or between husband and wives, even amongst children and others. According to Adekola and Falase (2001), domestic violence is a common feature in polygamous homes, either between husband and wife (wives), among wives, between half-brothers and half-sisters, among siblings. Wikipedia (2010) defines domestic violence thus: Domestic violence also known as domestic abuse, spousal abuse, child abuse or Intimate Partner Violence (IPV) can be broadly defined as a pattern of abusive behaviours by one or both partners in an intimate relationship such as marriage, dating, family, friends or cohabitation. Domestic violence or abuse is a pattern of controlling behaviours that are purposeful, and directed at achieving compliance from and over a victim without regards for his or her rights... Domestic violence is a combination of physical force or terror designed to cause physical, psychological, social, religious, economic, mental and emotional harm to victims.

From the above definitions, it can be deduced that violence is perpetrated by intimate partners (adults, youths/adolescents) against their intimate partners. Are we perpetrators of violence in our homes, communities and society at large?

What is Family Violence?

UNICEF (2000) defined family violence as violence perpetrated by intimate partners and other family members, and manifested through physical abuse such as slapping, beating, arm twisting, stabbing, strangling, burning, choking, kicking, threats with an object or weapon, and murder. It also includes traditional practices harmful to women such as female genital mutilation and wife inheritance (the practice of passing a widow, and her property, to her dead husband's brother); sexual abuse such as coerced sex through threats, intimidation or physical force, forcing unwanted sexual acts or forcing sex with others; psychological abuse which includes behaviour that is intended to intimidate and persecute, and takes the form of threats of abandonment or abuse, confinement to the home, surveillance, threats to take away custody of the children, destruction of objects, isolation, verbal aggression and constant humiliation; economic abuse includes acts such as the denial of funds, refusal to contribute financially, denial of food and basic needs, and controlling access to health care, employment, etc.

Family violence is also described as physically or emotionally harmful acts between individuals in families or in intimate relationships. The term family violence covers a wide range of behaviours and includes domestic violence (sometimes referred to as spouse abuse), child abuse, and abuse of the elderly. Violence between adult partners can include threats and coercion, physical and sexual assault, and murder. Child abuse ranges from physical or sexual assault to neglect of a child's basic needs. Violence toward elderly involves physical, psychological, or financial abuse or neglect (Microsoft Encarta, 2007). According to Gelles (2009), domestic violence or spouse abuse is physically or emotionally harmful acts between husbands and wives or between other individuals in intimate relationships. It includes emotional or verbal abuse, denial of access to resources or money, restraint of normal activities or freedom (including isolation from friends and family), sexual coercion or assault, threats to kill or to harm, and physical intimidation or attacks. Child abuse is intentional acts that result in physical or emotional harm to children. The term child abuse covers a wide range of behaviour, from actual physical assault by parents or other adult caretakers to neglect of a child's basic needs. Adegoke and Oladeji (2008) opined that information on the amount of violence shows that it is not a rare phenomenon. Family violence, of course, represents a rather extreme example of the failure of supportiveness, it is found in every kind of family and it can reach extreme levels.

Theories of Violence

There are some theories associated with violence in our society. An understanding of the theories of violence will go a long way in reducing/eliminating the incidence of violence in schools, homes and in the society at large. According to Bandura (1981), Walker (1979), cited in Okobiah and Okorodudu (2003, 2004), and Dekeseredy and Perry (2006), the following theories explain violence. They are sociobiological, social learning, sub-cultural, patriarchal, power and control, evolutionary, psychodynamic, personality, exchange, psychosocial, learned helplessness, psychopathological, pathological conflict, and so on. Some of these theories will be discussed below:

Socio-biological theories are used to explain some types of domestic violence such as rape, child abuse, infanticide, child neglect as reported by Dekeseredy and Perry (2006). The understanding is that individuals with these tendencies are most likely to transmit these violent behaviours which are genetic. What can we do about such individuals? As counsellors/psychologists, we know that conducive environment can elicit inherent traits in man to act violently. It therefore, behooves on the parents, teachers, church and society to provide non-violent environment – for the child so that he/she cannot be motivated externally to act violently.

The social learning and patriarchal theories of violence postulate that violent behaviours are learned. Such violent behaviours are "precipitated by a combination of contextual and situational factors" (O' Leary, 1988 as reported by Dekeseredy and Perry (2006). In a dysfunctional family where there are batteries, lack of respect, humiliation, love, money, etc., there is usually aggression, stress and exhibition of violent behaviours. In families where there is drug abuse, alcohol abuse, infidelity etc., there are exhibitions of one form of violent behaviour or the other. The children from such homes who have been exposed to such aggressive behaviours while they were growing up are likely to be more violent in their homes and schools than their counterparts who grew up in non-violent homes (Okobiah, 2010).

Psychopathological theories of violence posit that individuals who suffer from some "kind of physiological and/or psychological imbalance(s) expressed by combinations of obsessive ideation, compulsive repetition, poor impulse control, rapid desensitization to violence, diminished effect reactivity failure to changing stimulus – reinforcement association, hyper dependence, depression or anxiety, low self-esteem, paranoia, disassociation from their own feelings, antisocial tendencies, failure to sympathize, fear of intimacy, etc. have personality and psychopathology traits that are unique to violence assailants (Dekeseredy and Perry, 2006).

Pathological theories posit that individuals are violent when there are differences among individuals who are attached to others; they are rejected, abandoned, alienated and humiliated. They become angry and such anger usually lead to violent actions.

Violence in the Home

Parental upbringing provides an indispensable guide to the child in all that he/she does in the future. Actually, if there is zero violence tolerance in homes, violence in the society, churches and schools will be reduced to the barest minimum. One gets to know from the children in schools, staffrooms, churches and from members of the households. The cases even if reported, are not treated with all the seriousness they deserve. Those (police, family members, friends) who get the reports would always believe that it is a family issue and, therefore, do not see the violence presented as a serious matter. The perpetrators are usually intimate individuals to the victims. Violence is a very serious problem and I make bold to say that domestic violence occurs in pastors, rich men, professors, lawyers, doctors, petty traders; etc. homes simply stated, violence does not discriminate (Okobiah, 2010).

What Constitutes Domestic/Family Violence in the Home?

Domestic /family violence of course, is the major basis of child violence. Family violence takes a number of forms: physical and psychological and occurs not only between spouses but across members of unhealthy families. According to Egwu (2004), the most common examples of family violence are the following:

- Wife battering
- Physical abuse of children (physical violence)
- Child neglect and rejection (emotional violence)
- Child victims of sexual abuse
- Family homicide cases
- Elder abuse
- Marital rape
- Incest
- Alcohol, alcoholism, drug and family violence
- General parental irresponsibility, such as family abandonment by husbands.

Where these occur, the family is readily unhealthy, thereby jeopardizing the development of the Nigerian child, most especially educational development. Violent children in our educational institutions come from unhealthy, violence homes and families, have parents with criminal and violent history, anti-social personality, lack parental supervision leading to the development of conduct behaviour problems such as juvenile delinquency, experience parental support of the use of aversive and aggressive behaviour and are also victims of divorce or separation (Egwu, 2004).

In the main, family violence can be categorized into two: (i) physical violence and (ii) emotional violence.

i. **Physical Violence:** This involves the administration of noxious stimuli that are likely to cause bodily harm or bring about lasting damage to children (Nwachukwu, 2004). Family members who lack an understanding of the process of development in children hold unreasonable expectations for the abilities of such children. They wish to ascribe adult qualities and role to very young children and are easily frustrated when their wishes are not met. They do resort to brute force (violence) when everything else fails because they see these children as stubborn, uneducable and morally deprived, which is not good for the educational development of the Nigerian child. It is also the intentional use of physical force with the intent of causing injury, harm, disability or death.

ii. **Emotional Violence:** This also involves the use of stimuli that do not involve bodily harm. Emotional violence is a disservice to the educational development of the Nigerian child as well as educational enterprise. Onete and Imona (2008) described emotional violence as any attitude or behaviour which interferes with a child's mental health or social development. This includes yelling, screaming, name-calling, shaming, negative comparison to others, telling them they are bad, no good, worthless or mistake. According to Nwachukwu (2004), emotional violence is in different forms viz: (a) use of invidious language (b) language that has the potential to ridicule someone. It described the first of these forms as the use of language by the family members that is likely to cause resentment, provoke ill-will and unintended behaviour. Expression of preference for a particular child, whether in overt or disguised manner have but one consequence, which is that of withdrawal on the part of those that are not the family members' favourite. The long-term effects include loss of self-esteem, the development of negative self-concept and a likely desire to withdraw from the influences that are administered by the family members. In extreme forms, children may develop irreparable dislike for the school and all that it stands for (Nwachukwu, 2004).

The second group consists of words and expressions that cause or have the potentials to cause mental, spiritual, and moral pain. Nwachukwu (2004) opined that words such as "idiot, I did not expect anything better, teach him/her how to do it, enjoyment officer, latecomer, glutton" lead to belittling, denigrating ridiculing, scaring, and discrimination against the child. He said that the net effect of this approach is to alienate the child and create the impression that the school is engaged in an undeclared battle with the child as well as arousing phobic feelings in the child, leading ultimately to the abandonment of the school. Emotional violence is manifested in verbal attacks, belittling, harassment, isolation of partner and children, deprivation of physical and economic resources, withholding affection, ignoring victim, name calling and use off derogatory language, etc (Mowaiye-Fagbemi and Idowu, 1997).

From the discourse so far, one can deduce that a child from this type of environment is already emotionally drained before getting to school. The resultant effect is that the child may not pay attention to what the teacher teaches, may be withdrawn, may hate the teacher and may be disillusioned about life. So, if the child is a pupil, chances are that he/she may drop-out because of poor academic performance. The child may be violent towards other children due to transfer of aggression. Some children from such homes where there is violence may not want to go home when school closes. They may want to hang around the school premises and this exposes them to 'bad boys or bad girls' who would offer conducive homes to them.

Family Violence and Its Effects on the Education of the Nigerian Child

Families affected by violence touch all service systems and lives in every community. Children exposed to family violence are in our schools and daycare centers. Though, family violence cuts across the economic spectrum, poor families are more likely to be affected. In fact, many families in which family violence is present, struggle with multiple problems, including poverty, substance abuse and exposure to other forms of violence. According to Imhonde, Aluede and Oboite (2009), Adegoke and Oladeji (2008), Adeniyi (2006), Haggai and Mang (2006), Nwachukwu (2004), Isangedighi (2004), Omoniyi (2004) and Arifayan (2004), the following are the serious negative and long term effects of family violence on Nigerian child;

- Development of irreparable dislike for the school and all that it stands for.
- Late coming to school, high absenteeism.
- Impairment of cognitive development especially in terms of intelligence and intellectual functioning at school.
- Poor academic performance and low level of problem solving skills.
- Development of negative self-concept
- Higher risk for maladjustment both in school and at home.
- Development of behaviourial problems such as aggression, phobias, insomnia, low-self esteem, and disobedience, low level of social competence, and tendency toward substance abuse.
- Development of emotional problems such as fear, anxiety, depression, anger, hostility and poor self-esteem.
- Nightmares and physical health complaints.
- Replication of parental aggressive and abusive behaviour in schools thus creating a vicious cycle of family violence both at home and educational institutions.
- Impairment of physical, social, emotional and mental development.
- Withdrawal on the part of those that are not the family members favourite.
- Sexual abuse which could lead to adolescent premarital pregnancy, contraction of sexually transmitted disease (STD) and the universal scourge known as HIV/AIDS.

Children from violence family bring their baggage of experience straight to classroom. They act out their searing pain in disruptive, annoying and frustrating ways through behaving aggressively, deliberately hurting and annoying other children and other dysfunctional behaviours. They are all susceptible to the above effects and they can prevent the Nigerian child from having the desired and best education in his or her life.

Strategies for Preventing Family Violence

Preventing family violence can be achieved through the following:

- Changing the individual's behaviour – through education, lectures, and counselling.
- Changing the environment – providing mentors who furnish positive role models.
- Changing the law – legal requirements for arrest and prosecution of offenders.
- A societal change in the acceptability of family violence (Branon & Feist, 2004).

Conclusion

This paper has been able to show that family violence is a problem that should be definitely confronted and condemned totally. Family violence, as discussed, has serious implications on the educational system in Nigeria. It presents a serious draw back on the Nigerian child's educational development and thus hinders societal growth and development. The problem requires adequate and efficient handling in order to improve educational development of the Nigerian child. Much needs to be done to create awareness and demonstrate that change is not only necessary, it is also possible. Now that strategies for dealing with it are becoming clearer, there is no excuse for inaction.

However, as counselors, psychologists, educationists, one can only give what one has. If one must make positive contribution to the elimination of violence in our educational system in Nigeria, one must start with oneself and must be able to identify and deal with (a) the violent tendencies in him/her (b) the behaviour one exhibits because it is cultural to do so. It is only then that one can provide a home devoid of violence in which our children grow up.

Recommendations

In the light of the serious consequences of family violence especially on the Nigerian child, it is therefore recommended that:

- Scholars (psychologist, counsellors, etc.) in Nigeria should come together to educate and sensitize Nigerians on the deadly effects of family violence especially on the education of the Nigerian child.
- Counselling should be provided to parents and the entire citizenry to evolve good parent-child relationship in order to reduce violence in the family.
- As much as possible, parents/caregivers should avoid the use of corporal punishment because it only teaches children that violence is the best way of maintaining control and it encourages them to hit other children.
- Parents should provide a nurturing and supportive child-friendly home, free from discrimination, violence and/or abuse of any kind.
- Parents should have sound inter-personal relationship with their children showing them love and affection.
- A child should not be disciplined when the adult's anger is out of control.
- Intense awareness should be created among Nigerian families using seminars, workshops and training programmes about what constitutes family violence.
- There should be penalty for those engaging in family violence against Nigerian child to deter others.

References

Adekola, G. & Falase, O. A. (2006). Domestic Violence and Women Participation in Community Development in Ibadan Metropolis; Nigeria. *African Journal of Education and Development Studies 3(1): 85-93.*

Adegoke, T. G. & Oladeji, D. (2008). Family Violence Variables Influencing the Psychosocial Wellbeing of Children of abused partners in Ibadan Metropolis, Nigeria. *Journal of flmacin Ecology.*

Adeniyi, E. F. (2006). Influence of Child Abuse on Emotional State and Academic Performance of Victims. *The Nigerian Educational Psychologist 4, (2), 212-222.*

Arifayan, T. (2004). Child Abuse: The Inhuman Games People Play. *Daily Times,* pp. 12. September 9

Branon, L. & Feist, J. (2004). *Health Psychology: An Introduction to Behaviour and Health* (5th Ed.) USA: Thomson Learning Inc.

Dekeseredy, S. & Perry, B. (2006), (Ed). A Critical Perspective on Violence in Advancing Critical Criminology: Theory and Application by Lexington Books.

Egwu, E. U. (2004). Family Psychology. In A. K. J. Ibanga, A. C. Mbanefo, Z. K. Dagona & E. U. Egwu (eds), *Introduction to Basic and Applied Psychology.* Lagos: Waptech Limited, 148 – 159.

Ezurike, C. I. M. (2004). Child Abuse in Contemporary Nigeria Society: Its Psychosocial Implications for National Development. In R. O. Nnachi & P. S. E. Ezeh (eds.), *Child Abuse and Neglect.* Awka: Erudition Printers, 224-232.

Gelles, R. J. (2009) Child Abuse. *Microsoft Encarta Online Encyclopedia.* Retrieved on August 8, 2015 from http://encarta.msn.com.

Haggai, M. P. & Mang, G. L. (2006). Incidence and forms of child abuse among foster and step children and their educational implications. *The Nigerian Educational Psychologist 4, (2), 328 – 336.*

Imhonde, H. O., Aluede, O. & Oboite, W. (2009). Domestic Violence and Adolescent Psychological Functioning among secondary school students in the Benin Metropolis of Nigeria. *European Journal of Educational Studies* 1(1). Retrieved on August 8, 2015 from http://ozelacademy.com/EJESv1ni2.pdf.

Isangedighi, A. J. (2004). Child Abuse. In R. O. Nnachi & P. S. E. Ezeh (eds.), *Child Abuse and Neglect.* Awka: Erudition Printers, 1-20.

Microsoft Encarta (2007). *Family Violence.* Microsoft Student 2007 (DVD). Redmond, WA: Microsoft Corporation.

Mowaiye – Fagbemi, O. & Idowu, A. I. (1997). Physical and Psychosocial Effects of Violence Against Women in Nigeria. *The Counsellor* 15(1): 13 – 20.

Nwachukwu, V. C. (2004). Child Abuse and the Education of the Child. In R. O. Nnachi & P. S. E. Ezeh (eds.), *Child Abuse and Neglect.* Awka: Erudition Printers, 21 – 27.

Okobiah, O. C. (2010). Keynoted Address Delivered at the Opening Ceremony of the Nigerian Society for Educational Psychologists during the 10th Annual Conference on Violence, Education and the Nigerian Child Held at the Delta State University, Abraka, Nigeria from 4th – 8th October.

Okobiah, O. C. & Okorodudu, R. I. (2003). A Study of Spouse Abuse Dimensions in Southern Nigeria. *Journal of Psychology and Education,* 1(7): 135-148.

Okobiah, O. C. & Okorodudu, R. I. (2004). Gender Differences in Spouse Abuse Dimensions in Southern Nigeria. *Journal of Educational Research and Development* 3(1): 180-191.

O' Leary, D. K. (1988). Physical Aggression Between Spouses: A Social Learning Theory Perspective. In N.V. Ibn Itasselt (ed) *Handbook of Family Violence,* New York: Plenum, 31 – 53.

Omoniyi, O. K. (2004). Eradicating Child Abuse in Nigeria: The Role of Educational Media. In R. O. Nnachi & P. S. E. Ezeh (eds.) *Child Abuse and Neglect.* Awka: Erudition Printers, 217 – 223.

Onete, U. O. & Imona, M. E. (2008). Child Abuse: Dimensional Perspective. *The Nigerian Educational Psychologist* 6, 30 – 37.

United Nations Children's Fund (UNICEF) (2000). Domestic Violence against Women and Girls. Innocent Digest, 6. Retrieved on August 10, 2015 from http://www.unicef-irc.org/publications/pdf/digest6e.pdf

Wikipedia, (2010). Domestic Violence, http:/www.womenhealth.gov/violence Retrieved on August 9, 2015.

19

Creating Environment for Inclusive Education Practice for Learners with Special Needs in Nigeria

Kingsley E. Nwachukwu *Ph.D*

Abstract

*T*he need to reposition and re-engineer the place of inclusive education in Nigeria cannot be overrated. No nation of the world can effectively claim adequate education of its citizenry without incorporating children with special needs. Thus, this paper discussed creating environment for inclusive education practice for learners with special needs in Nigeria. The paper discovered that for a successful education system in Nigeria, there must be a change of attitude, reorganization and employment of special needs staff, better curriculum, better teaching approaches, corroboration of all students and better classroom management must be revisited. Conclusion was that the notion that inclusiveness was only a concept for the disabled children should be discarded.

Key Words: *Academic Environment, Inclusive Education, Special Needs.*

Overview of Inclusive Education and Inclusive Classroom Environment

The trends away from segregated education has attracted various terms; integrated, mainstreaming normalization, open and now inclusive education. The term inclusive education has been conceptually defined by several authors and professionals in special needs education. Ozoji (2013) states that an inclusive classroom is one in which all students attend and are welcomed by their neighbourhood schools in age appropriate, regular classes and are supported to learn to contribute and participate in all aspects of the school. Encarta (2006) sees it as a process of allowing all children the opportunity to fully participate in regular classroom activities regardless of disability, race or either consideration, while UNESCO (2005) defines it as a process of addressing and responding to the diversity of needs of all learners through the increasing participation in learning and reducing exclusion within and from education.

Deinner (1999) stated that, mainstreaming, integration and inclusive are interchangeably used by some experts. She went further to indicate that there are fundamental differences in each of them. She opines that in mainstreaming, there is already existing programme and persons with special needs who were not originally part of the programme are being added to those in the programme with minimal support. She also quotes Salisbury (n.d.) who feels that integration goes a little beyond mainstreaming. Integration she says, is an interaction between two groups of children with adequate support so that all children can participate. It is thus an opportunity for children with special needs to participate in academic, physical or social activities with their non disabled peers.

She submits that inclusion as a latest concept appears to have taken care almost of all the criticisms of the earlier concepts. That inclusion means, that, all children, regardless of their developmental level or disability, are always included in whatever setting is appropriate and available to other children of their age. Inclusive education affords every child the opportunity to interact and learn from one another and hence there is speedy adjustment and elimination of negative labeling.

Centre for Studies in Inclusive Education (2002) states that inclusive education means that every child and young person with and without disabilities or learning difficulties learn together in the same class and institutions with appropriate networks of support. Ozoji (2003) stated that inclusive education is a transverse issue cutting across all education initiatives right from early childhood through primary, vocational, adult, teacher's education to curriculum developments. It is also to be found in spheres related to cultural and social developments. In all therefore, inclusive education has to do with giving education to both non disabled people in the same class with support and attention to realize the goal of learning. Okobah (2005) defines Inclusive education to be "providing specially designed instruction and supports for students with special needs in the context of regular education system".

When students with special needs are in your class, you must take extra care to plan because their ability to progress and their self esteem are influenced by classroom environment and how well you have arranged your class. If one of them needs a wheelchair, provide open rows and a place to sit. If they have problems with social interaction, place them within a group of students who work well with others. If they need to be in the front of the room, make a walking path around the classroom to influence students who need discipline, they should also be close to the teacher. Special Education Guide (2016), listed seven tips of classroom management from an experienced teacher to include establishing relationships, creating a positive learning climate, encouraging helpful hands, and teaching needed skills. Others include setting up structure and procedures, organizing the lesson, and using effective discipline.

In creating an inclusive environment, establishing a relationship becomes pertinent. As a teacher, your relationship with a student starts that moment you meet them. No matter how difficult a student may be, you need to embrace the challenge of getting to know him or her. Every child deserves the best, life had enough hard knocks in store for a child who struggles cognitively, physically, socially and you may be one of the few people that the child believes cares about him or her. This could make a difference in his or her life choices or at least in his or her decision not to disrupt your class especially children with Attention Deficit Hyperactive Disorders (ADHD) and others with behavioural and emotional needs.

Creating a positive learning environment/climate is one of the most important things you can do to be proactive in managing an inclusive class. Your class must establish a climate that encourages learning from all frontiers. Teachers need to be aware of students' intellectual, emotional, physical and social needs and establish rules and procedures to meet them. Students with special needs should be recognized as individuals, each of whom has something to offer. Arrange students seating strategically, group students by skill level or arranging them in a manner that is conducive to group work or sharing in parts. Also plan for patterns of movement within the classroom and hove your students practice until it is second nature, morning students in a structured timed way can enliven your classroom, while maintaining control and adding focus. Make sure that every student is welcomed in a group and expected to participate.

Teach need skills for success in the classroom. Often, teachers think about teaching content without realizing how important it is to teach other skills, such as social skills, thinking skills, study skills, test taking skills, problem solving skills, memory skills and self regulation. Many school issues disappear after a few lessons in anger management or another needed skill. Students can benefit greatly if you find small segments of time to teach and model a skill. However, you may need to be creative since not all students need instruction in the same skill.

Rationale for Inclusive Education Practice

Inclusive education has attracted the most diversified intellectual discourse among professionals than any other issue in special needs education. It is expected that views on inclusive education will be as polarized, varied, contentions, glamorous as there are interests on the subject (Ozoji, 2013). The Salamanca statement and framework for action provides more detailed guidance on inclusive education internationally. It came out of the Salamanca Conference organized by the United Nations Educational Scientific and Cultural Organization (UNESCO) Special Needs Department in 1994, in order to further the objective of Education for All (EFA). The conference considered the policy shifts required to promote inclusive education. Participants were concerned to develop ways for schools to serve all children, particularly those with special educational needs rather than to create separate facilities. They clearly stated that all children have unique learning needs and have the rights to attend their local schools (Part 2 of the Salamanca statement), these included:

- Education system should be designed and educational programmes implemented to take into account the wide diversity of these characteristics and needs.
- Those that have special educational needs must have access to regular schools, which should accommodate them within child centred pedagogy capable of meeting these needs.

Hence, inclusive education is a response to world declarations:

- Universal declaration of human rights 1948
- World pledge at the 1990 conference on education for all to ensure that right for all regardless if individual difference (Jomtiem Thailand)
- United Nations standards, rules on the equalization of opportunities for persons with disabilities are an integral part of the education system 1993.
- World conference on special needs education access and quality. Salamanca Declaration 1994.
- Education for All Dakar declaration (2000)
- The 48th session of the International Conference on Education (ICE), Geneva Nov (2008).
- No child left behind Act 2000 in United States of America.

Therefore, inclusive education according to the Salamanca statement is aimed at:

- Combating discriminative attitudes, creating welcoming communities and building an inclusive society.

- Be the norm for all children regardless of their physical, intellectual, social emotional and linguistic or other conditions.
- Place the individual needs of all children at the centre of the process and fit the learning to the needs for the child rather than the child to the system.
- Celebrate difference and individual abilities and welcome the unique contribution and participation of all.
- Provide equal opportunity for access to a quality education at all levels.

Learners Targeted by Inclusive Education

According to Ozoji (2013), ideally inclusive education targets all learners not just those with disabilities. Three groups are targeted:

- Learners in mainstreaming schools that are failing to learn due to barriers of whatever nature (e.g. language issues, poverty, inappropriate teaching, gender biases and disabilities).inclusive education also targets learners who have no disabilities and who are learning very well.
- Learners in special schools who have been placed in the school on the basis of their disability; children with significant disabilities. There are about twelve (12) categories of children with special needs, these include:
- Learning disabilities
- Attention deficit (hyperactivity disorder)
- Emotional and behavior disorders
- Intellectual disabilities (formerly mental retardation)
- Hearing impairment
- Visual impairment
- Low incidence disabilities such as traumatic brain injury, multiple severe disabilities deaf-blindness)
- Autism spectrum disorder
- Communication disorders (speech and language disorders)
- Gifts and talents
- Physical and health impairments
- Children at risk.

Finally the third group Ozoji termed learners of compulsory school going age who are out of school or who have never been enrolled in school due to barriers of whatever nature (children with or without disabilities).

Inclusive Environment and Learning

An inclusive learning environment is one in which all those participating feel able to actually engage, feel safe, and feel welcomed. An inclusive learning environment also acknowledges and celebrates difference as part of everyday life. The teaching-learning process in an inclusive environment is an inherent social act; hence teachers need to be mindful of the social and emotional dynamics of the classroom climate as research has documented the effects of a "chilly classroom climate" on some students or group of students (Hall, 1982).

According to Teaching Excellence and Education Innovation (2015), the classroom climate and environment can impact positively or negatively on learning on the following ways:

- Regulates the circulation and construction of knowledge for instance in an inclusive environment all students are more likely to volunteer different perspectives and thus enrich discussions.
- Impacts curricular and citizenship skills; an inclusive environment facilitates the development of skills such as leadership, communication and conflict resolution. While at the opposite spectrum non inclusive learning environments facilitates the perpetuation of stereotypes about students from other groups.
- Engenders emotions that impact learning in an inclusive environment, learning experience is characterized by excitement for discovery, joy, satisfaction and pride at ones accomplishments which has effect of motivating students for further learning (Ford, 1992).
- Can channel energies away from learning or towards it. For instance, a slow learner feels it is not in his best interest to be out of class, they tend to carefully monitor their participation for fear of inadvertently limiting their understanding and class performance.
- Communicates expectations placed upon students. People tend to perform in relation to the expectations placed upon them. When there is positive perception of learners, the meet expectations (Pygmalion effect). But if expectations conform to stereotypes, learners underperform regardless of actual capabilities (stereotype-threat effect) (Rosenthal and Jacobson, 1992; Steele and Aronson, 1995).
- Communicates poor dynamics. In inclusive classroom environment teachers need to use their authority to empower everybody to take ownership in the learning process as the ultimate form of resistance for learners who feel powerless in a hostile environment is refusal to learn (Kohl, 1994)
- Impacts students' persistence. When the cumulative direct and indirect messages students perceive in a learning environment communicates that they are not able as other students and don't belong, students are likely to be frustrated and dropout.

Strategies for Creating a Productive and an Inclusive Environment

- Examine your assumptions. It is very common for teachers to assume that learners share their own background, but this is not necessarily so.
- Learn and use students' names. Even in large classes, you can start with a few names and build up.
- Model inclusive language. For example avoid using masculine pronouns for both males and females.
- Use multiple and diverse examples; take care to include examples that speak to both groups able and disabled.
- Establish ground rules for interaction. This will assure that other learners are also being inclusive and respectful.
- Examine your curriculum; are certain perspectives systematically not represented in your course material (plus unique and minus or adapted curricular contents).

- Strive to be fair. Perception of unfairness can induce feelings of learned helplessness (Peterson, Maier and Seligman, 1995).
- Be mindful of low ability cues. These cues encourage attributions focused on permanent, uncontrollable causes which diminish students self efficacy.
- Provide accommodations for students with disabilities. Provide as required by law reasonable accommodations to learners with documented disabilities.
- Don't ask people to speak for an entire group. Learners with disabilities often report either feeling invisible in class. This experience is heightened when they are addressed as spokespeople for their whole group and can have implication on performance.
- Practice inclusive classroom behaviour. Recognize unconscious behaviours "micro inequalities" that certain learners may experience as they could add up and have a highly discouraging effect on the learners.

Issues in Environmental Re-engineering for Inclusive Education Practice

Inclusive education requires a fundamental and holistic environmental restructuring and re-engineering of the entire school system. These fundamental changes include, change of attitudes, school organization and staffing, the curriculum content and offering, teaching approaches, collaboration between regular and special education teachers and class organization and management.

Change of Attitudes:

Some basic attitudes that must change for inclusive education to succeed include the notion that there are some students who are "normal" and some others who are special and that the so called normal student should go to regular or "ordinary" schools while the so called special or disabled ones should be educated separately in special needs education schools. More so, they belief that only teachers who are specialized in the field of special needs education can teach students with disabilities and that regular class teachers are incapable of teaching or handling them and should not be used as an excuse. Other assumption is that people with special needs will either not benefit optimally from the curriculum and the teachings of the regular school or will adversely affect the schooling and learning rate of the normal learners needs to change.

These assumptions have given rise to negative attitudes which have serious implication in the management of the teaching learning programmes of the inclusive school. These changes will give rise to a more conducive and accommodating learning environment for both learners with or without disabilities and a more purposeful management of the school.

School Organization and Staffing:

The school management, the layout of the compound, classrooms and other facilities, staffing and the creation of timetables as they are normally operated in the regular schools will have to change considerably. There must be environmental re-engineering to make the roads, facilities, buildings and parts to them more accessible and environmental friendly for those with different forms, categories, types and kinds of disabilities/special needs conditions. In staffing, the uniqueness of special needs person needs to be considered. Specialists, para-professionals, support or helping professionals like medical doctors, Nurses, social work and sign language interpreters, braillist and mobility guides need to assist these with hearing/usual impairments and other special needs condition.

Classes and class organization need to be flexible as students who need special attention could be moved to one corner of the classroom to the special resource classroom for closer specialist attention. Those special units, activity corners, and resources rooms for various learning activities need to be created in order to appropriately cater for the various learning needs of learners with special needs. For instance, a child with reading problem (Dyslexia) may be taken to a corner or special rooms by specialists for attention and coached with simplified books.

The Curriculum Content and Offering:

Curriculum for the inclusive school is essentially the same as the one for the regular school system. Be it as it may, provisions have to be made for what is called the "Plus" and "Minus" unique curriculum. Plus curriculum have to do with adaptations and modifications to cater for the learning and other needs of those with disability including in recreation and sports such as Para soccer, adapted physical education and activities.

Unique curriculum have to do with additions to the curriculum to cater for learning needs of the different categories of the learners with special needs based on their uniqueness since no two learners with disabilities are the same. The unique contents include sensory training, Braille reading and writing, use of abacus for mathematical operations, recording and use of recorded books (talking books, calculators), typewriting, orientation and mobility for the learners who are visually impaired. For those who are hearing impaired, sign language, total communication, lip and speech reading should be in cooperated as their unique curriculum content. While for those with physical impairments, mobility training by physiotherapist, speech and language training for those with speech disorders and for the intellectually disabled and so on should also be in cooperated as well.

Curriculum minus, implies the removal of regular curriculum contents, activities, skills and materials which people with disabilities cannot practically and meaningfully take part in and or benefit from due to their disability or other special needs conditions and limitations. For example, close visual activities such as colouring, colour separation and screening in fine art or in practical experiments involving visual observation in science laboratory and home economics for learners with visual 9mpairment. Oral language exercises, debates and phonetics for the hearing impaired. Obani (2006)

Teaching Approaches:

Variability and flexibility is the watchword. Since different lessons and different subjects to a certain degree, demand different methods and approaches. More so, bearing in mind the different learners, their learning needs and the different conditions and experiences they bring to school (some with disabilities, some learn faster while others slowly, some average, others above or below average in class work). Interest and aptitudes likewise differ in learners and types of experiences brought from home also count. All these need to be considered in the approach or approaches that a teacher adopts in his/her classroom. See instructional strategies or approaches the teacher need to adopt in an inclusive classroom as discussed earlier.

Collaboration between Regular and Special Education Teachers:

For a high level of success to be achieved in the education of all learners in the inclusive class(es) or schools, there must be a high level if structure contact and collaboration between the regular class and special education teachers. This collaboration, according to Obani (2006), should involve the whole school organizations, classroom organization; curriculum developments, instructional approaches and teaching methods. Obani further stated that some of the peculiarities of the regular school, the regular class and even of the special education teachers themselves would have to be traded off and adjustments made and accepted in order to produce situations that will provide appropriate and adequate education for all learners.

Class Organization and Arrangement:

Classroom organization and arrangements should be such that provide responsive and conducive learning environment for all pupils, taking into consideration their needs and peculiarities. A regular classroom with a number of learners with visual, hearing or physical impairments with wheelchairs, on crutches or other appliances should be arranged in such a way that movement within and around the classroom is easy. Space should be created between rows of desks to all for easy movement and unnecessary furniture or any other obstruction to easy movement removed.

Seating arrangements for an inclusive class should have learners with hearing impairments, low vision and partial sights should seat in the front rows. Learners with physical disabilities could be placed anywhere in the class as they may not have extra trouble maneuvering to the middle or the back seats in the classroom. Furthermore, for some particular lessons or class activities, the class maybe re-arranged, adopting a zoning formular. Under this arrangement, some disabilities or special needs groups are assigned to one part of the class for some particular activities which if carried out in the general group, would be disruptive to the other groups and not lead to optimal learning in disadvantaged groups. Examples, in sign language instruction for the hearing impaired and Braille reading and writing for visually impaired.

Conclusion

This paper has examined the importance of inclusive education to the overall academic achievements of students. It is also very clear that the notion that inclusiveness entails only children with one disability or the other has been laid to rest, considering the fact that all school age-going children need inclusiveness in order to get them better equipped in this competitive and fast technologically shifting society, hence the call for a better and more acceptable planning of an enabling school environment for inclusive education.

References

Encarta Premium (2006). *Microsoft co-operation.*

Ford, M. (1992). *Motivating humans: Goals, emotions and personal agency beliefs.* Newbury Park: CA Sage.

Knight, B. A. (1999). Towards inclusion of students with special needs in the regular classroom. *Support For Learning* 14 (II).

Kohl, H. (1994). *I won't learn from you and other thoughts on creative maladjustment.* New York: The New Press.

National Teachers Institute (2012). *Special Needs and Disabilities (SENDs)*. Lagos: Axiom Learning Solutions Ltd.

Obani, T. C. (2006). Organization and administration of regular (UBE) schools with Special needs children. In T. C. Obani (Ed). *Teaching Pupils with Special Educational Needs in the Regular (UBE) Classroom*. Ibadan: Book Builders.

Ozoji, E. D. (2013). Implementing inclusive education in FCT, Abuja. Abuja; FCT Universal Basic Education Board and UNIJOS Consultancy Ltd.

Peterson, C., Maier, S. F. & Seligan, M. E. P. (1995). *Learned Helplessness: A Theory for the Age of Personal Control*. New York: Oxford University Press.

Rosenthal, R. & Jacobson, L. (1992). *Pygmalion in the Classroom; Teacher Expectation and Pupils' Intellectual Development* (2nd.ed) New York: Ardent Media.

Steele, C. M. & Aronson, J. (1995). Stereotype threat and the intellectual test performance of African Americans. *Journal of Personality and Social Psychology*, 69(5), 797-811.

Special Education Guide (2016), Behaviour and Classroom Management. www.specialeducationguide.com.

Teaching Excellence and Educational Innovation (2015) www.cmu.edu/teaching/Eberly.

The University of Auckland (2010). How do I create an inclusive learning environment? www.teachingandlearninghub-Addressinddiversity.com.

Unachukwu, G. C., Ozoji, E. D. & Ifelunni, I. C. S. (2008). Opportunities for Inclusive Education in Nigerian Primary Education. A Research Report submitted to the Nigeria Educational Research and Development Council.

UNESCO (1994). World Conference on Special Needs Education: Access and Quality. Salamanca: Author.
www.specialeducation.com-management/classroom-management-7-tipsfrom-an-expereinced teacher/.

20

Guilt-Feelings, Emotional Imbalance and Anticipated Good Health Care as Consequences of Premarital Sex in Secondary Schools in Akwa Ibom State

Agbaje A. Agbaje *Ph.D* & Efon U. Inyang

Abstract

*I*n developing countries of the world premarital sex has become a great concern to many stakeholders as mortality morbidity is very high compared with developed countries. Besides, premarital health knowledge and access on quality of care of premarital health services in developing countries are poor with significant health consequences. Counseling psychology logistics are assured to have appropriate directives to premarital sex health knowledge, beliefs and will power of women to access quality family services which are essential for improvement. The study, therefore, aimed to access premarital sex, health knowledge, beliefs and influential factors of contraceptives use among secondary schools girls. Thus the study was cross sectional in nature involving 600 randomly selected respondents out of 3,150 of the entire respondents among students. The questionnaire was administered by the researcher and his assistants. Analysis of Covariance (ANCOVA) and the questionnaire prepared by the researcher were used to analyse the data. Only sixty six percents of the respondents believed that premarital sex can occur while thirty four believed that having sex with a woman once with a man would not result in pregnancy. The study revealed that premarital sex is dominant in senior secondary students in Akwa Ibom State and that Guilt feeling and Emotional Imbalance act as consequences to premarital sex in senior secondary schools. The paper concluded that we must persistently insist rather in maintaining that sex education is really meaningless unless it can be related to the meaning, the role and the importance of sex in the modern world.

Key Words: *Guilt-feeling, Emotional Imbalance, Health Care, Premarital Sex*

Introduction

The hormonal changes, the alterations in body form, and the psychological correlates naturally play a major role in adolescent personality development. We have referred to these characteristics of pubescence as the consummator factors in precipitating the transitional personality phase of adolescence. They accomplish this not only through the effect on cultural expectations but also endogenously by their impact on the individual. The adolescent reacts to his adult body form, his newly acquired reproductive capacity and his mature sexual drives by raising his aspirations for volitional independence and earned status. However, just because pubescence is the consummator catalytic phenomenon that initiates the adolescent period of development, sexuality cannot, therefore, be regarded as the central problem of adolescent.

Newly acquired sexual urges have a significant obstacle to personality maturation since they are the chief source of hedonistic need during adolescence. The control and regulation of the new physiological drive creates an emergent problem of adaptation that had not arisen since early childhood. It is true that the individual is now holder, more experienced in self-control, more responsive to moral obligations, and more highly motivated by status considerations to postpone the need for immediate hedonistic gratification. But, by the same token, he is also more self-assertive and restive to adult standards and direction.

Insistent sex needs not only threaten other long-range goals, but also threaten the individual's newly acquired volitional independence (Hawkins, 2003). Genuine affection relationships imply considerable self-surrender and imitation of personal antonomy. These can be avoided either by ascetiasm or by entering into numerous and superficial psycho physiological sex relations (promiscuity)., it is an important area of adolescent adjustment. Whether existing sex needs are gratified or denied, affects the total balance between frustration and satisfaction, and hence, the overall stressfulness of adolescence. This is also influenced by conflict or guilt feelings about sex and impinges on the individual behavioural reactivity, emotional stability and anticipated good health care.

Frustration of sex needs may result in preoccupation with an over valuation of sexuality bothersome distractions and compensatory attempts at self-entrancement in other directions by symbolizing his sub-adult status or by instigating guilt producing substitute sex outlets. These frustrations may impair self-esteem because of the intense psychological conflict until relatively recently about sex in middle class boys (and now also in middle class girls) in our society and because of the unrealistic cultural "avoidance and depreciation of the subject of sex in the face of their positive knowledge of its actual importance", adolescents subjectively over-value the relative importance of sexuality in the total scheme of things. But regardless of its actual intrinsic importance, there is no gainsaying the phenomenological reality of this over-valuation to these adolescence. In a much different category, is the social scientists' interpretive over-valuation of the importance of sexuality in adolescent adjustment. Much of this interpretive over-evaluation can be attributed to deficiencies in the type and source of information about sex behavior. Before Kinsey and Coworkers (1998) and (2008) monumental study of the sexual expression of the American male, most valuable and available conceptions of adolescent sex activity where conjectural. Previous studies were superficial and did not sample large or representative enough segments of the population and in keeping with their psychoanalytic orientation, many psychologists and psychiatrists were too liable to over generalize from case histories drawn from middle class patients and from their own middle class backgrounds. Pornographic and over-explicit sex in the media has had much the same over-evaluating effects on adolescents.

Among those who were concerned with the theoretical interpretation of adolescent psychology in our culture, the point of view had been steadily gaining ground until relatively recently that the American adolescent owed the greater part of his characteristic emotional instability to the inordinate amount of sex frustration he experienced. This opinion was customarily bolstered by citing MEAD'S SAMDAN, DATA, which was over generalized to support the hypothesis that an invariable, one to one casual relationship prevailed between the stressfulness of adolescence and the degree of cultural repression of adolescent sex activity. When we consider all the evidence, however, it becomes apparent that sex frustration is the only one of many factors in adolescent status deprivation and actually one of the less crucial factors leading to a stressful adolescence., there is no simple relationship between the severity of cultural restrictions on sexual expression and the degree of psychological conflict from sex. Such conflict develops only when simultaneous sex drives are generated and moral prohibitions again their expression are internalized. In our society, therefore, psychological conflict about sex is hardly characteristic of adolescents generally, since as early as 1998 studies led by Kinsey established that 85 percent of American male adolescents accepted premarital intercourse as natural and desirable and despite the existence of formal expectations to the contrary, exercised this conviction almost as freely as SAMOAN Adolescents. Further twenty-eight studies of premarital sex behavior conducted since Kinsey's report in 1993 on female sexual behavior indicated that there has been an increase in the percentage of young people engaging in premarital sexual intercourse. Moreover, this change has been more revolutionary for women to the extent that even two decades ago there was almost no difference in the proportions of young men and women who engage in such behavior (Agbaje, 2005). Psychological stress from sex is relatively impressive only in some middle class youth and not because of psycho physiological tensions produced by repression per se (since such tensions are relieved by masturbation, petting and sexual intercourse) but because of the psychological ambiguity of the situations, the guilt feelings engendered and the invidious reflections on self-esteem.

Secondly, there is little relationship between experienced degree of conflict about sex and the total stressfulness of adolescence because other non sexual factors are more crucial in determining that stressfulness. Depending on the operation of these other factors, absence of sex repression and lack of psychological conflict about sex can co-exist with relatively unstressed adolescence (as in Sanwan) or an extremely stressful adolescence (as among present day youth in our own culture). Whenever adolescence is simultaneously non-stressful and unaccompanied by little mental conflict about sex, other more compelling reasons unrelated to sexuality can usually be found for the idyllic nature of adolescent development. Samoan, for example, adopted an extremely casual approach to life and does not engage in any frantic struggle for status, and Avapesh adolescents are warmly accepted and eagerly integrated into a benevolent non-productive culture.

Thus in primitive cultures in which a stressful adolescence co-exists with considerable conflict about sex, there are also other reasons for the experienced difficulty of adolescence. In the Mundugumor, Manus and Kwoma cultures, with greater emphasis placed on status, the culture as a whole is more competitive and aggressive, the adolescent has a more marginal position in society and status is more persistently withheld from him. Although, sexual problem was undoubtedly added to the stressfulness of adolescence in the Manns (Mead, 1989) and other primitive cultures, greater weight must be given to the traumatic potential of these non-sexual factors. If this proposition holds true for primitive cultures, it can be applied with even greater validity to our own culture for the differences among primitive cultures in non-sexual determinants of adolescent stress, are relatively minor in comparison with the corresponding difference between primitive and complex cultures. When so many important variables contributing to a stressful adolescence are simultaneously operative, the presence or absence of sexual conflict is a relatively negligible factor. Thus, the lower class adolescent male in our society is spared by the trauma of psychological conflict about sex, his adolescence on the whole is no less stressful than that of his middle class contemporary.

Teenage Pregnancy

Adolescent pregnancy has increased world-wide by leaps and bounds in the post-world war II decades. Thus, it has tended to stabilize recently, the frequency is still high enough to constitute a serious public health, family and social problems: one million adolescent pregnancies annually yielding approximately 500,000 live births. About 40 percent of the original pregnancies are terminated by abortion (Marchbanks, 1999 and 2002). The current trend, however, is for the adolescent mother to keep and raise her baby rather than resort to abortion or adoption. The beginning of the adolescent pregnancy problem in the post-world War II (in developed as well as in developing countries) largely reflects the outcome of an interaction between the sexual revolution on the one hand and an extension of his phenomenon from most African – African, ethnic and minority group adolescent girls in whose case regular premarital sex relations were traditionally very prevalent but whose out-of-wedlock pregnancies were not significantly socially stigmatized. This in the course and aftermath of the war, and the accompanying, sexual revolution, the more casual and permissive sexual attitudes and practices of the latter adolescent girls spread to their middle-class counterparts, resulting in their becoming sexually drive and in producing their share of the annual crop of one-half billion babies.

Contributing Causes of Adolescent Pregnancy

"The Epidemic" includes the following:

- A very large number of the adolescent girls having premarital sexual relations apparently believed to some extent the widespread fable that they were invulnerable to becoming pregnant after unprotected sexual intercourse.
- Most of the girls were not knowledgeable about the various uses of contraceptives and even if they decline to use them.
- The great increase in female sexual activity (and consequent contact with males) leading up to premarital sexual intercourse, greatly increased the number of conceptions followed by pregnancy.
- The much earlier occurrence of female pubescence naturally increased the amount of time in which the more sexually active adolescents were exposed to make impregnation.
- The failure of emotional and intellectual maturation of lower-and-upper class adolescent girls to keep pace with sexual maturation is responsible in part for the lack of adequate control of the sex drive and its implementation in casual and permissive sexual activity.
- Exclusively casual and permissive sexual activity on the part of the adolescent girls often serves a compensatory function in relieving the hopelessness, poverty and drabness of their existence. This activity is not socially expected by the community and accepted by the adolescent girls and pregnancy ensues little or no stigma is attached to it. In fact their self esteem is often enhanced by the pregnancy.
- In premarital adolescent girls, the occurrence of pregnancy sometimes causes a non-specific and reactive retaliatory or vindictive behaviomal response against the presumptive father.

Premarital Intercourse

It is argued by those who favour premarital sexual intercourse as the preferred sexual outlet for adolescents, that it is the most "natural" sexual activity for all sexually mature human beings.

Naturalness, however, is a very slippery argument because in the course of civilization's advances, man had learned to inhibit and curb many "natural" drives and impulses, the expression of which would have jeopardized his well-being and welfare. The more germane questions therefore, are: what are the necessary preconditions for extending this marital practice to adolescents prior to marriages? What are its advantages, disadvantages and perhaps its hazards. The first option preconditions are that the adolescent must have already attained sufficient psychosexual maturity to be able to express a psycho-affectional form of sexuality, that is, to express in his sexual activity love, affection and a deserve for enhanced intimacy with his sexual partner not merely sensuality, hedonism and sexuality as an end in itself. Implied also in mature sexual intercourse is a certain degree of exclusiveness, of affinity, fidelity and permanence otherwise the individual in question is dealing merely with casual, permissive and promiscuous sex, this will be a reasonable assumption both in later marriage and in a serious current liason.

The unfortunate reality of the situation among "sexually active" adolescents, however, is that only a very small minority of those adolescents who have been evaluated psychiatrically and of other teenagers meet this precondition. This age limitation is relevant, of course, because the earliest one could typically expect all of the essential facets of psychosexual maturity to be sufficiently developed under current cultural and familiar conditions to make premarital sexual intercourse a reasonably affectionate and loving experiences, is at the end of adolescence or the beginning of early adulthood. The consequences to a psychosexually immature young adolescent engaging habitually in casual and purely hedonistic and promiscuous intercourse are far from innocuous: through the psychological mechanism of canalization, this kind of sexual expression could become the only and pre-emptive type of sexual outlet that he would find gratifying, even in marriage. He tends to become conditioned and sensitized by this habitual orientation to sexual experience and thus to become unresponsive to the psycho-affectional aspects of sexuality both the receiving and expressive ends. When such an individual marries therefore it is only reasonable to expect his psycho physiological orientation to prevail. This the psychosexual level at which he operates martially is qualitatively lowered rendering impossible of fulfillment a basic function of the marital relationship in the indeo-Christian tradition.

Furthermore, there is the high risk of pregnancy and sexually transmitted diseases that do not exist in the alternative strategy of abstinence. Not only are condoms unreliable for both purposes but if distributed by the state or by the school the official approval of this type of sexuality by these agencies would also be implied. Really, from a secular and religious standpoint, adolescents and young adults are traditionally expected to practice abstinence from intercourse until they are married. Although this ideal is no longer honoured very much in practice today, it still has much to recommend it. On the negative side it is still the best preventive against unwanted out-of-wedlock pregnancy and sexually transmitted diseases and it also avoids the canalizing and sensitizing effects of an immature approach to sexual expression becoming permanent and persisting into marriage. On the positive side, it saves the most affectionate and intimate aspects of sexuality for sharing with one's spouse – the person whom one professedly loves most deeply and to whom one has a permanent commitment of love. Finally, for those adolescents who have professed sincere religions convictions, abstinence from premarital intercourse avoids the troublesome moral conflict and guilt feelings and perhaps anticipated good health care in pregnancy. It is certainly a psychologically tenable and morally supportable position in the modern world – even if an increasingly lonely one. The current major ethnics – religions minority view on premarital sexual intercourse that this act should be reserved solely for the marital relationship is largely based on the same moral and practical grounds as the psychological and physiological positions just considered above with one significant exception. All Christian religious doctrinally proscribe sexual intercourse for all persons except with their only married spouses. This procedure from the standpoint of everyday morality, is somewhat arbitrary but it avoids all negative social judgements as well as all adverse criticism of the newly married pair and imputations of sins. More importantly, this position rules out unmarried sexual intercourse that satisfies all of the preconditions of premarital intercourse specified above except for the current impossibility of marriage for pressing practical reasons.

Need for Sex Education in the Schools

To be satisfactory and un-offensive to parents of different moral beliefs and persuasions, the schools should offer only a very general sex education. Such education would be concerned with physiology and psychology of normal sexual development and with the emotional and ethical goals of sex expression. It would lead to individual guidance, specific problems and various sexual practices. Any effective programme of sex education would also have to be geared to "developmental changes in the form of children's concern as they move from the early adolescent into the late adolescent period". It is ironic to recall that when boys and girls are most eager to make an approach to each other, to discover what a man and woman mean to each other and how they should act toward each other, we can only offer them sex education, that is, teaching about reproduction. We must persistently insist rather in maintaining that sex education is really meaningless unless it can be related to the meaning, the role and the importance of sex in the modern world. To separate these questions from the province of sex education is to make of it a meaningless jumble of isolated facts, merely to substitute fire-syllable for four-letter words. The researcher, in other words, cannot accept the point of view that sex education must be fully factual and descriptive in nature and cannot presume to tell an individual how to behave in an activity that is primarily personal rather than social in nature.

What is forgotten in all such arguments is that every culture accepts an implicit set of ethical values for significant behavior and proceeds as a matter of self-preservation to educate the young to accept these values. Does anyone after all object to the "one side" advocacy of the virtues of democracy, honest, truthfulness and kindliness in our schools? Since it is impossible to conceive of any directed behavior which is devoid of either purpose or moral content, how can sex education neglect either aspect? The individual still retains his right of self-determination by being free to accept or reject the goals and standards offered him, providing his behavior does not infringe on the rights or interests of others. It is also unnecessary too avoid comparative moral judgements with respect to alternative approaches to sexual experience and type of orientation to sameness or difference in gender of the sexual object from the person seeking sexual gratification.

Objectives against such judgements are frequently made by advocates of and apologists of homosexuality and permissive sexuality on, the grounds that they (the judgements) are authoritarian, absolutistic and repressive of freedom of choice and of legitimate human variability. They would merely have us state that either heterosexual or homosexual, psycho affectionate, or physiological forms of sexual expression are only different from each other but are equally meritorious and desirable, rather than better and worse. However we have already taken the position that every culture has an indisputable right to adopt certain central moral alternatives on an absolutistic basis and to inculcate them exclusively in the socialization of the young, without being accused of authoritarianism or the abridgement of freedom.

This concept of sexuality presumes a high degree of ego involvement which disallows a casual attitude toward sex activity such as that which underlies sexual promiscuity, experimentation and filtration. The goal toward which it strives is the monogamous type of marital relationship which we have already adopted in our society. The difference however would be that marriage would be advocated as the best possible medium for enhancing a psycho-affectionate sexual partnership rather than as the factor which in itself legitimizes something inherently shameful. If our culture would adopt and teach this point of view, "psychosexual development would proceed according", and adolescent boys and girls would really feel this way about sex. The problems associated with psycho-physiological sex needs would for the most part vanish, and if marriage could occur at a reasonably early age, the sexual turmoil which now characterizes adolescent development in so many individuals would be a thing of the past. Teenagers who engage in premarital sex at an early age place greater value on independence, express less concern about academic achievement are less religious and report that they happen to be influenced by the opinions of those who are friends to them by those of their family (Craig & Kitchen and Stuydom (2006). Premarital activity is also more likely among the teenagers who view dating as important in their lives and express strong desires for a partner. Newcomb and Huba (2006) observed that the importance of dating was associated with:

- Confidence and being popular with an attractive to the opposite sex.
- A positive and accepting, view of oneself and
- More experiences involving stressful physical or family related events.

Thus the importance of dating, a predictor of premarital sexual activity was correlated with both positive factors and negative experiences. According to Greathead, Darenish and Gallingan (2008) teenage mothers are a norm in many societies and countries now. Teenage pregnancy began to become as a problem to the society of United States of America around the 1970's. Although the number of overall births was deluding teenage pregnancy rates reached sky high as the new generation engaged more in sexual activity at younger ages and greater acceptance of premarital childbearing.

Proximal Social Influences

Factors impacting on adolescent sexual behavior include personality make-up, sex, cultural and religious background, racial factors, family attitude and sexual education and prevention programmes, Sadock and Sadock (2007). Personality factors have been linked to sexual behavior, as well as sexual risk-taking. Individuals with higher levels of impulsivity are associated with younger age at first experience of sexual intercourse; higher number of sexual partners; sexual intercourse without the use of contraception, including condoms; and a history of sexual transmitted diseases. Historically, male adolescents have been found to have initiated sexual intercourse at a relatively younger age compared to female adolescents. The younger the teenage is when she first has sex, the more likely she is to have unwanted or non-voluntary sex. Close to four of teenage girls who had first intercourse at 13 or 14 years of age reported it was either not voluntary or wanted (Sadock and Sadock, 2007).

Sex Guidance

The advocated programme of sex education is concerned with general problems on sexual development and expression and with a long-range attempt to redirect psychosexual development in accordance with certain specified cultural value judgements on the goals of sexuality. Sex guidance on the other hand, deals with individual problems of sexual adjustment and can be handled effectively only within the framework of a counseling relationship. This does not mean that guidance (any more than education) must take place in an amount setting, that the counselor is concerned only with clarifying the sex problems of his client or with helping him adjust his inner sex needs to the limitations imposed by the environment cannot be overstated. In counseling relationship, sexual problems must first be placed in an ethical context of meaning and objectives. It is the counsellors' right and duty to communicate his own moral formulations and judgements to the client. He cannot of course, insist that the client accept his position, but he can give him the benefits of reaching to a set of mature moral expectations representative of the culture at large and in so doing he encourages the individual to approach his sex problems from the standpoint of some system of moral values rather than from the standpoint that one way is as good as another provided it reduces tension or yields satisfaction.

Two persistent ethical problems arise in modern sex needs:

The management of existing psycho-physiological sex needs and the management of psycho-affectionate sex needs before marriage is very important. Adolescents might very well be able to accept the proposition that society should so regulate psychosexual development in the future that individuals will develop only psycho-affectionate sex drives. But what are they to do in the meantime with their own psycho physiological drives? The only answer consistent with the sex philosophy advocated above is that the reduction of physiological sex tensions by authoritarianism is more in keeping with the psycho-affectionate ideal than with the use of a "socio-sexual outlet such as petting or intercourse. If this principle is acceptable, what are we to tell the adolescents who are genuinely in love, but unable to marry, about the ethics of premarital intercourse?

To remain consistent we would have to admit that although premarital sex relations are obviously less satisfactory that marital relations, they are nevertheless compatible with one psycho-affectionate approach to sexuality if they meet the structures already discussed. Realistic sex guidance however, cannot ignore the social reality in which the adolescents live. By the time they appear for guidance, depending on their sexual millien, they have already incorporated a vast array of sexual attitudes, urges, inhibitions, taboos and morally weighted opinions about the desirability and legitimacy of various forms of sexual activity. One can only present certain moral considerations to them and point how they can be applied in practice, but because of the course which psychosexual development has already taken, one cannot expect that these precepts will be either acceptable or realistically applicable in every case. In practice, therefore, after a counseling psychologist has put the quest of sexuality in its proper context of moral values, goal and purpose the best he can do is to equip the boy or girl for intelligent self-determination. To do this, he must supply precise and reliable information about the advantages and disadvantages, the issues and the implications of the various forms of sexual expression and to the meaningful and helpful, answers to such questions must be specific and applicable to the adolescent's actual problems.

Concerns of fostering moral development:

Moral issues are usually intertwined with societal standards already existing within the society. If the educational sectors do commit to moral education, such education should emphasize the importance that students should know the results or consequences of engaging in morally acceptable behaviours. According to Nucci (2000) and Wood (2006) presenting students with scenarios that engages both morality and societal standards, ask them to consider both the moral and conventional aspects of such issues this in turn helps them to be able to understand the relationship between the two.

Purpose of the Study

Realistically, shame is the sharper of symptoms and it strongly affects the self esteem and results in hiding, denial and addictions to keep the bad feelings at bay. Shame is associated with feeling incompetent, different and less worthy, victim of indecision and care-free than others. The typical body posture that accompanies this emotion is holding the head and avoiding eye contact. Feelings of being ashamed and humiliated, criticized, teased or bullied, rejected, ostracized or during sexual and physical abuse. Causes of shame might include a betrayed by others or a broken trust through disapproval. Harsh, critical parental, behavior produces shame prone children, parental high expectations of behaviour, criticism and disapproval for failure create shame. Parental humiliation and punishment for failure or for distress or eyeing creates the need to hide vulnerability. Parental withdrawal rejection or favouritism of a sibling cause deep fears of abandonment. The child feels that he must be really bad or his parents would love him. The trauma of physical and sexual abuse imprints major feelings of being devalued and unworthy in the victim.

Repressed shame leads to substituting more acceptable emotions such as anger, depression and anxiety to reduce the internal tension. Other defences of shame include matching behavior, inlettectualisation and sharing down feelings, controlling, blaming, criticizing or feelings superior to others are other common defences against feeling shame. Engaging in excessive use of alcohol, substances and addictive behavior may be an indication of shame. Besides engaging in behaviours that the society frowns at, it creates more shame which then has to be repressed. Patterns of dysfunctional behavior in relationships in a person's life can indicate a strong internal shame core. It is the measurement of the effectiveness of moral teaching strategies in the absence of evaluation, the teacher may feel he has done a successful job and may not be able to explain when the end becomes a failure; lack of intricacy and connection to others indicates a lack of trust and shame can cause a lack of trust to others and a deep breach or separation from others or real self.

Statement of the Hypotheses

Based on the objectives of the study the following hypotheses were formulated and tested at 0.05 alpha level.

1. There is no significant relationship between premarital sex and guilt feelings among senior secondary school girls in Akwa Ibom State.
2. There is no significant relationship between premarital sex and emotional imbalance among senior secondary school girls in Akwa Ibom State.
3. There is no significant relationship between premarital sex and anticipated good health care among senior secondary school girls in Akwa Ibom State.

Design

The survey design was used for this study because it seeks to examine people and their attitudes and opinions on educational and psychological phenomena such as the consequences of premarital sex on the personality development.

Participants

The participants for this study consisted of 500 senior secondary school girls from 5 senior secondary schools in Akwa Ibom State. The schools are:

- Uyo High School, Uyo
- Saint Joseph Secondary School, Ikot Ekpene,
- National High School, Odobo, Okobo
- Community Secondary Commercial School, Okon Eket
- Community Secondary Commercial School, Ukpap Ikono

All the experimental schools were mixed schools made up of both boys and girls, their age ranged between 12 and 19 years with a mean age of 15.5 years and standard deviation of 4.4 years. All the experimental participants were fully engaged and the control groups were not given any treatment. The experimental groups received treatments and were compared with the control group to test the treatment effects.

Instrumentation

Two instruments used in this study are: Consequences of premarital sex and self expression inventory (CPSSI) and Decision-making self-efficacy scale was developed Nwagwu 1998 and Adeyemo 1999 respectively. The former scale consists of five factor inventory with a total of 23 items. The need for Girls awareness of consequences of premarital sex and self expression which represent education factors were utilized for the study. Typical items on the subscales are:

1. Before I start premarital sex, I still need to talk to people about sex education,
2. Before entering sex education, I still need to attempt to answer "who am I". The responds format of the scale ranges from 'strongly agree' to 'strongly disagree'.

The two subscales have a total of eleven items. The whole instrument has a list-re-test reliability values ranging between .79 and .84 and Cronbach Alpha index between .73 and .86. The internal consistency for the total inventory was .87. As it is spelt out by the author a client CPSSI profile configuration might suggest specific intervention for enthusiasm towards becoming sex educated.

The second scale has give subscales namely

1. Self-appraisal
2. Sex education information
3. Making plans
4. Problem solving
5. Goal-setting

It has a total of thirty-eight items with responsive format ranging from "Not sure (1) to very much sure (5). The instrument has a theoretical value of between 38 and 190. The self appraisal subscale has a total of nine items with a co-efficient Alpha of .75, sex education information scale has eleven items with .85 making plans subscale also has six items with .85 and goal-setting subscale has five items with .77. The overall scale has a cronbach alpha level of .79. The instrument was used to identify levels of self-efficacy of the participant.

Procedure

Having secured the permission of the school authorities, the students were addressed at the school halls. The focus of the speech was "Emotional Imbalance, Guilt Feelings and Anticipated Good Health Care and Challenges to premarital Sex in Secondary Schools in Akwa Ibom State". A random sampling technique was used to select participants for the study. Researcher and his assistants worked in conjunction with the school teachers and the captains representing all the classes to distribute the questionnaire copies to the participants. This system was adopted because it has helped to have effective control of the participants during preparation both before and after the participants were randomly assigned into experimental and control groups.

The study was carried out within twelve weeks in different parts of Akwa Ibom State. Later experts in psychology, Nurses in women affairs and Gynaecologists were invited to give speeches in Emotional Imbalance, Guilt Feeling and Anticipated Good Health care in premarital sex at different times to enlighten the students. Each refine has two sessions served as experimental groups while the other group was used as control group. Two instruments "Emotional Imbalance Guilt-Feeling and Anticipated Good Health Care Inventory and Questionnaire on Guilt Feelings scale were administered on the participants as pre-test while Girls awareness and anticipated good health care inventory training while experimental group was treated with Emotional Imbalance inventory course. However the control group was not treated but was given a brief study skill counseling after the pest-test.

Data Analysis

Analysis of co-variance (ANCOVA) was used to analyse the data. It was because of its capacity to take care of initial differences among the participants, it equally enables the researchers to make predictions with some degree of certainty, (Denga, 2009, Joseph and Udoh, 2011).

Table 1: Total number of questionnaire distributed and duely returned to the researcher.

No of questionnaire Administered	No of Questionnaire Returned	Percentage % Returned
600	580	100

Results
Hypothesis 1

There is no significant relationship between Guilt feelings and premarital sex among senior secondary school girls in Akwa Ibom State.

To establish relationship between guilt feelings and premarital sex, analysis of co-variance was performed on the scores of items measuring effective consequence as a model of premarital sex.

Table 2: Analysis of Covariance (ANCOVA) on Guilt Feelings and Premarital Sex

Variable	Source	Sum of square	Df	Mean	F	P
Guilt	Row	742.94	2	371.47	1225.42	< .05
Feelings	Columns	18.71	2	8.35	30.86	< .05
Premarital	Interactions	5.87	4	1.47	4.85	< .05
Sex	Within	1036.73	171	.303		

As it is shown in Table 2, the analysis of covariance of participants post-test scores on Guilt feelings shows that there was significant main effect of treatment (FCI.114) = 2443/67.(<0.05). Consequently, the null hypothesis which posited that there will be no significant relationship between guilt feelings and premarital sex senior secondary school girls was rejected. The inference that could be drawn from this result is that significant relationship existed in the Guilt feelings and the premarital sex of the treated participants and the control group. It is also identifiable that there is moderating effect of opinions, lifestyle and self-efficacy on participants guilt feelings (1.114.57 = 30.86 P<0.05). The interaction of treatment with awareness of personality progress and self development cum self-efficacy was also significant F(4,171 = 4.85 P<.05).

Table 3 presents the results of the second hypothesis which postulated that there is no significant relationship between Emotional Imbalance and premarital sex among senior secondary school girls in Akwa Ibom State.

Table 3: Analysis of Covariance (ANCOVA) showing the effects of Emotional Imbalance on Premarital Sex

Variable	Source	Sum of square	Df	Mean	F	P
Emotional	Row	632	1	632.11	3443.90	< .05
Imbalance	Columns	20.62	2	10.31	42.95	< .05
Premarital	Interactions	15.81	2	7.91	33.95	< .05
Sex	Within	601.00	200	.29		

The result in Table 3 indicates that there was significant effect of Emotional Imbalance of the participants (fC114) = 3443.90 P<0.05) sequel to this result, it is concluded that Emotional Imbalance was superior to control. Besides both personality progress, moderation of opinions, and self expressions technique influenced the relationship between Emotional Imbalance and Guilt feelings about premarital sex. The participants clearly expressed their feelings and experience about premarital sex in which they were involved, this also influenced the relationship between the causal variable and criterion measure (F(2,114)=42.95, P<0.05).

The results of the data analysis for hypothesis three which posited that there is no significant relationship between anticipated good health care and premarital sex among senior secondary school girls in Akwa Ibom State.

Table 4: Analysis of Covariance (ANCOVA) showing the effects of anticipated Health care on premarital sex

Variable	Source	Sum of square	Df	Mean	F	P
Good	Row	543.10	1	543.30	2060	< .05
Health Care	Columns	6.71	2	3.35	12.74	< .05
Premarital	Interactions	4.28	2	2.14	8.13	< .05
Sex	Within	600.83	114	.26		

Table 4 indicated that there was significant relationship in the scores of the participants exposed to good health care and premarital sex and control (F(2114) = 2060, P<0.05). This shows that social life and cultural values course was effective in fostering information seeking behavior of the participants. Anticipated good Health care and Guilt Feelings moderated the relationship between treatment and the criterion measure (F(2114) = 12.74, P<0.05). There was significant interaction effect of treatment and columns (F(2114) = 8.13, p<0.05).

Table 5: Multiple Classification Analysis (MCA) of Guilt-Feelings Emotion Imbalance and Anticipated Good Health Care

Variable + Category	N	Unadjusted Deviation	ETA	Adjusted for Covariance Deviation	Beta
Levels					
GFS	205	5.71		4.22	
AGH	205	54		.84	
ETE	205	6.36	.46	-470	
Treatment					
WASI	205	6.44		6.44	
DMSE	205	6.43		6.43	
Control	205	-12.87	.84	012.56	.84
Gender					
Female					.16
	600	4.36	.9		
Multiple 2					.959
Multiple					.979

This table 5 shows the Multiple Classification Analysis (MCA) of the adjusted independent variable plus the covariate. The adjusted deviation value of 6.52 is an indication of the effectiveness of girls' awareness of moderated opinions inventory in enhancing information and self expression intervention demonstrated superiority over decision making moderated opinions and control group, groups with adjusted deviation values of 6.34 and -12.86 respectively. Decision making and self expression were effective in fostering information and the treatment of the participants when compared with the control group. The MEA also indicated that there was high degree of consideration between Guilt feelings and Emotional Imbalance as the treatments as evident by the multiple R2 value of .959. By implication 95.9% of the variance (Guilt feelings and Emotional Imbalance is attributable to girls' awareness and self expression intervention.

Discussion of Findings

The participants in the treatment groups openly scored significantly higher on measure of operated opinions than their counterparts in the control group. Realistically this finding corroborate the assertion of Agbaje (2002) that information is basically a form of investment in human capital, and the rate of developments of a nation is related to passing correct information and this is also related to its investment in this human capital. This also occurs with that of Adeyemo (2006) who posited that policy makers and employers not only need to place women's employment in the centre of social and economic policies, they also need to recognize that the challenges faced by our young women in the world require intervention tailored to specific needs.

An explanation for the effectiveness of (WASI) in improving and actualizing gate way to good healthy life of our young women is that it exposed the participants to various avenues through which they could look for information gathering existing in the societies and elsewhere. This attempt had gone a long way to remove the veil of ignorance, "I do not know that it would be like that" among the participants. EMIM effectiveness could be instituted to that fact that it was presented as another interesting phenomenon which is characterized by good interaction among the participants and this gives the freedom to express their opinions, had their misconception corrected and new information was given to broaden their knowledge about fairly planning is all about. Agbaje (2008) and (2010) stated that women have made steady progress in all area of family planning. The effectiveness of EMIM in enhancing family planning was supported by the study of Denga (2011) who discovered young women students who were given training in Emily planning and were able to take appropriate decision than the comparison group.

The second hypothesis result clearly shows that there is a significant relationship between the Guilt-feeling and Emotional Imbalance (EMIM) and the control group. Openly the result attested to the effectiveness of the treatment programme. The finding is in line with Denga (2006), Adeyemo (2006) and Agbaje (2006), in that these researchers concluded that knowledge exploration produces favourable result in terms of education on health care and health as a gateway to a healthy life. The finding was also in agreement with Sacvickas (2003) and Welbel (2004) who attested that knowledge exploration on health has a significant impact on health maturity self concept on crystallization. They further explained that health impact on the decision making process in health search. It would have been a great surprise had the control participants performed better than those participants treated with emotional imbalance since it has been confirmed in the first hypothesis that the two treatment strategies were superior than control group. Thus how performance of the control participants was due to that fact that they were not exposed to the treatment.

The result of the third hypothesis proved that there was a significant difference/relationship in the Guilt feelings Emotional Imbalance scores of the participants exposed to EMIM when compared to those in the control group. Thus the significant relationship is noted in the fact that the treated participants were exposed to comprehensive EMIM treated programme. The control was not exposed to any form of treatment. The finding corroborates Adeyemo (1997), Aremn (1999) and Agbaje (2007) who established that health training programme could be effective in broadering the experience outlook as well as improving the maturity of the participants.

Once other peculiar aspect of the study is the moderating influence of opinions on the causal link between the intervention programme and the criterion measures. Opinions have been established as a crucial factor in health decision – process. In this, process, tasks are involved and the real appropriateness of such decision would be a large extent influenced to what extent which a person believes in himself to execute purely health tasks.

Conclusions

An increasing plurality of sexual attitudes, values and lifestyles and an increased awareness of problems related to sexuality such as venereal diseases, AIDS, unwanted pregnancies among adolescents and numerous yearly abortions make sex education in schools an urgent need. Given the urgency of adolescents' sex-related problems and anxieties, the extent of their ignorance and misinformation about sex, and the reluctance of parents to provide sex education because of embarrassment, lack of rapport, of sufficient relevant knowledge, and of pedagogic skills in presenting it, the school obviously has an obligation to counteract the existing paucity of knowledge and ratio information, and to forestall risky experimentation prompted by curiosity, ignorance, and perplexity.

Realistic sex education would also deal with the problem of preventing, adolescent pregnancy and sexually transmitted diseases. Such education would be concerned with the physiology and psychology of moral sexual development and with the emotional and ethnical goals of sex expression. It would leave to individual guidance specific problems about various sexual practices. We must persistently insist rather in maintaining that sex education is really meaningless unless it can be related to the meaning, the role and the importance of sex in the modern world.

Recommendations

In view of the research findings the following recommendations are proffered with the hope that they would solve some of the problems associated with this research.

- Unfortunate parental attitudes and parent-child relationships
- The example of an unhappy marriage in the home, the parents' depreciation of sex or of the sex of the adolescent parental changing to the adolescent child or preventing him from marking heterosexual contacts with his peers, parental ridicule of early heterosexual ineffectiveness, unwholesome family relationships needs to be addressed.
- Personality traits associated with social tendencies (excessive introversion, timidity, insecurity, anxiety impaired self-esteem, asceticism and over intellectualization) and with inappropriate differentiation of biological sex role (narcissism or over identification with the sex role of the parent of opposite sex.
- Insufficient opportunity for learning experiences, due to extreme physical unattractiveness, isolation from peer group or from members of the opposite sex and lack of social skills.

References

Adeyemo, D. A. (2006). *Policy-Makers on Adolescent Development.* Ibadan: Oxford University Press.

Adeyemo, D. A., Avemu, S. and Agbaje, A. A. (2001*). Health Training Programme – Aid to effective broadening of the experience outlook.* Calabar: Wusen Press.

Agbaje, A. A. (2002). *Adolescent Information on Self Development and Future Anticipation.* New York: Basic Books.

Agbaje, A. A. (2008/2010). *Young Adolescents and Family Planning, the way forward.* New York: McGraw-Hill.

Ansubel, P. F. (2006). *Children Approaching Adolescence.* Calabar: Centre Press.

Danga, I. D. (2011). *Young men and Appropriate Decision-making on knowledge exploration.* Calabar: Centre Press.

Hawkins, C. A. (2003). *The skilled helper: A Systematic Approach to Effective Helping.* Pacific Grove, CA: Books/Cole Publishing Co.

Kinsey, A. I. and Coworkers (1998). The Normal way to Adolescent Adjustment. Annual workshop of Psychology Department, University of Uyo, Uyo - Nigeria

Leighton, S. A. and Klukhoum P. O. O. (2007). *Differentiation on social sex Roles.* London: Macmillan Press.

Manna, C. A. (1989). *Primitive cultures in non-sexual determinants of adolescent stress.* Calabar: Wusen Press.

Merchabanks, T. O. (1999/2001). Prevention of Teenage Pregnancy in our Secondary Schools in Nigeria, Workshop of the Women Association in Nigeria.

Merand, P. J. (2009). *Status world of the children and adolescents – What the parents should know.* Calabar: Centre press.

Nunci, J. P. and Wood, T. O. (2006). *Issues and implications of various forms of sexual expression.* Jos: Fab Education Books.

Nwangu, H. and Adeyemo, D. A. (1998). *Consequences of premarital sex and self expression inventory.* Ibadan: Claverion Press.

Parsions, C. T. (2002). *Girls are more selfless in trapping.* Ibadan: University Press Ltd.

Parsions, C. T. (2006). Essential nature of men and woman in social sex roles, Itasca II F. E. Peacocks.

Sacvicks, P. O. (2003). *Knowledge exploration on health maturity,* Ibadan: University Press Ltd.

Sadock, A. O. (2007). *Proximal social influences, sexual education and prevention programmes.* Ibadan: Calvenium press.

Sulmons, O. A. and Rosenberg, T. P. (2005). Adolescents and future educational opportunity. Faculty of Education, University of Calabar, Calabar.

United States of America (1970). A positive and accepting view of oneself.

GLOBALISATION ISSUES

21

Building Capacity through Cross-border Higher Education: Prospects and Challenges for Public Universities in Ghana

Deborah Afful & Collins Owusu-Ansah

Abstract

*C*ross-border education has the potential to help expand quickly a country's tertiary education system and to increase the country's stock of highly skilled human capital. This is significant in the sense that it will be a benchmark to academics and universities as institutions on the quality and relevance of their services which can lead to organisational learning through academic partnerships, franchising, opening of branch campuses, staff and student exchanges. The paper seeks to examine the relevance of cross border tertiary education, capacity building, and the various types of internationalization. It concludes on the challenges and the way forward for maximization of the gains of capacity building through cross border higher education.

Key Words: *Capacity, Cross-border, Higher Education*

Introduction

Tertiary education in Ghana has provided the avenue for the training of technocrats and professionals for both the private and public sectors of the economy. It has been the backbone of the various sectors of the economy by providing avenues for the development of the required human capital for development. As education has been recognised as a human right by the international community with "basic education for all" as one of the internationally agreed Millennium Development Goals, the importance of education for development hardly needs discussion. Tertiary education is also important in an education capacity building strategy because it supports the primary and secondary levels of education. A strong tertiary education is thus necessary for quality primary and secondary education sectors.

Over the past decades, access to tertiary education in sub-Saharan Africa has expanded at an unprecedented rate. While there were fewer than 200,000 tertiary students enrolled in the region in 1970, this number soared to over 4.5 million in 2008. In effect, the growth enrolment rate for tertiary education for each year was 8.6% between 1970 and 2008 as compared to a global average of 4.6% over the same period (UNESCO Institute for Statistics, 2010). Despite the rapid growth, only 60% of the tertiary education age cohort was enrolled in tertiary institutions in 2008 compared to the global average of 26% in the sub-Saharan Africa. Today, the data reveal that only 12% of the population of tertiary age in Ghana is enrolled (The Forum for Education Reform IMANI, 2013). This goes to buttress the point that many developing countries still face problems of unmet demand for tertiary education due to insufficient domestic provision. Such countries can use cross-border higher education to rapidly improve access to tertiary education for domestic students.

In a paper on cross border higher education in Ghana, Oduro and Senadza (2005) reported that, in 2002 to 2003, Ghana ranked third in terms of the number of African students enrolled in the U. S. Universities, with majority of them pursuing undergraduate studies. According to Effah and Senadze (2008) the unavailability of coherent data on international students in Ghana makes it difficult to gauge trends in inward mobility accurately. However, available data indicate that international students are becoming an important part of Ghana's higher educational system in recent times though on a smaller scale than the number going abroad. The current data reveals that foreign students' enrolment in the private Tertiary Education Institutions (TEIs) in Ghana stands at 11,978 while that of the public Tertiary Education Institutions (TEIs) stands at 3,207. A relatively higher proportion of students in the Private TEIs, as compared to Public TEIs, are foreign students. Foreign students comprise 18% of all students in Private TEIs. On the other hand, foreign students constitute 1% of the total student population in Public TEIs (National Accreditation Board Report, 2015).

Definition of Cross-border Tertiary Education

Organisation for Economic Cooperation and Development (OECD) and International Bank for Reconstruction and Development (IBRD)/World Bank (2005, 2007) define cross-border tertiary education as the movement of people, programmes, providers, curricula, projects, research and services in tertiary education across national jurisdictional borders. It further sees cross-border education as a set of educational internationalisation and can be part of development cooperation projects, academic exchange programmes and commercial initiatives.

Cross-border tertiary education also refers to situations where students, teachers, programmes, institutions/providers or course materials cross national borders. It can take several forms, such as students (and teachers) travelling to study (teach) in foreign countries, educational institutions partnering with foreign institutions to offer joint educational programmes or degrees, educational institutions operating abroad, and educational courses being supplied across borders through e-learning or distance learning (Knight, 2003, 2005,2008).

What is Capacity Building?

The United Nations Development Programme (UNDP) (2003) defines capacity as the ability of individuals, organisations and societies to perform functions, solve problems set and achieve goals. It further states that it is about promoting learning, boosting empowerment, building social capital, creating enabling environments, integrating cultures, and orienting personal and societal behaviour. According to Vincent-Lancin (2007), capacity building is based on learning and acquisition of skills and resources among individuals and organisations. The acquisition of skills should be seen in opposition to transfer of technology or technical assistance. According to OECD and IBRD/ The World Bank (2007), capacity development is the process whereby people, organisations, and society as a whole, create, adopt and maintain capacity over time, that is, the ability to arrange their affairs successfully.

Relationship between Higher Education and Capacity Building

Generally, education for emphasis and higher education, play a significant role in any capacity building strategy. The ultimate goal of institutional development strategy is to achieve progress and development. It is noteworthy that education has a unique privilege as a built-in feature of any capacity development strategy. Whatever the sector, capacity building relies on the strengthening of individual capacity through training and learning, in order to raise the institutional stock of human capital in a specific field. This is usually done by setting up specific educational programmes in the formal education system or by other forms of learning. Although, some of the necessary skills would typically be acquired on-the-job or through learning-by-doing, developing countries characterised by less efficient organisations of work or by obsolete technologies might need to rely more on formal vocational/professional education and training.

Types of Internationalization
Campus-based Internationalization

Nilson (2003) opines that the campus based or "at home" internationalisation puts more emphasis on the intercultural aspects of the teaching/learning process and the curriculum. Knight (2008) puts the elements of campus-based or "at home" internationalisation as follows:

- **Curriculum and Programmes**
  This involves new programmes with international themes, foreign language study, area or regional studies and, joint or double degrees.
- **Teaching/Learning Process**
  This refers to active involvement of international students, returned study-abroad students, and cultural diversity of classroom teaching/learning processes. It can also include virtual student mobility for joint courses and research projects and the use of international scholars and reference materials.
- **Extracurricular Activities**
  These activities involve student clubs, international campus events and peer support groups and programmes.
- **Research and Scholarly Activity**
  This covers joint research projects, international conferences and seminars, published articles and papers, international research agreements, research exchange programmes, international research partners in academic and other sectors and Integration of visiting researchers and scholars into academic activities on campus.

Cross-border Education or Education Abroad

Tefera and Knight (2008) refer to cross border or education "abroad" as the movement of people, programmes, providers, knowledge, ideas, projects and services across national boundaries. Delivery modes range from face-to-face to virtual. This term is often used interchangeably with "Transnational" "Offshore", and "borderless" education.

Current Trends in Cross-border Education

OECD/IBRD/The World Bank (2007) identifies three trends as follows:

- **Staff and Student Mobility**

  Vincent-Lancrin (2007) sees student and staff mobility as an effective way to build capacity in tertiary education at the individual level. He asserts that students and academics can access better quality courses and research facilities abroad and return with enhanced skills and experience. Encouraging and supporting domestic students to study abroad is arguably the best way to get a well-trained international workforce which can improve the quality and quantity of human resources in the economy. This is true for faculty too. They would be able to access international academic network in which many developing countries have little involvement, although it is growing (Vincent-Lancrin, 2007).

- **Programme Mobility**

  Knight (2005a) describes cross-border mobility of programme as the movement of individual education or training courses and programmes across national borders, either face-to-face, by distance delivery, or as a combination of these modes. Credits towards a qualification can be awarded by the sending foreign country provider or by an affiliated domestic partner or jointly. Among the more popular methods of cross border programme mobility are franchising, twinning, double/joint degrees, and various articulation models.

- **Provider Mobility**

  Teferra and Knight (2008) describe cross border mobility of providers as the physical or virtual movement of an education provider (institution, organisation, company) across a national border to establish a presence in order to offer education/training programmes and/ or services to students and other clients. Credits and qualifications are awarded by the foreign provider (through foreign, local, or self-accreditation methods) or by an affiliated domestic partner. Knight (2005b) identifies different forms of cross border provider mobility as branch campus, independent institution, acquisition/merger, affiliation/networks, Study Centre/ Teaching Site and Virtual University. According to Vincent-Lancrin (2007), programme and institution mobility can provide another way of improving the quality of domestic educational provision. Foreign programmes delivered at local institutions or foreign institutions operating in the country can in specific fields offer students a better education or training than some domestic institutions are able to.

The Strengths and Prospects of Cross-border Education

The mobility of professors, students, knowledge and even values has been part of higher education for centuries but it has recently grown at unprecedented pace. From the Presentation by Eugenio Cetina Vadillo at OECD/Norway Forum on Trade in Education Services held on November 3-4, 2003, Mexico is an example of a country using academic mobility to improve the quality of its higher education. Between 1998 and 2002, the percentage of Mexican full-time academic staff with degree rose from 30 to 65. Universities have achieved this increase through the "Institutional Enhancement Integral Programme" (PIED) aiming, amongst others, at improving the quality and qualification of the faculty through new recruitment and in-service training. The latter included the possibility to study abroad, particularly at doctoral level.

Given the resource constraints facing higher education institutions, it is no longer possible to release staff and students on study leave for longer periods. The preferred option is split-site programmes which enable students to have relatively short periods abroad during which they review literature, broaden their horizons and analyse data, particularly in science and technology-based programmes where appropriate equipment and laboratories may not be available in their institutions.

According to Effah & Senadza (2008), Cross-border Education is not new to Ghana.

- At the Kwame Nkrumah University of Science and Technology, for example, collaboration with the University of Dortmund in Germany has been running for more than 20 years in a postgraduate programme in Development Planning and Management (SPRING).
- The Faculty of Education of the University of Cape Coast has a joint agreement with the Florida Agricultural and Mechanical University to mount a doctoral degree programme in educational leadership funded by USAID to promote the development of faculty staff. Ten students have been admitted into the programme since 2001 when it began.
- Three public Universities-University of Cape Coast, University of Education, Winneba, and University of Ghana – collaborated with Simon Fraser University of Canada in a six-year project which began in 2004 to strengthen the institutional capacity of the three Ghanaian Universities to design, develop, and deliver HIV/AIDS worker programmes aimed at reducing stigma and transmission among children and out-of-school youth.
- The University of Ghana entered into five-year agreement with Harvard University in staff development in 2004. Under the agreement, known as the University of Ghana-Harvard University split Ph.D programme, faculty of the University of Ghana who are enrolled in its Ph.D economics or economics – related programmes are admitted at Harvard for one academic year to take core courses in their areas of specialisation. Additionally, the visit offers these scholars the opportunity to work on their dissertation at Harvard. The programme has benefited six PhD students.
- The University of Education, Winneba, also offered a joint postgraduate programme in Physical Education with SUNNY – Brockport, New York. This programme benefited four PhD students who came back to beef up the staff strength of the department.
- The University of Cape Coast collaborated with the Sasakawa Foundation in Japan providing facilities for farmers' training programmes and the School of Agriculture's Extension facilities. These initiatives have brought immense benefits to the collaborating institutions.

Cross-border education in summary facilitates the building of international networks, which are essential to academic expertise as well as to the creation of national innovation systems and international business. It also leads to increased access to higher education, strategic alliances between countries and regions and expansion of human resources and institutional capacity. It stimulates appreciation of intercultural differences and ethnic diversity.

Critical Issues and Challenges

- **Brain Drain**

The period spent abroad is supposed to be temporal rather than permanent and the experience and skills acquired through this will eventually benefit the developing country's faculty and economy. However, in practice this does not always happen, particularly as an increasing number of developed countries are trying to retain skilled foreign students, academics and more generally professionals to join the labour market (OECD, 2004a). In the Ghanaian context, brain drain occurs in two forms:

- students trained abroad fail to return home, and
- people trained within the country, especially professionals like doctors, and nurses, emigrate abroad.

Data on the emigration of Ghanaian medical personnel indicate that the situation is alarming. Current data on the rate of emigration of other professionals such as academics are however hard to come by. However, it is unlikely that such a high rate of emigration can be attributed to internationalisation. Consequently, the internationalisation of higher education per se may not be a cause of the brain drain in Ghana especially when it takes the form of academic faculty moving from higher education institutions. The greater threat to brain drain on academia is from within. Thus, well-trained faculty may leave the academic environment to take up jobs in the private and public sectors because of poor remuneration in higher education. They quit the lecture halls and accept political positions as Ministers of State or Municipal and District Chief Executive or join the national parliament which has become juicy in recent times. Internationalization may, however, facilitate such brain drain if inequalities in remunerative packages attract people to leave to seek better opportunities (Effah and Senadza, 2008).

- **Cost of Cross-border Education**

A limitation of Cross border higher education lies in its cost which may be unaffordable for students from developing countries. The ability to access student mobility partly depends on the host country's fee policy and standard of living. Given limited resources, most governments can only support a handful of students. Most students are self-funded and only a limited number of families are able to meet the costs.

Differences between the cost of living and studying in the country of origin and the host country mean that low-income or even average-income families in general cannot afford to send their children abroad to study. Even countries where international students do not pay tuition fees like Norway and Germany, or just a small amount like in France and Spain, the costs of living make access to higher education system difficult for students from middle-income families in developing countries (OECD, 2007).

- **Student Access**

As observed already, there have been rapid increases in student intake at tertiary institutions over the last decade. According to Educational Sector Performance Report, 2013, enrolment figures in tertiary education were as follows, 2009/2010-179,998; 2010/11-185,268; 2011/2012-202,063; 2012/2013 - 389,897; and 2013/2014 - 414,460. Still, access to tertiary education in Ghana is low, because competition for the limited vacancies is so keen, given the large number of qualified applicants. Efforts of universities to attract international students are seen as having negative impact on an already bad situation. The steadily rising number of international students in Ghana's public universities provides both an element of internationalisation and also a major source of revenue.

However, it also reduces the number of places available for indigenous Ghanaian students. While this point is valid in the short term, cross border education could be seen as enlarging opportunities for higher education abroad especially in the area of graduate training and in various forms including distance education (Effah & Senadza, 2008). Again, cross-border education has the potential of increasing the number of providers within the country and thereby providing greater access (Oduro & Senadza, 2005). In this regard, cross-border education would not only increase student access but also, has the potential of lowering costs for students through local provision rather than requiring them to travel abroad (Mohamedbhai, 2002, cited in Oduro & Senadza, 2005).

- **Accreditation and Quality Assurance**

One of the results of cross-border education is the emergence of numerous campuses and influx of diverse providers. Ghana also has few international private institutions providing academic programmes and courses on fee-paying basis. Such cross-border education calls not only for national accreditation and quality assurance systems but an internationally harmonious framework as well (Knight, 2003). There is the need for comprehensive frameworks for coordinating various initiatives at the international level. The absence of this will make students and other stakeholders more vulnerable to low-quality provision of this type of provision (OECD/World Bank, 2007). Rogue providers could use the foreign crest to operate more easily (OECD and IBRD/World Bank, 2007).

Ghana already has in place an accreditation authority, the National Accreditation Board (NAB) to ensure that institutions are properly accredited and that quality is assured. To ensure that quality is not affected by cross-border education, the National Accreditation Board must be more vigilant and better resourced so that it can fulfil its responsibilities in a more efficient manner (Effah & Senadza, 2008).

- **Recognition of Degrees and Study Periods Abroad**

The issue of recognition of degrees and credits obtained abroad or through foreign institutions operating in the home country is also important. Recognition can facilitate study abroad and will allow students with foreign qualifications to work in their home country or in the international market. Students' options for undertaking further study abroad may also be limited if their domestic qualifications are not recognised by the foreign institutions either for the purpose of enrolling in higher education or further training (OECD)/World Bank, 2007). Non-recognition of study periods abroad causes waste of time for students, extending the overall duration of study and producing extra study load and examinations.

The Way Forward

Having identified the above as the challenges to the prospects of cross border higher education towards capacity building, the following are worth considering. As a way of tackling the brain drain, the universities must create a favourable working environment that will constrain and motivate staff to return to the institutions after their sponsored training abroad. Also, some of the programmes could be run on split basis so that part of the course could be run locally in order to make it unattractive for staff to stay away after the completion of their course. Again, due to high cost involved in the provision of cross border education, universities find it difficult to sponsor an appreciable number of staff for studies abroad. There is therefore the need for the institutions to explore more opportunities for sponsorships from corporate organisations, foundations, and donor agencies to enhance capacity building through cross border education. The universities can as well explore the promotion of joint programmes in building capacity between their staff and institutions in both developing and developed countries.

In addition, there is the need to expand facilities on our campuses in order to increase student access to universities. This will improve intake of both local and foreign students. Furthermore, education today is increasingly becoming international and the increasing use of Information Communication Technology (ICT) is one way to achieve this outcome. ICT holds the key to moving education from where it is now to where it needs to be. Therefore, the public universities must use online education facility to increase their accessibility to as many students as possible both local and foreign without the limits imposed by physical or socio economic circumstances. Lastly, the universities must position themselves to take advantage of capacity building opportunities which are made available through globalisation. In this way, Ghanaian Public universities can have more fruitful collaborations with other accredited institutions abroad.

Conclusion

Building capacity will often be an important concern particularly in developing countries and young universities in Ghana for several reasons. Primarily, young universities are often isolated or not connected with broader marketing spheres. Secondly, to participate in these broader spheres, the young universities may need education and training programmes concerning enhanced quality management for high-value products. In addition, the selection of countries and institutions on which to focus capacity-building depends upon the resource endowment of the institution and country concerned. Globalization has permitted countries to reach beyond the limits of their natural boundaries in order to obtain resources.

References

Effah, P. & Senadza, B. (2008). Ghana. In Teferra D. and Knight J. (Eds.), *Higher Education in Africa: the International Dimension* (pp.209-237). USA. Center for International Higher Education, Boston College.

Knight, J. (2003b), GAT Trade and Higher Education. Perspective 2003: Where are we? *Observatory on Borderless Higher Education, URL*. Retrieved from www.obhe.ac.uk/products/reports/publicaccesspdf/May2003.pdf. Last Accessed 7th March 2005.

Knight, J. (2005). New Typologies for Cross border Higher Education. *International Higher Education, 38*.

Knight, J. (2005a). *Borderless, Off-shore, transnational and Cross border Education: Definition and data dilemmas*. Report for observatory for Borderless Higher Education. London: Observatory for Borderless Higher Education.

Knight, J. (2005b). "An internationalisation Model: Responding to new realities and challenges". In H. de Witt, I. C. Jaramillo, J. Gacel-Avila, & J. Knight (Eds.), *Higher Education in Latin America: The International Dimension* (pp.1- 38). Washington, DC: World Bank.

Knight, J. (2006c). *Higher Education Crossing Borders: A guide to the implications of GATS for cross-border education.* Paris: Commonwealth of learning and UNESCO.

Knight, J. (2008*).* Internalisation of Higher Education: Complexities and Realities.

In D. Tefera & J. Knight (Eds.), *Higher Education in Africa: The International Dimension* (pp 1 - 43). USA. Center for International Higher Education, Boston College and Association of African Universities.

Ministry of Education Sector Performance Report, August 2013.

National Accreditation Board (2015). Tertiary Education Statistics Report 2012/ 2013 Academic year. October, 2015.

Nilson, B. (2003). *Internationalisation at Home: Theory and Praxis. European Association for International Education Forum.* Monograph No.12.

Oduro, A. & Senadza, B. (2005). Cross border provision and the future of higher Education in Africa: A case study of Ghana. Paper prepared for the 11th General Conference of the Association of African Universities (AAU), Cape Town, South Africa.

OCED /IBRD and World Bank (2007). Developing capacity through Cross border Tertiary Education – Executive Summary – 11 Paris. www.oecd.org/edu/highereducationandadult learning/39169515.pdf

Romer, P. M. (1993). Two Strategies for Economic Development: Using Ideas and Producing Ideas, Processing of the World Bank Annual Research Conference 1992, Supplement to the World Bank. *Economic Review*, 63-91.

The Forum for Education Reform IMANI Ghana (2013). Post on myjoyonline.com 20/12/13.

UNESCO Institute for Statistics (2010). Trends in Tertiary Education: Sub Saharan Africa. UIS Fact sheet, No. 10.

UNESCO/OECD (2005). Guidelines on quality provision in cross border higher education. *Higher education and adult learning.* www.oecd.org/education/highereducationandadultlearning/unes cooecdguidelinesonqualityprovisionincross-borderhighereducation.htm.

United Nations Development Programme (2003). *Ownership, Leadership and Transformation: Can we do better for Capacity Development?* (Eds.), C. Lopes & T. Theisohn, Earthscan. London.

Vincent –Lancrin, S. (2007). Developing capacity through cross border tertiary Education. In R. Kagia & B. Ischinger (Eds.), *Cross Border Tertiary Education: A way Towards Capacity Development.* OCED/World Bank: CERI.

22

Role of Curriculum in Combating Climate Change in Nigeria

Mahmud HalliruBakori & Inuwa Magaji

Abstract

The purpose of this study was to investigate the role of curriculum in combating climate change in Nigeria. To achieve this, the authors looked at the concepts of curriculum and climate change as perceived by several authors. Human activities and natural phenomena were identified as the two major causes of climate change. The authors further mentioned some consequences of climate change and the role of curriculum in combating the negative effects of climate change. The paper concluded that the growing awareness of the negative effects of climate change on all aspects of our lives can only be adequately addressed through education empowered by a relevant curriculum. The paper recommended, among other things, that climate change should be integrated into secondary school curriculum and teachers should be trained on how to handle climate change related lessons.

Key Words: *Curriculum, Climate Change*

Introduction

Education is the bedrock for meaningful development in any country. It is the wheel on which other developmental effort revolves. A country cannot develop beyond the level of education of its citizens. The cardinal role education plays in nation building informs the reason why many nations of the world invest heavily in education, and educationists all over the world are constantly carrying out research on how to improve the quality of education in order to meet the ever growing and changing needs of their societies. Unfortunately, education sector in many developing countries, such as Nigeria, is beset with many challenges which mar the efforts of the government and educationists in providing quality education.

The issue of climate change came up in the early 19th century when it was suspected that natural changes in pale-climate had occurred just as at the same time the natural greenhouse effect was identified (Pembina Institute,2012). By the 20th century, scientists had argued that human emissions of greenhouse gases could change the climate. While the details of the calculations were being disputed in 1950s and 1960s, the calculation of the warming effect of carbon dioxide emissions became increasingly convincing. According to Pembina Institute (2012), some scientists pointed out that those human activities in the form of atmospheric aerosols such as pollution could have cooling effects as well. These scientific opinions increasingly favored the warming view point in the 70s. By

1980s, consensus was reached that human activity was in the process of warming the climate, leading to the modern period of global warming science. That is the basis of the phenomenal climate change which is today a serious educational concern.

Concept of Curriculum and Climate Change

The two concepts were defined by different scholars in different ways. For example, Offorma (1994) viewed curriculum as the organized knowledge presented to learners in a school which covers every element in the learning environment such as the subject matter to be learned, the students, the teachers and the physical environment. But Toffler (1971) defined curriculum as the planned and guided learning experiences and intended learning outcomes, formulated through the systematic reconstruction of knowledge and experience under the auspices of the school for the learner's continuous and purposeful growth in personal social competence. Mkpa et al (2004) saw curriculum as a body of knowledge that is sacrosanct, a plan for actors, a race experience, a guide learning experience, a learning structure and a reconstruction of knowledge and experience. Curriculum can therefore be defined as a highly organized body of knowledge reconstructed to guide both learning experience and intended learning outcome.

Climate change, on the other hand, is the variation in global or regional climates over time. Offorma (2010) defined climate change as a continuous, rapid, and prolonged alteration of climate in one direction which reflects changes in the variability or average state of the atmosphere overtime, ranging from decades to millions of years. Wikipedia, the Free Encyclopedia (2012), defined climate change as a significant and lasting change in statistical distribution of weather patterns over a period ranging from decades to millions of years. World Meteorological Organization (2012) defined the concept as a significant and lasting change in the statistical distribution of weather patterns over period of time. Similarly, Cummings (2012) defined climate change as the average weather of the statistical description in terms of the mean and variability of relevant quantities over a period ranging from months to thousands or millions of years. These qualities are most often surface variables such as temperature, precipitation, and wind.

Causes of Climate Change

Human activities and natural phenomena have been identified as the two major causes of climate change. The human activities include: bush burning, deforestation, desertification, burning of fossil fuels, and industrial pollutions. These activities of man, cause the release of excess carbon dioxide (CO_2) and other heat trapping emissions such as methane (CH_4), Nitrous Oxide (N_2O), chlorofluorocarbons (CFCS) and Ozone (O_3). These green-house gases contribute to the depletion of the Ozone layer in the atmosphere leading to global warming. The natural phenomena that contribute to climate change include: Solar output, variations in earth's orbit, volcanic eruptions, and ocean variations. Ekpo (2009) stated that every system, whether human or otherwise is tied to climate and that changes in climate affect many related aspects of where and how people, plants, and animals live.

Consequences of Climate Change

Commenting on the adverse effects of climate change, the Union of Concerned Scientists (2012), stated that climate change put our food and water supply at risk, endanger our health, jeopardize our natural security and threaten other basic human needs. Agriculture has been adversely affected by climate change. Many farmers in Nigeria have lost their farm lands and farm produce due to flood. Flood has increased the salinity of farm lands in affected areas, rendering them unfit for crop production. Farmers in some areas not affected by flood experience drought, which leads to low yield of crops. This condition has led to shortage of food supply in the country. Different species of animals and plants need certain type of climate to survive. People's health has also been adversely affected by climate change. Climate change has resulted to increased diseases that lead to loss of lives, some of whom are the students as well as parents and guardians that sponsor the education of their children and wards. The economic life of the people in Nigeria has not been spared by climate change related problems. Farm lands, business premises, factories and offices are destroyed by flood thereby impoverishing the people.

Climate change-related problems directly affect punctuality and attendance to school among teachers, students and school supervisors. Other direct effects of climate change on teaching and learning include: disruption of school calendar, destruction of school structure and learning materials, incompletion of curriculum content, and consequently, poor performance of students in examinations. According to Asian Disaster Preparedness Center (2008), there is evidence that flooding inhibits completion of school programme with schools located in flood-prone areas subject to at least one and a half months of closure due to flooding. Bangay and Blum (2010) asserted that school absenteeism and drop out are higher in flood-prone areas. Zaidi in Blessing (2014) stated that many children enrolled in secondary schools do not complete their education due to challenges that make it difficult for them to attend and participate in school, of which climate related hazards are inclusive. Climate change also indirectly affects teaching and learning by adversely affecting the health of teachers, students and food production, thereby jeopardizing the efforts and resources expended by government on eradication of illiteracy and provision of quality education as well as other Millennium Development Goals (MDGs) projects.

According to UNDP in Bangay and Blun (2010), climate change is hampering efforts to deliver the MDG promises. Looking to the future, the danger is that it will stall and then reverse progress built-up over generations not just in cutting extreme poverty but in health, nutrition, education, and other areas.

Other effects of climate change can be seen in the following areas;

- Increased incidence of extreme high sea level
- More frequent hot days and nights
- Increase in global areas affected by drought
- Increase in intense tropical cyclone activity.
- Increase in diseases associated with floods and droughts.
- Heavy precipitation leading to flooding.
- aridity and desertification in northern Nigeria
- Erosion
- Rising sea level

Role of Curriculum

Human race seems to be at the verge of extinction if nothing tangible is done to checkmate the incidence of climate change. There may be no better way of fighting this issue than through education. The school serves the society. It is one of the major institutions through which the society meets its needs, solves its problems, and achieves its aspirations. The school contributes its own quota in tackling the challenges posed by climate change via the provision of quality education in Nigeria. Through schools, curricular could be used to help in tackling the problem posed by climate change. Most nations of the world appear to be doing something resolute to combat this menace. Cummings (2012) wrote that the United States of America would urgently design primary school curriculum on climate change. A similar curriculum had been designed for its post primary and tertiary education levels (Cummings, 2012). In Nigeria, climate change calls for the restructuring of our education system towards surmounting them. There should be a curriculum at all levels of education to offer knowledge on climate change. Climate change and environmental science should be integrated into secondary school curriculum, workshops, seminars and conferences on climate change should be organized for teachers and students and resource persons should be engaged to teach both teachers and students adaptation and mitigation measures.

A number of curricular measures can be applied to tackle these challenges. According to Mumuni and Amadi (2013), climate change draws knowledge from diverse disciplines and sub-disciplines of science. They stress that a holistic understanding of climate change does not rely on knowledge from only one discipline or subject matter but amalgamation of subject matter with their diverse knowledge. Education is a veritable tool for tackling societal problems. International Council on Human Rights Policy (2008) observed that education is as important as health and that a well-educated populace is better equipped to recognize in advance the threats posed by climate change and to make preparations. According to Bourn (2008), learning, which inculcates skills such as critical thinking and problem solving, is key to addressing climate change and sustainable development. It is therefore, imperative that both teachers and students keep abreast with current issues and particularly on climate change related issues in order to acquire the necessary knowledge and skills that will help them proffer solutions to the problems of climate change.

Conclusion

There is growing awareness of the adverse impacts of climate change on many aspects of our lives. These effects could only be adequately addressed through education empowered by a relevant curriculum. The curriculum presently available to Nigeria educational system was seen as lacking in the area of knowledge of and how to tackle the problem of climate change. A curriculum on climate change would fit this present period as discussed in this chapter.

Recommendations

Based on the discussions above, the following recommendations were made:

- Climate change should be integrated into secondary school curriculum.
- Seminars, workshops and conferences should be organized for teachers, students and school administrators on adaptation.

- Government should, as a matter of urgency, set up a committee whose membership are curriculum experts to draw a befitting curriculum on climate change for all levels of the nation's education system.
- Teachers should be trained on how to handle climate change related lessons.
- Government should ensure that instructional materials necessary for implementing climate change curriculum are available.
- Nigeria citizens should be given proper orientation on how to avoid activities inimical to the environment.

References

Asian Disaster Preparedness Center (2008). A Study on Impact of Disasters on the Education Sector in Cambodia. Bangkok: Asian Disaster Preparedness Center.

Bangay, C. & Blum, N. (2010). Education Responses to Climate Change and Quality: Two parts of the same Agenda. *International Journal of Educational Development,* 30(4), 335-450.

Blessing, A. (2014). Challenges on Provision of and Accessibility of Quality Education in Nigeria. *Journal of Education Learning and Development* 2(2), (www.eajpurnal.org).

Bourn, D. (2008). *Global skills.* London: Learning and skills. improvementservice.http://www.isis/ org.UK/libraries/documents/globalskills%20NOV08WEB.Sflb. Accessed on 15th August, 2013.

Cummings, M. (2012). *Climate and the Society.* Retrieved on 10/08/2012 from http://www. willwtegerfoundation.org/summer-institute.

Ekpo, E. C. (2009). Introduction: Debating Policy Options for National Development. Enugu Forum Policy Paper 10; *African institute for Applied Economics (AIAE).* Enugu, Nigeria: 13-18. http:// www.aiaenigeria.org/publications/policypaper10.pdf. Accessed 28th August, 2013.

International Council on Human Rights Policy (2008). *Climate Change and Human Rights: A Rough Guide.* Versoix, Switzerland: International Council on Human Rights Policy.

Mkpa, M. A. & Izuagba, A. C. (2004). *Curriculum Studies and Innovation.* Enugu: Book-Konsult.

Mumuni, A. A. & Amadi, C. P. (2013). Secondary School Teachers' Conceptual Knowledge of Climate Change and Implications for Curriculum Knowledge Organization. Paper Presented at the 26th Annual Conference of Curriculum Organization of Nigeria (CON) at University of Port Harcourt, Nigeria held on 18th – 21st September, 2013.

Offorma, G. C. (1994). *Curriculum implementation and instruction.* Onitsha: Uni-World Educational Publishers (Nig.) Ltd.

Offorma, G. C. (2010). Climate Change and the Need for New Curriculum Development in Nigerian Universities. *Nigerian Journal of Curriculum Studies,* 17(3), 265-270.

Ogundipe, O. (2006). *Introduction to Environmental Issues: Causes, Effects and Solutions.* Lagos: Ikofa Commercial Press.

Pembina institute (2012). The Climate Change Awareness and Action Education Kit. Retrieved 10/08/2012 from http://www.pembina.org/publicationitem.asp?id=9.

Toffler, A. (1971). Future shock. London: Pan Union of Concerned Scientists (2012). Global warming. http://www.UCSUSa.org/globalwarming.101. Retrieved on 25th March, 2014.

Wikipedia, The Free Encyclopedia (2012). Climate Change. http://www.en.wikipedia.org/wiki/climatechange. Retrieved 25th March, 2014.

World Meteorological Organization (2012). Global Weather and Climate Extremes, Retrieved on 24/08/2012 from www.wmo.int/../index-en.html.Tweet

SCIENCE ISSUE

23

Biological Variations in Population of Living Things

Martha O. Egbro

Abstract

*T*his paper discussed biological variations in population of living things. It then identified the morphological and physiological variations and further measured the variations in population of the organisms. In the end, the paper spotted the sources and causes of variations as genetic and environmental differences. The paper concluded therefore that while the genetic differences are passed from parents to offspring, the environmental differences are acquired traits which cannot be inherited from parents by offspring.

Key Words: *Biological, Variations, Population, Physiological, Morphological*

Introduction

Organisms that make up a population differ in characteristics or traits; even closely related organisms. A trait is a distinct structural or functional feature of an organism. Structural features describe the physical appearance or form of an organism while functional features emphasize the functioning of the different body parts. Differences resulting from these features in organisms bring about variation and also form the basis for the different types of variation.

Definition of variation

Variation is defined as the difference in traits or characteristics that exist in organisms of the same species.

Types of Variation

Variation can be classified into two types based on the presence of structural and functional features in organisms namely:

- Morphological variation
- Physiological variation

Morphological Variation: Morphological variation is the difference that exists in the structural features (physical appearance or form) of organisms of the same species. Differences in size (height, length, weight and width), colour, texture, fingerprint, shape, body type etc. are some morphological variation which could either exist in plants or animals. Some examples of morphological variation include:

	In plants	In animals
a)	Height of plant	Colour of skin
b)	Shape of leaf	Colour of hair
c)	Shape of flower	Colour of eyes
d)	Shape of root	Circumference of head
e)	Shape of stem	Shape of head
f)	Width of fruit	Shape of ear lobe
g)	Mass of seed	Shape of face
h)	Shape of pod	Shape of feet
i)	Shape of seed	Shape of nose
j)	Length of stem	Shape of jaw
k)	Length of branch	Shape of mouth
l)	Length of root	Height of body
m)	Length of leaf	Length of arm
n)	Width of stem	Width of body
o)	Width of root	Length of tail
p)	Texture of fruit	Length of index finger
q)	Colour of flower	Number of gills
r)	Number of peas in pod etc.	Shape of fingerprint etc.

Fingerprints

A striking variable feature in humans is the pattern of fingerprints. No two individuals have the same pattern of fingerprints; fingerprint is a tool for identification.

Classification of finger prints

Fingerprints are unique patterns, made by friction ridges and furrows, which appear on the digits (fingers and toes), the palm of the hand or the sole of the foot, consisting of one or more connected ridge units of friction ridge skin. Friction ridge patterns are grouped into four basic distinct types:

1. Arch: Ridges enter on one side and exit on the other side.
2. Loop: Ridges enter on one side & exit on the same side.
3. Whorl: Consists of circles, more than one loop, or a mixture of pattern types.
4. Composite or Compound: Composed of two or more different patterns, separate and apart exclusive of the arch.

The patterns of these four types of fingerprints are on display in figure 1.

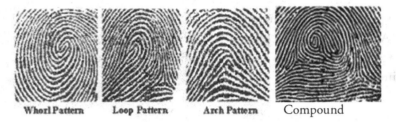

Figure 1: Basic types of fingerprints

Other sub-types arise from these four types of fingerprints. Patterns of some sub-types of the four basic types of fingerprints are shown in figure 2 below.

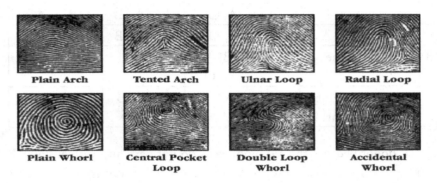

Figure 2: Sub-types of the four basic types of fingerprints

Physiological Variation: Physiological variation is the difference that exists in the functional features (functioning of the different body parts) of organisms of the same species. For this type of variation, it is either the organism possesses a particular trait or does not. There are no intermediate forms of the trait.

Examples of physiological variation in animals and plants

1. Ability to taste phenylthiocarbamide (PTC) - tasters and non-tasters.
2. Ability to roll the tongue – rollers and non-rollers.
3. Ability to move the ears without moving the head or not
4. Ability to close one eye and leave the other eye partly open or not.
5. Behavioural patterns such as intelligent or dull, aggressive or non-aggressive, brave or timid etc.
6. Baldness – either you have bald head or do not.
7. Sex – male or female.
8. Sickle cell anaemia or normal blood genotype.
9. Haemophilia – ability to clot or not.
10. Wing and wingless plants.
11. Round and wrinkled skin of a pod.
12. Differences in blood groups either you belong to blood group A or B or AB or O etc.

Blood Grouping System

There are four distinct blood groups A, B, AB and O in humans as indicated in Table 1. They can be identified on the basis of the presence of two antigens, A and B, attached on the surfaces of red blood cells and antibodies, anti-A and anti-B in the plasma. These antigens are natural proteins that stimulate an immune system to produce antibodies while the antibodies are proteins which can combine with antigens to produce immunity.

Table 1: The Antigens and Antibodies in Blood Groups

Blood groups	Antigens in red blood cells	Antibodies in blood plasma	Can receive blood from	Can donate blood to	Blood Genotypes
A	Antigen A	anti-B	A, O	A and AB	AA or AO
B	Antigen B	anti-A	B, O	B and AB	BB or BO
AB	Antigens A and B	none	A, B, AB and O	AB	ABO
O	none	natural anti-A and anti-B	O	A, B, AB and O	OO

Group O is called a universal donor because the red blood cells do not have any antigens which will react with the antibody in the recipient's plasma. Group AB is regarded as a universal recipient because they lack anti-bodies which would react with the donor's antigens.

Blood Transfusion

Blood transfusion is the transfer of blood from donors to recipients intravenously or orally. The blood of the donor and recipient must match to prevent clumping of red blood cells. In the blood transfusion process, the following happen:

1. Individuals with blood group A can donate blood to recipients with blood groups A and AB while blood from individuals with blood group B can be administered to recipients with blood groups B and AB.
   Reason
   If blood from blood group A is transfused into the circulation of an individual with blood group B, for example, then the anti-A present there binds to the A antigens. The donor erythrocytes marked in this way are recognized and destroyed by the complement system leading to death.

- Blood from the AB group can only be administered to recipients with the AB group and they can receive blood from all the blood groups.
   Reason
   The individuals with blood group AB lack antibodies that would react with the donor's antigen.

- Those with blood group O can donate blood to all the blood groups but can receive only from individuals with blood group O.

  Reason

  Individuals with blood group O do not possess any antibodies and therefore do not react with anti-A or anti-B in the recipient's blood Otherwise, the red blood cells in the blood of the donor may be caused to agglutinate (clump) by the antibody in the plasma of the recipient.

Therefore, before blood is transfused, an agglutination test must be carried out.

Agglutination

Agglutination is the clumping of the red blood cells due to reaction of similar antigens and antibodies in the plasma of an individual. In the test tube, agglutination of the red blood cells can be observed when donor and recipient blood are incompatible. The recipient's serum should not contain any antibodies against the donor red blood cells, and the donor serum should not contain any antibodies against the recipient's red blood cells as shown in Table 2 below.

Table 2: Agglutination Reactions in the Blood Grouping Systems

Blood group (antibodies) \ Blood group (antigens)	Blood group A (Antigen A)	Blood group B (Antigen B)	Blood group AB (Antigens A and B)	Blood group O (None) Universal donor
Group A (anti-B)	no clumping	clumping	clumping	no clumping
Group B (anti-A)	clumping	no clumping	clumping	no clumping
Group AB (no antibodies) Universal recipient	no clumping	no clumping	no clumping	no clumping
Group O (natural anti-A and anti-B)	clumping	clumping	clumping	no clumping

Agglutination forms the basis for several laboratory tests. Agglutination makes the blood of the recipients unable to flow within the blood vessels. Death may result.

Forms of variation

- Continuous variation
- Discontinuous variation

Continuous Variation: Continuous variation is a gradual transition from one extreme to another of a particular trait. Examples of continuous variation include height, weight, colour, shape and width of organisms. It could also be regarded as quantitative variation since the traits are quantitative.

Characteristics of Continuous Variation

The following are the characteristics of continuous variation:

- The traits show a complete graduation from one extreme to another without any break.
- Traits exhibiting continuous variation are controlled by the combined effects of many genes (polygenes).
- Traits exhibiting continuous variation could be affected by environmental factors.
- Intermediates are formed with individuals produced having traits exhibiting continuous variation.
- The frequency distribution for a trait exhibiting continuous variation is a normal distribution curve/bell shaped curve/Gaussian curve.

Discontinuous Variation: Discontinuous variation is a clear graduation from one form to another of a particular of a trait. It could be regarded as qualitative inheritance since the traits are qualitative. Examples of discontinuous variation include blood groups, sex, ability to taste PTC, ability to roll the tongue, tasters and non tasters to PTC (phenyl thiocarbamide), blood groups, sickle cell anaemia, haemophilia, skin pigmentation (normal skin colour/albinism), normal eye colour or colour blindness etc.

Characteristics of discontinuous variation

The following are the characteristics of discontinuous variation:

- The traits produced by discontinuous variation show a clear-cut graduation from one extreme to another of a particular.
- Traits of discontinuous variation are controlled by one or two genes.
- Traits exhibiting discontinuous variation could be unaffected by environmental factors.
- No intermediates are formed with individuals produced having traits exhibiting discontinuous variation.
- It could be represented on histograms, bar graphs and pie charts.

Similarities between Continuous and Discontinuous Variation

- Both are controlled by genes.
- Both could be measured.
- Both are heritable.
- Both could be represented on histograms.

Differences between Continuous and Discontinuous Variation

	Continuous Variation	Discontinuous Variation
1.	There is a gradual transition of a trait from one extreme to the other.	There is a clear graduation of the trait from one extreme to the other.

2.	It is affected by environmental factors.	It is not affected by environmental factors.
3.	It is controlled by the combined effect of many genes or polygenes.	It is controlled by one or two major genes.
4.	There are intermediate forms.	There are no intermediate forms.
5.	The genes show incomplete dominance.	The genes show complete dominance or co – dominance.
6.	Traits produced are quantitative.	Traits produced are qualitative.

Measuring Variation in Population

Discontinuous variation produces qualitative traits that fall into discrete intervals or categories not a continuum. The qualitative traits cannot be measured but analyzed by counts and ratios. They can be represented on histograms, bar graphs and pie charts. Examples of qualitative traits include round/wrinkled skin in pea pods, winged or wingless plants (e.g. fruit fly), albinism, sex, humans' ABO blood groups (as seen in Figure 1) etc.

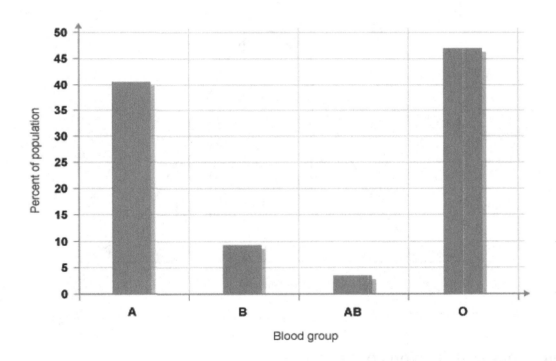

Figure 1: A histogram showing frequency distribution for a qualitative trait (blood group).

Continuous variation produces traits that are quantitative and in a continuum. These quantitative traits can be measured to observe their place relative to others. Quantitative traits have numerical values, hence, are also referred to as quantitative variables. They are represented on normal distribution curves, histograms (as in figures 2 and 3) as well as bar graphs and pie charts. Examples include height, intelligence, skin color etc.

251

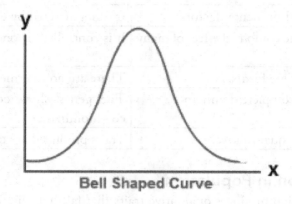

Bell Shaped Curve

Figure 2: A bell-shaped curve of a normal distribution

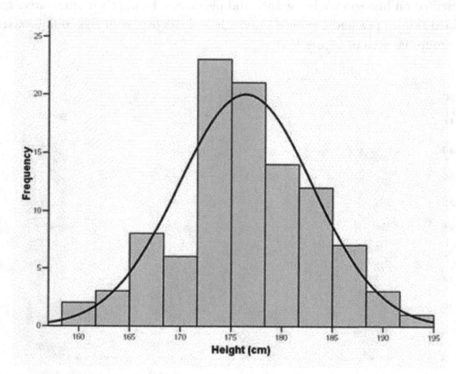

Figure 3: A normal bell-shaped curve on a histogram for a quantitative trait (height).

Frequency distributions of variation

Every population has a distribution of values for every quantitative variable. This reflects the number of individuals possessing each value for the trait. These distributions are frequently expressed as histogram and normal distribution curves with frequency on the vertical axis (y- axis) against trait values on the horizontal axis (x-axis) as shown in figures 1, 2, 3 and 4.

Variation in a trait occurring in a large number of organisms within a population, such as height in humans, can be measured. Height is an example of quantitative trait. Individuals can have a complete range of heights, for example, 156 – 160 cm, 161 – 165 cm etc. as shown in figure 4 below. These values could either be graphed with respect to frequency distribution resulting in normal distribution curve that is bell-shaped or plotted as histograms.

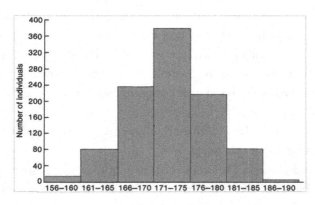

Height class (cm)

Figure 4: Frequency distribution on a histogram for a quantitative
trait (height) showing continuous variation.

Sources/Causes of Variation

- Genetic (heritable) differences.
- Environmental (acquired) differences.

Genetic differences: Genetic differences cause genetic variations which are heritable (passed on from parents to offspring) and are made possible by gene reshuffling as a result of the following events:

- **Crossing over of genes between chromatids of homologous chromosomes during** meiosis resulting in genetic recombination of alleles and formation of new linkage groups.
- Independent assortment during meiosis which involves the segregation of alleles located on non-homologous chromosomes independently resulting in different chromosome combinations.
- Random fusion of gametes during fertilization whose alleles have been separated resulting in new gene combinations.

Environmental differences: These refer to differences among organisms of the same species due to the different environmental factors they are exposed to. Examples include exposure of organisms to different temperatures, light, humidity, nutrients, loss of body parts via accidents, dehorning of cattle by man, lightening of the skin using cosmetics, lifestyle etc. These environmental differences result in variations. Environmental variations that result in acquired traits cannot be inherited from parents to their offspring. Some environmental factors such as cosmic rays, can cause mutations which result in genetic variations. Therefore, interactions between genetic and environmental differences cause variation.

Application of Variation

- **Crime detection:** Finger prints are applicable in crime detection since the technique of making them is simple and inexpensive. Criminals who leave their fingerprints at the scene of their crimes have their fingerprints collected and matched with those of potential suspects and past criminals and/or filed away and used to solve the various crimes that occur in the country. DNA fingerprinting technique is employed in developed countries to solve crimes such as rape. The rapist whose body cells are left at the scene of the crime are collected and the DNA pattern is analysed and compared with the suspect's DNA pattern, possibly identifying the rapist.

- **Mark of identity:** It provides a clear mark of identity between organisms of the same species. Finger prints can be applicable here.
- **Variation in blood groups:** Differences in the blood groups ensure that blood is not given at random but the blood of the donor matches that of the recipient before there is transfusion.
- **Determination of paternity:** Differences between organisms can be used to determine paternity, i.e. to show whether a man is the actual father of a child or not. Blood group tests are usually done to determine paternity but this test is not conclusive as someone with same blood group could also be the father. Therefore, DNA fingerprints are used since they can conclusively prove if a man is the father of a child or not.
- **Classification of the human race:** The human race can be classified into four groupings; Caucasoid (people with white skin), Negroid (people with black skin), Mongoloid (people with yellow-brown) and Australoid (people with brown skin) based on the differences in skin pigmentation.

References

Hickman, C. P., Roberts, L. S., Keen, S. L., Eisenhour, D. J., Larson, A. & I'Anson, H. (2011). Integrated Principles of Zoology. In *Organic Evolution*. (15th ed.). McGraw-Hill, New York. Pp. 127 – 129.

Hoover, J. E. (2006). Federal Bureau of Investigation. *The Science of Fingerprints: Classification and Uses*, Project Gutenberg eBook.

Idodo-Umeh, G. (2004). College Biology. In *Genetics and Variation*. (2nd ed.). Idodo Umeh Publishers, Nigeria. Pp. 429 – 432.

Iloeje, S. O. (2007). Senior Secondary Certificate Practical Biology. In *Heredity, Variation and Evolution*. (Ist ed.). Longman Nigeria PLC. Pp. 152 – 153.

Kent, M. (2000). Advanced Biology. In *Variation*. (2nd ed.). New York: Oxford University Press, Pp. 414-415.

Lyle, D. P. (2008). Fingerprints: A Handy Identification Tool. *Forensics: A Guide for Writers* (Howdunit), Writer's Digest Books, Cincinnati. Pp. 269–284.

Taylor, D. J., Stout, G. W. & Green, N. P. O. & Soper, R. (2008). Biological Science. In *Variation and Genetics* (3rd ed.).Cambridge University Press, India.

Sarojini, R. T. (2003). Modern Biology for Senior Secondary Schools. In *Variation and Genetics*. African First Publishers Ltd. Nigeria. (2nd ed.). Pp. 503 – 509.

Spiegel, M. R. & Stephens, L. J. (2008). *Statistics*. (4th ed.). McGraw-Hill. New York.

Printed in the United States
By Bookmasters